Perspectives on Korean Unification and Economic Integration

Perspectives on Korean Unification and Economic Integration

Edited by

Young Back Choi
Professor of Economics
St. Johns University

Yesook Merrill
Assistant Director/Senior Economist
US General Accounting Office

Yung Y. Yang
Professor of Economics
California State University – Sacramento

Semoon Chang
Professor of Economics
University of South Alabama

Edward Elgar
Cheltenham, UK • Northampton, MA, USA

Published by
Edward Elgar Publishing Limited
Glensanda House
Montpellier Parade
Cheltenham
Glos GL50 1UA
UK

Edward Elgar Publishing, Inc.
136 West Street
Suite 202
Northampton
Massachusetts 01060
USA

A catalogue record for this book
is available from the British Library

Library of Congress Cataloguing in Publication Data

Perspectives on Korean unification and economic integration / edited by Young Back Choi, ...[et al.].
    p.cm
  Includes index.
  1. Korea (South)—Foreign economic relations—Korea (North) 2. Korea (North)—Foreign economic relations—Korea (South) 3. Korean reunification question (1945–) I. Choi, Young Back, 1949–

HF1602.5.Z4 K783 2001
337.519505193—dc21   00–067190

ISBN 1 84064 418 4

Printed and bound in Great Britain by MPG Books Ltd, Bodmin, Cornwall

Contents

Figures

Tables

Contributors

Bradley O. Babson is a consultant on North Korea for the World Bank. He recently retired after 26 years, with a concentration on East Asian affairs, including serving as the Bank's first Resident Representative to Vietnam from 1994–97. He received his BA degree from Williams College in 1972, and MPA degree from the Woodrow Wilson School of International and Public Affairs at Princeton University in 1974.

Young Back Choi is Professor of Economics at St. John's University. He has been a visiting fellow at George Mason University, Washington University, the Social Philosophy and Policy Center, Max-Planck Institute for Comparative Economic Systems, and Kokugakuin University. He received his Ph.D. from the University of Michigan. Choi has published extensively including *Paradigms and Conventions* (University of Michigan Press, 1993.)

Oknim Chung is a research fellow at the Sejong Institute. She was a visiting fellow at the Brookings Institution and the Hoover Institution. She has taught at Stanford University, Korea University, and Hanyang University. She was a post-doctoral fellow at the Asia Pacific Research Center of Stanford University. She is a member of the Junior Advisory Group for the NSC of the Presidential Executive Office of Korea and a co-project director for the Council on Foreign Relations–Seoul Forum Project on Managing Change on the Korean Peninsula. Chung received her Ph.D. in Political Science from the Korea University. She has written extensively including *Five Hundred and Eighty-Eight Days of North Korean Nuclear Crisis*.

Xinshen Diao is a research fellow at the International Food Policy Research Institute. She was previously an Assistant Professor of Applied Economics at the Minnesota University and stationed at the Economic Research Service, US Department of Agriculture. Diao was also a consultant in the agricultural and natural resource department of the World Bank, senior research fellow, assistant director-general, and division chief in the Economic Reform Institute of China, and research fellow in the

Research Center for Rural Development of the Chinese State Council. Diao earned her BA and MA in Economics and Ph.D. in Agricultural Economics from the University of Minnesota.

John Dyck is Senior Agricultural Economist with the Economic Research Service at the US Department of Agriculture. He studies at Cornell University. His research interests are in the areas of agricultural trade in Asia. One of his tasks since 1980 has been to monitor food and agricultural issues surrounding North Korea. His chief assignments are the agricultural trade of Japan and South Korea.

Donald Gregg is the Chairman of the Board of the Korea Society in New York City. He had a long and distinguished public service including almost 30 years with the Central Intelligence Agency. He served as Vice President Bush's National Security Advisor and the US Ambassador to Korea (1989–93). From 1980–89, Gregg was a professorial lecturer at Georgetown University. He earned a BA in Philosophy from Williams College and received honorary degrees from Green Mountain College in Vermont and from Sogang University in Korea.

Tony P. Hall has been US Representative for Ohio's Third District since 1979. He has been an outspoken advocate for combating world hunger, protecting human rights, and promoting humanitarian causes. Hall has visited numerous poverty-stricken and war-torn regions, including six trips to North Korea. He has received numerous honors and been nominated three times for the Nobel Peace Prize. He serves on the House Committee on Rules and chairs the House Democratic Task Force on Hunger. He graduated from Denison University.

Sang Taek Kim earned his Ph.D. in Economics from Columbia University. He joined KISDI (Korea Information Society Development Institute) in 1995. He specialized in pricing, interconnection charge, antitrust, and other policy issues as well as North Korean issues. He has published many papers related to telecommunications policies in many academic journals including *Information Economics and Policy*, *Seoul Journal of Economics*, *Journal of Economic Theory* and *Econometrics*. He is now an Assistant Professor of Economics at Ewha Women's University.

Youn-Suk Kim holds a BA degree in Business Administration from Seoul National University, and MA and Ph.D. degrees in Economics from the New School (University) for Social Research. He is Professor of Economics at Kean University. Kim has also taught at Fairleigh Dickinson University, Seoul National University and Hankuk University of Foreign Studies. He is a member of the editorial board of Human Systems Management. Kim has published over 60 articles including "Inter-Korean Business Economics" and seven books including *Economics of the Triad: Conflicts and Cooperation among the United States, Japan and Korea.*

Haksoo Ko is a Lecturer in International Affairs at Columbia University School of International and Public Affairs. A graduate of Seoul National University, he studied at Columbia University to earn J.D. (Law) and Ph.D. (Economics) degrees. His main areas of research include economic analysis of legal and institutional arrangements in Korea.

Chinkook Lee is Senior Agricultural Economist at the Food Markets Branch, Economic Research Service of the US Department of Agriculture. He is a specialist in input–output analysis. He holds a Ph.D. from Washington State University,

Young-Sun Lee received his Ph.D. in Economics from the University of Maryland. He worked for the Korean International Economic Institute from 1978 to 1981. Since then, he has been Professor of Economics at Yonsei University, Seoul, Korea. His main research interests cover international trade, the political economy of economic policy, and the economic effect of Korean unification. He once served as Director of the Institute for Korea Unification Studies at Yonsei University and now he is Director of the Office of University Planning and Development.

John Merrill is Acting Chief of Northeast Asian Division in the US Department of State's Bureau of Research and Intelligence. He has held teaching and research positions at Georgetown University, the George Washington University, the Center for Strategic and International Studies, Lafayette College, Korea University, and University of Delaware. Besides numerous journal articles and book chapters, Merrill has authored several books including *Korea: The Peninsular Origins of the War* (University of Delaware, 1989). He has an MA in East Asian Studies from Harvard and a Ph.D. in Political Science from the University of Delaware.

William Newcomb is Senior Economist in the US State Department's Bureau of Intelligence and Research. He has written extensively on developments in China, Vietnam, and North Korea for US policymakers. Prior to joining the State Department, he followed East European and the Asian economies for the Office of Economic Analysis, US Central Intelligence Agency. Newcomb did his graduate work in Economics at St. Mary's University and at Texas A&M. He specializes in the analysis of command economies and economics reform and has studied developments in North Korea for more than 20 years.

Marcus Noland was educated at Swarthmore College (BA), and the Johns Hopkins University (Ph.D.). He is currently a Senior Fellow at the Institute for International Economics and an Associate of the International Food Policy Research Institute. He was a Senior Economist at the Council of Economic Advisers in the Executive Office of the President of the United States. He has held research or teaching positions at the Johns Hopkins University, the University of Southern California, Tokyo University, Saitama University, the University of Ghana, and the Korea Development Institute. He has been the recipient of fellowships sponsored by the Japan Society for the Promotion of Science, the Council on Foreign Relations, and the Council for the International Exchange of Scholars. Noland has authored or coauthored numerous books, including *Avoiding the Apocalypse: the Future of the Two Koreas* (IIE, 2000). In addition, he has written many scholarly articles on international economics, US trade policy, and the economies of the Asia-Pacific region.

Kongdan (Katy) Oh is a Research Staff Member at the Institute for Defense Analyses (IDA), a public policy think tank conducting research for the Office of the Secretary of Defense. She is also a non-resident senior fellow at the Brookings Institution. In Korea she received her BA degree at Sogang University and her MA at Seoul National University. She subsequently earned an MA and Ph.D. in Asian studies at the University of California, Berkeley. Her most recent publications include *Korea Briefing 1997–1999: Challenges and Change at the Turn of the Century* (editor) by M.E. Sharpe and *North Korea Through the Looking Glass* (co-author) by Brookings.

Leon V. Sigal is Director of the Northeast Asia Cooperative Security Project at the Social Science Research Council in New York. An adjunct professor at Columbia University's School of International and Public Affairs, he was a member of the editorial board of *The New York Times* from 1989 until 1995. He taught at Wesleyan University and Princeton University's Woodrow Wilson School in 1988 and in 2000. His book, *Disarming Strangers: Nuclear Diplomacy with North Korea*, published by Princeton University Press, was nominated for the Lionel Gelber Prize and was named 1998 book of distinction on the practice of American diplomacy by the American Academy of Diplomacy. He has numerous other publications.

Agapi Somwaru is Senior Economist at the Economic Research Service of the US Department of Agriculture. Her research interests are in the areas of modeling production, development, trade, and risk in agriculture. She received her Ph.D. in Economics from the University of Connecticut.

Acknowledgement

We wish to express our deepest appreciation to all those who helped to make the conference the success it was: all the participants in the conference and those who provided generous support, financial or otherwise, including the Korea–America Economic Association, Korean Economic Association, Korea Society, Korea Foundation, KDI, KERI, KEIA, KDI School of International Policy and Management, the East–West Research Institute, Maeil Business Newspaper, SK Telecom, Korea Electric Power Corporation, and Yong-Kang Foundation.

Foreword

Tony P. Hall

Hindsight now makes it clear that the Korea–America Economic Association's (KAEA) conference came at a momentous turning point in North Korea's history. Whatever happens to the fledgling ROK–DPRK relationship next – whether it continues to pleasantly surprise Koreans and Korea experts alike, or whether it meets some other fate – the events since KAEA examined the two Koreas' progress toward one economy will not soon be forgotten.

Any economic association can be forgiven its tendency to see current events through a "macro" lens. Certainly, the economy of North Korea in recent years is prima facie evidence of the need to open its markets and change its ways. But what in 2000 made that need greater than it was in 1999, or 1998, or any other year of this decade?

As someone who focuses on humanitarian concerns, I can be expected to see most situations differently than an economist might. I believe it is the "micro" situation that helped persuade North Korea to shift gears, and not just the microeconomic one. What has been happening in the country's homes and factories – and the world's response to its people's suffering – is doing a great deal to change individuals' attitude toward outsiders throughout North Korea.

I was astonished to see how ordinary people's reaction to the sight of outsiders shifted between 1995 and 1999. Where children and adults we met on rural roads ran away in 1996, by 1998 they were beginning to wave back – and in 1999 some were starting the friendly greeting before we could. And it wasn't just Westerners: many Koreans from the south or Japan stand a head taller than their brothers in the north, a sight that's hard to miss and drew a lot of curious attention.

I believe this change in ordinary citizens' thinking played a key role, both permitting – and forcing – North Korea's leaders to reach out. As difficult as that step was, though, history suggests that it was the easy part of the task ahead. Countries in transformation hear a lot of advice about what not to do; it is harder for many to figure out an affirmative course to follow.

Koreans' strong culture, and the wide experience many Koreans have had with economic hardships similar to those the DPRK has suffered, may help ease this transition. The ROK and DPRK are blessed with friends among the Korean American community and others who presented papers at the October 1999 conference, whose insights remain timely.

Food shortages probably sparked the DPRK's initial turn toward the international community. Political, cultural and family issues no doubt encouraged its continuing outreach. In the end, economics certainly will be the measure of this initiative's success – but I am equally sure that compassion will be a critical touchstone on the road ahead.

It was an honor to address the gifted group of people KAEA assembled last fall. I wish them, those who share their commitment to helping the two Koreas, and the Korea–America Economic Association all the best in the coming months.

Foreword

Donald Gregg

Major events in foreign affairs, even those long anticipated in advance, usually come as a surprise. I remember having dinner with former German Chancellor Willy Brandt in Seoul, in October 1989. He had just visited the demilitarized zone (DMZ), and was deeply shocked by what he had seen. He referred to the DMZ as "a time warp" and predicted that when it was at last penetrated, the psychological adjustments required by North and South Koreans in order to relate positively with each other would be far greater than those the Germans would have to deal with when the Berlin Wall came down. Brandt was immediately asked when he thought the wall would be eliminated, and his reply was "not in my lifetime." In fact, the wall was down within 60 days.

Last October, I made some informal remarks at the conference, "Two Koreas: Toward One Economy," that this book documents and said, "We have a long, long way to go with North Korea." I went on to quote American historian Catherine Weathersby who, in a retrospective article on the Korean War, had said that North Korea, as a result of the Soviet Union's collapse, had no foreign aid, no close ally and no sense of how normal diplomatic relations are conducted. If there was a consensus at the conference it was that North Korea was stuck in a posture of extreme isolation, that it was terribly fearful of change, and that no breakthrough in the near future was at all likely.

No one at October's conference predicted the kind of breakthrough that has taken place, starting at the summit meeting in Pyongyang last June. President Kim Dae-jung's diplomatic accomplishment and Kim Jong-il's daring emergence from isolation certainly have come as a surprise to virtually everyone. What has been even more surprising is the pace of follow-up actions between North and South Korea, as well as North Korea's rapid expansion of relations with other countries. A paradigm shift is taking place in Northeast Asia, and the United States will be called upon to re-examine our objectives in the region, and how best to achieve them. (This might be the subject of another conference.)

The Pyongyang summit is only the beginning of a long and difficult process of adjustment and reconciliation between North and South Korea. Nothing has as yet been finally solved or decided. Thus, the many questions raised and discussed at last October's conference remain pertinent, and are potentially helpful as a new era in Northeast Asia begins.

Readers of this book will soon discern that some conferences were more prescient in their predictions than others. The book as a whole, however, serves both as a clear reminder of where we were in terms of thinking about North Korea in October 1999, and as a guide for the many issues relating to unification that now have to be dealt with.

Introduction

During the last decade of the twentieth century the Korean peninsula was the stage for non-stop, dramatic news events, the highlights of which include the death of Kim Il-Sung, the faltering economy and nuclear crisis in the North, and the 1997 financial crisis and the upset victory of President Kim Dae Jung in the South. Perhaps, the most alarming of these developments were the growing economic gap between the two Koreas and the North Korean famine that may have claimed as many as a million lives.

The Korea–America Economic Association's October 1999 conference on "Two Koreas: Towards One Economy" assessed some of these fast-paced developments. Set in Washington, DC, the conference assembled a diverse group of economists and analysts from academia, government, and think tanks from both South Korea and the US. Topics ranged from philosophical to practical policy matters, with participants differing on the basis of political persuasion, philosophical orientation, and analytical approach. We recognize the importance of such differences, and in compiling this book, have made no attempt to downplay them. Based largely on the conference papers, this volume brings together an unusually broad range of perspectives on US policy towards North Korea, the North Korean economy, and North–South economic cooperation. The following is a brief summary of each author's message.

Despite recent positive developments toward peaceful coexistence of the two Koreas, Oknim Chung believes that North Korea may still wage war if driven to desperation. She prescribes "management of tension" and "muddling through" rather than once-and-for-all solutions as a reasonable course to take for long-term peace and stability in the region and suggests that such policy direction would also be palatable to major powers surrounding the Korean peninsula.

Leon Sigal argues that the most important determinant of the North Korean economy is security, not economics. Economic reform will not stand in the way of security interests and the best way to assure peace on the Korean peninsula is to move beyond the 1994 Agreed Framework and seek a deal to end North Korea's missile program.

Katy Oh's assessment of the Clinton administration's policy toward North Korea is less than enthusiastic. Rather than seeking a new comprehensive agreement (as outlined in the Perry Report), she suggests that the US negotiate tough, limited agreements to achieve short-term goals, while simultaneously pursuing an aggressive game plan to unseat the current North Korean regime, informing the North Korean people directly about the reality of their government and the outside world.

Bradley Babson assesses the similarities and differences in the experiences of Vietnam and North Korea, two countries in Asia that have experienced wars followed by isolation from the international community. He discusses the influences of historical context, nationalism, culture, colonial experience, civil war, and crisis, on the dynamics of change. While the Vietnamese experience in opening up to the outside world provides lessons that are relevant to policies appropriate for North Korea, Babson emphasizes the equal importance of recognizing differences between the two countries.

William Newcomb and John Merrill argue that even if North Korea adopts a solidly conceived opening policy coupled with strong efforts at reform, the chance of success remains slim unless outside help is substantial. The choice facing Washington, Seoul, Tokyo, and Beijing is whether or not to try to raise the potential payoff of opening to induce Pyongyang to commit to the bolder course. Newcomb and Merrill suggest that the South and others must make some "uncertainty" calculations of their own. They must balance the risks and the costs of a North Korean collapse with those of bolstering an opening that may not succeed.

Youn-Suk Kim is optimistic about various signs of the two Koreas' economic cooperation. Increased diplomatic and economic exposure to the international community encourages North Korea to deal directly with South Korea. Kim stresses, however, that political gestures and diplomatic compromises must be accompanied by inter-Korean economic engagement to create meaningful development.

Diao, Dyck, Lee, and Somwaru consider North Korea's shortage of food a symptom of comparative disadvantages in agricultural production and the sharp decline of the controlled economy. They argue that North Korea can best solve its food problem by importing food, paying for this solution by expanding its existing export-oriented light industry based on processing materials for South Korean firms, exporting their finished outputs.

Sang Taek Kim describes how to develop pre-unification North–South Korean cooperative projects in information and telecommunications. He outlines both the current status of the South Korean telecommunication industry and the services in North Korea, and presents a framework for analyzing post-unification regulatory issues like entry and price regulations, competition, and relations with foreign companies.

Haksoo Ko observes that North Korea's previous lack of success in bringing in foreign investors may be attributable to ambiguities in legal provisions and the absence of well-functioning institutional infrastructure. He argues that developments during the past decade in laws and regulations on foreign investment in North Korea have gradually improved the investment environment.

Young-Sun Lee estimates the cost of unification under two different scenarios: gradual and sudden unification. The total cost of sudden unification – including substantial crisis management costs – is predicted to be about 60 percent of South Korea's 1990 GNP; a gradual unification can reduce both costs and financial difficulties.

Marcus Noland presents the economic implications of economic integration of the two Koreas under alternative scenarios: through trade and through factor market integration. Under the trade scenario, due to the sheer size difference between the two economies, integration brings great benefit to the North, with little impact on the South Korean economy; under the second scenario, however, it can have a major impact on the economy of the South without necessarily bringing about rapid equalization of income levels.

Young Back Choi questions the fundamental assumption of unification. He argues that the expected benefits of unification are overstated, while the costs are understated. He further asserts that "no unification" may be a superior alternative, both on political and on economic grounds. Such a policy induces the North Korean rulers to worry less about their survival – thereby reducing their erratic behavior – and, instead, to become more concerned about their long-term prospects for peaceful coexistence and prosperity.

The year 2000 opened a new chapter on the Korean peninsula; the North–South summit in June was no doubt a historical milestone that could lead to major changes on the peninsula. But the fundamental issues herein addressed are still relevant and important. No overnight solutions or magic bullets exist. Essential ingredients for North–South economic cooperation, ranging from regional security matters to policy nuts and bolts, remain little changed.

1 Security Outlook of the Korean Peninsula

Oknim Chung

ANALYSIS OF SECURITY ENVIRONMENT

The "North Korea" factor occupies a big part of the security outlook in Northeast Asia, and the Korean Peninsula is still considered the last area of the Cold War legacy on earth. Despite the excitement and high expectation of the inter-Korean summit held in June 2000, the possibility of resolving the entire Korean conundrum is slim. As witnessed in the issues of nuclear suspicion and missile launch tests by the North, tension and potential conflict characterize the security situation in the Korean Peninsula. Given North Korea's ballistic missile, artillery, and chemical weapons capabilities, no one thinks that peace will come easily. With Seoul and its allies having constantly to guess the real intentions of the heavily armed and inscrutable communist regime, the Korean Peninsula remains a major flashpoint of the post-Cold War era. The variables that determine the future of North Korea and the Korean Peninsula include North Korea's own policies and domestic development, North–South Korean relations and the major powers' policies and bilateral relations.

Comparatively speaking, the security environment in Northeast Asia centering on the four major powers – the United States, China, Japan and Russia – is more benign and less threatening than it has been in decades, in spite of its uncertainty and volatility. The likelihood of a new war between the two Koreas has been on the decline. And the balance of forces among the major powers appears reasonably stable despite some possibility of tension such as potential conflict between the US and China, US concern over a possible movement toward a strategic partnership between China and Russia, and China's worry about US–Japanese–Taiwanese Theater Missile

Defense (TMD) build-up. So far, security issues in Northeast Asia have largely centered around the Korean Peninsula and the Taiwan Straits, and have been characterized as uncertain and unpredictable. Spiraling events between the US and China, like the bombing of the Chinese Embassy in Yugoslavia, the Cox Report criticizing China for stealing nuclear weapon-related technology, and Taiwan's posture on its independence, create diplomatic tension and conflict. This is not a desirable phenomenon, particularly from South Korea's viewpoint: the US–Chinese tension may easily be coupled with the US–Chinese divergence of interest on the North Korea issue.

Cleavages in national perceptions and interests, lack of mutual trust, the historical legacy, and the arms race combine to make regional cooperation in security a tough challenge, with or without increasing regional economic interdependence. However, and strangely enough, there has been no war in the region since the 1953 armistice was signed on the Korean Peninsula. In other words, a state of passive peace has been maintained for almost five decades in this tension-ridden area. In analyzing the regional security in Northeast Asia, this uniqueness must be recognized. There is a balance of power, yet not in the traditional sense of Great Britain in eighteenth to nineteenth century Europe. The US, as the sole post-Cold War hegemon, is playing a role as stabilizer, not balancer, in the region. The so-called second-tier powers, China and Japan, have neither the willingness nor the capability to challenge the US hegemony, as there is little possibility of their colluding to challenge its power. Rather, both are eager to have a positive relationship with the US, and thus stray from the classical balance-of-power behavior.

Despite the argument that the Northeast Asian security system is mainly bilateral in structure, an in-depth observation of security in Northeast Asia reveals many folds of triangular relationships. The US–China–Japan triangle is at their core. The US–Russia–China, China–Korea–Japan, ROK–US–DPRK, ROK–China–DPRK, and US–Taiwan–China combinations are the second-tier triangles. An explanation for such interweaving complexities is that there is no single common enemy against which the others would ally in regional cooperation, with the exception of the ever-present troublemaker, North Korea. It also means that there is little common interest among the parties. The Chinese–Japanese version of the Franco–German closeness is currently too premature to state. The only common interest between them thus far is maintenance of the status quo, and this permits incremental and cost-effective change at most. The interested parties in this region realize the price of abrupt change and the costs of tension, not to mention the vanity of military clashes. They have maintained a relatively long spell of peace or, perhaps more precisely, lack of war in this region, and have done so by upholding the tenets of prudence that stem from neo-realism, and of economic interdependence and cooperation that stem from neo-liberalism. However, this situation does not completely exclude the possibility of rapid change in the region, such as the collapse of the Kim Jong Il regime or a China–Taiwan clash across the Taiwan Straits.

As outlined previously, the four big powers can play an important role in the future of the Korean Peninsula. From South Korea's viewpoint, insuring their participation in Seoul's engagement diplomacy is critical. Through the Korean Peninsula Energy Development Organization (KEDO), Japan is already engaged. China is engaged in the Four Party Talks process, which exhibits at least step-by-step progress. For such a vulnerable yet strategically important and dynamic region as Northeast Asia, the absence of a multilateral mechanism through which regional powers can consult over security problems is most unusual. Something like the Northeast Asian Security Dialogue (NEASD) could fill the void and engage Russia, not to replace the bilateral security framework but rather to complement the existing security mechanism for peace and prosperity in this region.

The South Korean government, which has pursued the dismantling of the Cold War structure for peace and stability on the Korean Peninsula, now pushes ahead with the so-called six-party talks that include Japan and Russia. However, despite the rhetoric, the proposed formula itself creates controversies at home as well as abroad, and mentions no specific action plans. Despite the differences in ideas and interests between its proposed members, the six-party formula clearly has merit in its potential to promote and provide to each potential member country both ever-present involvement in Korea-related issues and exchange of ideas and intelligence. The magnitude of the North Korean nuclear and missile issues not too long ago provides more impetus for divergent interests to converge in some way. Such feats are necessary to achieve peaceful coexistence and ultimate resolution of the separation of the two Koreas.

On the other hand, North Korea is unlikely to show much interest in the six-party security framework, as it fears being isolated in a de facto "Five plus One" formula. Still, North Korea's expression of intent in joining the ASEAN Regional Forum (ARF, a security dialogue forum encompassing Asia and the Pacific), as well as the historical summit between North and South Korea is cause for optimism, albeit guarded. Research should be undertaken to figure out the feasibility of the mechanism and methods both to activate the formula and to make it complementary to the current bilateral security structures that link the United States to Japan and Korea. Dealing with other important issues that are not covered under such dialogues as the US–DPRK missile talks, the Missing in Action (MIA) talks, and the four-party peace talks, is also an important component.

INTERESTS OF THE FOUR MAJOR POWERS IN THE KOREAN PENINSULA

The United States

South Korea enjoys good or improving relations with all of its large power neighbors – Japan, China, and Russia – as well as a continued strong alliance with the United States.[1] Although the interests of major powers in this area tend to converge with respect to stability and cooperation, their roles and interests regarding the Korean Peninsula exhibit some differences as well. Accordingly, before touching upon the North Korea issue as the most significant key security problem, it is necessary to address the interests of the so-called big powers surrounding the Korean Peninsula.

The United States, while more distant geographically than the others, has been deeply involved in the Korean issue since the end of World War II. US interests concerning the Korean Peninsula in the late 1990s include the following: preventing the proliferation of weapons of mass destruction (WMDs), including missiles; preserving peace and stability on the Korean Peninsula; securing dominance in the development of Korea; maintaining US troops as a forward base; containing Russia as well as China; protecting Japan; and maintaining South Korea as a showcase of democracy and economic development. The US also has long-term interests related to Korea, interests that include preventing the rise of hostile hegemony in Asia, ensuring freedom of navigation and open lines of communication, and maintaining access to open markets.

North Korea's ability to pose a military threat to the region, as seen in its multi-stage missile launch in August 1998, is the major source of its leverage over the United States. It is believed that North Korea has nearly perfected a missile capable of carrying weapons of mass destruction to Hawaii or Alaska and that long-range missiles could strike the continental United States in just a few years. The US administration, which suspects Russia is selling missile technology and components to North Korea (Gertz, 2000), is pressing for tight constraints on the full range of North Korean missile activities: exports, production, deployment and flight-testing. Moreover, North Korea's missile-led provocation provided ample justification for the US pursuit of the National Missile Defense (NMD) and Theater Missile Defense (TMD) programs, the response to which was criticism from China and Russia. The short-term objective of the US negotiations with the North is to prevent Pyongyang from further flight testing of long-range missiles and additional exports of missiles or related equipment and technology. The Berlin Agreement in September 1999, which freezes the missile program of North Korea as long as negotiation between the US and DPRK continues, was a good starting point for this purpose. Shortly after the Berlin accord, in October 1999, the US Administration launched the so-called Perry Initiative of comprehensive and integrated two-path strategy toward North Korea. According to this engagement packet, continuous humanitarian aid through international organizations including the World Food Program (WFP), higher-level talks between the US and DPRK, and US easing of sanctions against the North (particularly the removal of North Korea from the list of state sponsors of terrorism) would be conducted in exchange for North Korea's good behavior regarding the issue of tension reduction on the Peninsula.

The advent of the post-Cold War era has created an awkward triangular relationship among the two Koreas and the US. The North Korea factor is the most important element in the South Korea–US relationship. During the Kim Young-Sam government, South Korea advocated a hard-line stance, while the US wanted a bit more accommodation. It is probably difficult for the US to understand the emotional side of the issue. For the US, its alliance with South Korea exists mainly as a safeguard against the North Korean security threat. For South Korea, the alliance is more than a simple security guarantee. It is the symbol and substance of the US siding with and supporting South Korea in a family feud that transcends the security dimension. Any step toward befriending North Korea by the US may well be viewed in South Korea with misgiving and concern, even if a new balance of power between the two Koreas clearly indicates that both time and luck are on the side of the South. With the Kim Dae Jung Presidency, the roles of the US and South Korea have been completely reversed. The Kim government took a new approach in the name of the Sunshine Policy, encouraging the US to engage Pyongyang, while also winning support from Pyongyang's erstwhile friends for Seoul's policies. The US–ROK policy coordination is quite significant not only in handling North Korea but also in influencing the domestic public in South Korea, because the Northern regime has always been trying to drive a wedge between the two allies, and the South Koreans suffer from a "wedge complex" whenever they witness progress in US–DPRK relationships.

Meanwhile in the current US–ROK relationship, many harbingers of change may weaken the long-term alliance despite the common purpose and shared interest. Obstacles to the constructive alliance continue to include South Korea's eagerness to develop longer-range ballistic missiles and US restrictions on this development; Status of Forces Agreement (SOFA) issues[2]; and the emerging ROK debate over the future of relations with China, including whether or not South Korea should participate in the development of TMD. With the missile threat from the North, South Korea made an agreement with the US to develop and manufacture missiles ranging 300 kilometers (about 180 miles); it is also looking for a way to develop and test missiles ranging 500 kilometers (about 310 miles), to cover the border with China and counter North Korea's missiles.[3] However, the US administration pressures South Korea not to develop the longer-range missiles, warning of possible arms races in the region. In the wake of the successful inter-Korean summit, the South Korean missile issue subsided, whereas the appearance of improved relations between the two Koreas concerned the US in that it might divert international attention away from the issues of North Korean WMDs. Moreover, the moves to end North Korea's strict isolation and drum-beating belligerence challenge some of the rationale for the limited national missile defense system being proposed by the US, which has the ostensible goal of preventing any attack by countries such as North Korea (Struck, 2000).

Economic globalization poses another new challenge that will provide both opportunities and new potential conflicts. The emergence of the younger generation, with its different perspectives, may also have an important social and political impact on the bilateral relationship.[4] Some younger South Koreans view the joint command structure and South Korea's continued military dependence on the United States as institutional reflections of dependency rather than as a structure of shared responsibility for security. In addition, the inter-Korean summit and the emerging mood for peace provide the context for another debate on whether the US should and can maintain the presence of its troops in Korea after unification. To maintain a balance of power and prevent an arms race in Northeast Asia, the US is keen on keeping troops on the Korean Peninsula. It remains to be seen whether the centrifugal forces of complicated social, demographic, and economic change in Korea and the US will be sufficiently countered by the centripetal forces of shared core values so that both sides will look beyond short-term interests and cooperate in adapting to new circumstances (Snyder, 2000).

China

China shares many of the same objectives as the US regarding the Korean Peninsula. It too wants to keep Korea nuclear-free. It too wants stability. And it also wants to prevent armed conflict or any other disruption that could draw China into action. China does not want millions of North Korean refugees pouring across the North Korean border into its own Northeast. The Chinese are not eager for a rapid reunification of Korea. To Beijing, a stable, peaceful and friendly, but divided Korean Peninsula is more desirable than rapid Korean unification or the denuclearization of

North Korea. China's attitude toward the US troops in Korea is ambivalent. As a result of overall Chinese security considerations, Beijing appears to have quietly accepted the US–ROK alliance as part of the favorable status quo in Northeast Asia. China recognizes the positive effect of reassuring and restraining Japan. Indeed, the US military presence in Japan has been seen as a necessary, though not desirable, "cap" on Japanese military power. This perception, however, began to change early in 1996, when Clinton and Hashimoto signed the Joint Declaration regarding the Security Treaty. From China's perspective, the Joint Declaration gives Japan a broader, more active, and more flexible role in defining and meeting any perceived threats to its security from the Asia-Pacific. Moreover, the joint TMD program between the US and Japan is extremely worrisome to China, due to the possibility of Japan's military might and Taiwan's eagerness for joining the project.

Privately, Beijing authorities criticize the North's failure to take appropriate economic actions and disparage its political system, even if such terms as "lips and teeth friendship" may be invoked publicly.[5] On average, China has provided close to one million tons of unmonitored and unconditional food aid to the North per year. The Chinese government restarted high-level dialogue with Kim Young Nam's visit to China, and urged the North Korean delegation to try economic reform. North Korea is seen as a burden to China. The North Koreans have asked for too much, requesting that all their debt be forgiven and millions of tons of new assistance be provided before Kim Jong Il's visit to Beijing, but the ties between China and the North are still meaningful to both parties. Meanwhile, since diplomatic normalization in 1992, economic relations between the PRC and the South have expanded rapidly.[6] From China's point of view, South Korea has become an important source of investment, technology and imported goods as well as an export market. Indeed, South Korea has developed a substantial trade surplus, some $5 billion, with China.[7] On the political front, the rule among the major powers is "live and let live," with controversy generally avoided. For the most part, China has played a constructive role on the Korean Peninsula, as seen in the North Korean nuclear issue in 1994 and the missile issue in 1999. Kim Jong Il's visit to China in May 2000, only a few days before the inter-Korean summit, underscored China's political and economic leverage over the North.[8] In the short to medium term, China has the most to gain diplomatically from radically improved relations between North and South Korea.

In fact, the movement toward the Theater Missile Defense (TMD) between the US and Japan worried the Chinese, who are already vocally critical of TMD cooperation. Thus, the relationships among these larger countries are turning contentious. South Korea sees the Sino-American relationship as critical to regional security in general and efforts to contain possible North Korean adventurism in particular. China may have put pressure on the North Koreans as a way to slow down or stop work on TMD. Contrary to conventional beliefs, Beijing does not appear to have a negative view of closer relations between North Korea and the United States. On the contrary, China has been urging Washington to improve its relations with Pyongyang. Its attitude toward issues on the Korean Peninsula can be briefly characterized as sensitive toward US–Japanese military relations, watchful of US–Japanese–South Korean relations, benign toward improvement of US–North Korean relations, and reasonably positive toward North–South Korean relations.

Japan

Japan is becoming more active in the security arena; indeed, 1999 may be regarded as another turning point in its defense posture. First of all, North Korea's missile test so seriously shocked the Japanese that they finally agreed to commit funds for joint research and development (R&D) of a TMD system with the US. Until North Korea's missile launch on August 31, 1998, Japan's attitude to the TMD issue was guarded. After the launch, Japan decided to develop indigenous reconnaissance satellites, despite Washington's behind-closed-doors efforts to dissuade Tokyo from doing so.[9] Although Koreans suspect that Japanese supporters of the strengthened military power have taken advantage of North Korea's missile provocation, somehow the country's focus on self-reliance and its greater tolerance for strong military capacity seem irreversible. Redefining its alliance with the US as documented in the April 1996 Joint Declaration on Security and the September 1997 Guidelines for bilateral defense cooperation; rearranging related domestic laws regarding the activities of the Self-Defense Force; and moving toward the revision of the Peace Constitution, including Article IX, are the gradual steps Japan has taken for a more assertive role in regional security dynamics. Japan's possible TMD deployment may require integrating anti-missile defense command and control systems between Japan and the United States, with far-reaching implications for both sides.

Changes in Japan's military posture are clearly a wake-up call for China and South Korea. Not only has Japan been a fearsome enemy in the recent past, but the balance of power may shift in this region. The US–Japanese alliance is crucial to Korea's security even in a post-reunification setting. It can provide Korea with a certain degree of confidence that Japan will not become a future threat. Anti-Japanese sentiment is already proving to be a unifying force in Sino-ROK relations and could significantly affect the post-reunification security framework for Northeast Asia. But ROK–Japanese cooperation is important to long-term stability in Asia and, more immediately, appears crucial to the success of the US-initiated Agreed Framework and Korean Peninsula Energy Development Organization efforts to denuclearize Korea. With the North Korean issues, South Korea gradually begins to realize the necessity of cooperation with Japan. The newly defined roles and missions for the Japanese Self-Defense Forces in accordance with the Guidelines for Defense Cooperation cover contingencies in the "area surrounding Japan," which may also include the Korean Peninsula and the Taiwan Straits.[10] In fact, the first-ever joint military exercise between the two countries was conducted in the East China Sea in 1999,[11] and pending tasks will be to foster a more cooperative relationship between South Korea and Japan, enhancing mutual understanding, and developing common interests for a new chapter in the ROK–Japanese relationship.

When it comes to the North Korean issue, Japan does not want to be seen as toeing the US line and having to assume an excessive burden. Nor does it wish to bypass South Korea, which does not want to see Japan move too fast or too far. But it will be difficult to maintain this passive policy for long. Japan will want to become more active, perhaps in consultation with the US and South Korea, but not necessarily following in their footsteps. When North Korea fired a *Daepodong* missile in 1998, Tokyo reacted viscerally. In Japan, the launch was compared to that of Sputnik in terms of its impact on the public's views of security policy. (Abramowitz and Laney, 1999). The Japanese government suspended cooperation in KEDO for two months, though a cost-sharing agreement was eventually signed in November 1998 and the Diet agreed to funding in June 1999. With the resolution of the missile issue in Berlin, the Japanese government both eased sanctions against North Korea, including those on chartered flights and remittances by Korean residents in Japan, and embarked on normalization talks with the North. The two sides, however, are far apart on key issues like the alleged abduction of Japanese citizens by the DPRK and the DPRK's demands for reparations for damage suffered during Japan's colonial rule of the Korean Peninsula. North Korea may seek rapid normalization with Japan in anticipation of massive flows of economic assistance in the name of financial compensation. Yet, the Japanese government has been taking a scrupulous approach and is clearly conscious of its domestic atmosphere and bureaucratic scruple. Japan is also taking a cautious approach to the issue of North Korea's joining the Asian Development Bank (ADB). Japan will not only bear the largest share of the burden to aid North Korea if North Korea gains membership in the ADB, but will also automatically lose economic leverage over North Korea.

Although South Korea is a staunch ally of the US and a virtual ally of Japan because of this alliance, practically all security consultations used to be conducted bilaterally with the US as the linking pin rather than through a trilateral mechanism. Particularly with Japan, there had been many serious disputes and even more serious suspicions (Chung, 1998). It had thus been inevitable that the three-way security cooperation regarding North Korea was conducted in this fashion. However, the Kim Dae Jung government successfully strengthened the ties with these two countries by establishing and developing the Trilateral Coordination and Oversight Group (TCOG) in April 1999. This group effectively manages internal priority differences on specific issues, curbing the impulse for more emotional reactions to perceived provocations from North Korea. It also reduces the ability of North Korea to exploit differences in the policy stances of allies, as well as underscoring the importance of engagement strategy while containing North Korea's destabilizing behavior. Finally, it diminishes the possibility that precipitous unilateral action against North Korea by any single party will lead to the spread of broader conflict in Northeast Asia.[12] Meanwhile, South Korea faces the problem of having to maintain a strong security relationship with both the US and Japan while keeping its relations with China amicable and cooperative. Perhaps herein lies the explanation for its having officially ruled out any participation in the proposed TMD program, which appears to be directed against China or aimed at "containing" it, and hoping that the US and Japan maintain friendly relations with China.

Russia

Russia's main concern regarding the Korean issue is not to be left out of the process. It wants to prevent US or Chinese dominance on the Korean Peninsula. Hence, in 1994, it proposed an international conference in connection with the North Korean nuclear issue. Russia was not happy with the four-party proposal, from which it was excluded. DPRK relations with Russia were cool because of Moscow's decision to establish diplomatic relations with Seoul in 1990. Five years later, Moscow decided to scrap the 35-year-long bilateral treaty of mutual assistance with Pyongyang. However, in a move to recover its influence over North Korea, Moscow has tried to restore its balanced policy toward Seoul and Pyongyang. Since 1995, Moscow has been making efforts to mend fences. During a visit by Foreign Minister Ivanov to North Korea in February 2000, a new cooperation treaty was signed, emphasizing trade while insidiously leaving some room for military cooperation. Russia proposed that South and North Korea build a railway network connecting the divided peninsula and extending to Siberia. The Russian government also made an emphatic gesture of return to the Korean question by announcing shortly before the Korean summit the forthcoming visit by its president, Vladimir Putin, to North Korea.

Nevertheless, Russia has limited resources with which to help North Korea. North Korea, for its part, is concentrating its attention on the US as a source of support and aid. Meanwhile, the South Korean government has attempted to rehabilitate ROK–Russian relations, which were strained by Russia's expulsion of a South Korean diplomat and the subsequent diplomatic haggle. President Kim Dae Jung visited Russia in 1999 to place South Korean–Russian relations back on the right track. To South Korea, a truly effective arrangement of peace on the Korean Peninsula requires full support from Russia. President Kim has requested Russia's understanding of and cooperation in his engagement policy toward the North. He has also suggested that a six-party security framework be initiated in the future, and this recommendation received positive response from the Russian government. [13]

Russia is still in the process of difficult transition toward a more open and democratic society with a market economy. In geopolitical terms, after losing much of the European part of the former Soviet Union and facing determined NATO expansion,[14] Russia is forced to become more Asian (Zhebin, 1997). However, it faces tough competition in Asia, where Japan dominates in trade and investment, China commands diplomatic and political influence, and the US maintains military superiority. Russia knows it is advantageous to maintain good relations with the US, Japan and China. It seems to have become an object for, rather than a key actor in, regional politics. Especially because Russia's economic potential is noticeably below that of the former USSR, Russia is unable to ensure military parity in the Far East; its foremost task will therefore be to maintain its military presence in the area at a level adequate to preserve the status quo.

The four major powers prefer the status quo in the region because of the price they pay for any radical change. In general, they tend to be reactive rather than proactive regarding issues of the Korean Peninsula. Accordingly, the key factor that determines change on the Peninsula is North Korea's attitude and behavior. In a major departure from its decades-long isolationist policy, North Korea is rapidly returning to the international community by mending its relations with two traditional allies and making gestures of rapprochement to European and Asian nations. Included on the list of countries to which Pyongyang has made diplomatic advances are Italy, Australia, the Philippines, France, Taiwan, Thailand, Great Britain and Germany. Because North Korea cannot take advantage of such major power conflicts as the Sino-Soviet, Sino-US, or Sino-Japanese disputes which existed during the Cold War era, it sees improving relations with the

United States and Japan as the only way out of its diplomatic isolation and economic hardship. The North Korean leadership accepted South Korea's proposal of the summit partly because they wanted to put psychological pressure on the US and Japan to accelerate the improvement in relations with the North. North Korea also still depends on China for survival. As mentioned above, general cooperation among the major powers on the issue of the Korean Peninsula will create a convergence of interests. It requires increased consultations, discussions, and coordination between South Korea on the one hand and the major powers on the other.

ROK'S SUNSHINE POLICY

Military Threat from the North

The conservatives in South Korea believe that, even after the death of Kim Il Sung and despite its moribund economy and diplomatic isolation, North Korea has not abandoned its strategy to overthrow South Korea and finally to communize the entire peninsula (Ministry of Defense, 1999). Yet, because of its military and economic superiority, South Korea's deepest concern is not that it be overtaken by the North. South Korea is more anxious about the possibility that North Korea, feeling cornered, would desperately lash out with military provocation. This fear is not unfounded. Indeed, realizing that it cannot compete with the South using conventional military capabilities, the North has been focusing on developing weapons of mass destruction, and the possibility of its waging a suicide war cannot be discounted. Should leaders be pushed to the verge of regime collapse, there is no telling what threat to national security may result from the North's all-or-nothing attitude (Ministry of Unification, Republic of Korea, 1999); it is also possible for North Korea to initiate limited low-intensity warfare to dilute the seriousness of the conflict and leave little room for involvement by the United States.

North Korea's military strategy toward the South is short-term blitzkrieg. This aims at creating great panic in the South in the early stage of a war by launching simultaneous attacks in the forward and rear areas, plunging quickly and deeply into the South with maneuver forces to take the initiative in the war, and thus sweeping the entire South before the arrival of USFK reinforcements. Because of the US military capability, South Korea's human and material potential, the ROK–US alliance and joint military posture, and the sentiment of the UN and the international community, blitzkrieg is regarded as the only strategy it could use for a war. For the sake of this strategy, North Korea continues to reinforce its offensive military capability and deploys its main forces in an offensive posture that can easily be converted into a wartime military system when needed. In particular, the North would create a state of pandemonium in both front and rear areas simultaneously. In this fashion, it would attempt to invade the South by a coup de main using WMDs and special operations forces to attack areas with concentrated South Korean military units as well as metropolitan cities and major industrial facilities.[15] North Korea has recently decreased conventional weapons, increased mass-destructive asymmetric weapons that can be produced at a low cost, and modernized weapons.[16] In this regard, military threats against the South still remain as serious on the Peninsula. In fact, South Korea is already within range of North Korea's Scud and *Rodong* missiles. Even the *Daepodong* missile has grave implications for South Korea in that its development would lead to a shift in military balance in North Korea's favor. Some people express fear that if a second Korean War ignited, the US and Japan would not want to be involved because of the *Daepodong*'s ability to hold at least some US territory and all of Japan at risk.[17]

Yet, North Korea also has a fundamental dilemma. It cannot survive materially without economic reform. But if the regime begins any serious reform and becomes exposed to the outside world, its survival will be threatened. The same fear of undermining itself prevents the government from pursuing market-oriented economic reforms, even though it seeks a Chinese or Vietnamese formula of political recognition with economic resuscitation. After nine straight years of economic contraction, the economy of North Korea was considered the most disturbed in the world, all but ceasing to function. Yet, the DPRK economy began to register positive growth in 1999 for the first time in nine years. The DPRK's gross domestic product (GDP) grew by up to 3 percent in 1999. Its rebound from a nine-year contraction since 1990 was propelled by steady foreign aid and a recovery in agricultural and manufacturing output. North Korea officially declared that it would become an economically prosperous and militarily powerful state. Since the beginning of 2000, North Korea has been undertaking omni-directional diplomacy with European and Southeast Asian countries beyond the scope of the four major powers' diplomacy. This behavior reflects the urgency of economic rehabilitation and, in a sense, some psychological confidence on behalf of the leadership in dealing with domestic matters. Nevertheless, it is the conventional wisdom that North Korea may continue to muddle through for a considerable amount of time and, accordingly, amid all the discussion of "soft" and "hard landings" in recent years, the pattern of diplomacy has been one of "no landing," and just muddling through.

In order to tackle the North Korean nuclear and missile issues, and provide a more stable security environment on the Korean Peninsula, the Perry report in October 1999 articulated a comprehensive engagement with a two-path strategy. It accepts the existence of North Korea and the strong power grip of Kim Jong Il as a stark reality, urging the administration to concentrate more on peace and tension reduction instead of change on the Peninsula. It is a big departure from the assumption in the past that North Korea is teetering on the verge of collapse with a basket-case economy and that time is on the US and South Korea's side. Nobody can tell whether it will succeed, but all reasonable diplomatic options must be exhausted before moving to horrendous practices including military measure (Manning, 1999).

Gains and Losses of the Engagement Policy

Seoul understands the North's survival game plan well. The challenge, then, is to construct policies that protect the national security of the South against the North's belligerence while simultaneously coaxing the North to expand engagement with the international community. The core assumptions of South Korea's engagement policy are rather simple. Given the present level of mutual distrust and the long history of confrontation between the two Koreas, engagement will require patience and consistency to bear fruit. Individual acts of provocation must be firmly dealt with as national security threats. In brief, the Sunshine policy is a strategy with which to forge an environment suitable for leading the North to opt voluntarily for a path of reform and change. According to the South Korean government, this policy is inspired by the détente strategy counting on the emergence of the North Korean equivalent of Gorbachev, a regime shift in the North, and an end to the Cold War on the Peninsula. Based on these assumptions, the government has pushed the principle of separation between politics and business. On the business side, the Hyundai business tycoon, Chung Ju Young, is developing industrial parks and tourism at Mt Kumkang. Tourists at Mt Kumkang are numerous, as are South Koreans visiting other parts of the North. With all this inter-Korean exchange and the role of the non-governmental organization (NGO) sector in humanitarian aid increasing, North Korea is becoming dependent on South Korea even without state-to-state interconnectedness (Chung, 2000).

President Kim also made it clear that his own policies can succeed only in conjunction with the improvement of the North's relations with the US and Japan. Thus, the Kim government, for its part, has relaxed or even eliminated its linkage politics between North–South Korean relations and North Korea's diplomatic ties with the US or Japan. Kim assumed that improved ties with the US and Japan would eventually help bring North Korea out of isolation and that the sudden collapse of North Korea is not desirable for the ROK. In other words, the South Korean government, rather than pursuing containment of the North, is taking measures to transform the DPRK gradually through aggressive "engagement" policies. The Perry report was in fact reflecting much of South Korea's comprehensive engagement policy, as a way to tackle the pending missile issue in the near term and to reduce mutual threat in the long run.[18]

Although President Kim neither advocates nor predicts a collapse of the North, as Kim Young-Sam did, the Sunshine Policy has been frankly explained as a policy that will lead to reform of the North Korean system. "Reform," to North Korean leaders, however, means replacing the present leadership with new leaders beholden to the South as a result of dependent economic relations with Seoul. While useful in selling Kim's policies to South Korean and foreign audiences, the Sunshine Policy has had an extremely counterproductive impact on North Korea. For this reason, while Pyongyang is eager to get infusions of cash, investment and other economic help from the South, it scrutinizes each transaction suspiciously to minimize any resulting dependency (Harrison, 1999). North Korea has been pursuing a revised version of the separation of economics from politics. The major lesson of German reunification for Pyongyang has been to use barbed wire to inhibit person-to-person exchanges and cooperation, while allowing isolated projects that provide the foreign exchange necessary for its survival.

North Korea's hostility toward the Sunshine Policy reflects its fear of the policy itself; it was accordingly a big surprise when North Korea ultimately accepted the inter-Korean summit in April 2000. The acceptance was a response to President Kim's Berlin Proposal in which he unveiled the commitment to assist the North in rebuilding its ailing economy and supporting its agricultural sector if only DPRK accepted Seoul's proposal for resuming government-level contact in earnest.[19] Given the strategic dilemma Pyongyang faces, it is a mystery why North Korea finally agreed to the summit. North Korea is still caught helplessly between the necessity for an economic opening to salvage its faltering economy and the threat that capitalistic contamination could pose, leaving the regime's legitimacy in doubt. Its attempts to attract foreign investment were nullified in the past by the fear of capitalist contagion. From the North's perspective, the Sunshine Policy was merely a more subtle and clever way to achieve the goal of absorption than the cruder approach of Kim's immediate predecessor.

Having weathered the economic and famine-related crisis of the mid to later 1990s, yet still in dire economic straits, the North may view the summit and the anticipated South Korean "payoff" as a means to secure resources without fundamental economic reform. From North Korea's standpoint, after six months of meetings with the US to arrange higher-level talks to initiate the policy course recommended by the Perry Report, progress has come to a halt, perhaps because starting on the path that Perry has offered would require Pyongyang to make concessions, reducing its military threat, and particularly its ballistic missile program. Rather than taking these difficult steps Pyongyang views as making it lose face or compromising its interests, North Korea may have decided to look elsewhere for support. Such a move would not only hold the promise of obtaining additional free food and other economic assistance, but may also provide North Korean leverage on the US – or a cushion if a more conservative US administration emerges after the November Presidential election (Manning, 2000).

Whatever the motivations of the summit, and however slow and difficult it may be to implement the agreements, the summit at least opened a line of communication between the two leaders. But it is premature to believe that trust and confidence have been built all of a sudden and that an era of cooperation has arrived. Nor is it realistic to expect that unification is imminent. The large-scale economic assistance to the North that may result from the talks could help sustain the viability of the Pyongyang regime (Han, 2000). To South Korea, the summit is a dramatic breakthrough, a seizing of Korean diplomatic initiative after seven years of US-centered diplomacy on the Korean Peninsula. But the government has much work ahead. It must maintain the momentum established during the trip, and push for concrete agreements both in the area of economic cooperation, and more importantly, on a framework for peace and expanded people-to-people contacts, on the one hand. To critics, the summit announcement was a cynical pre-election political maneuver, or worse, a dangerous give-way. In fact, the way it was announced was criticized as a shameless trick to win votes because the announcement so closely preceded the April 2000 general election in South Korea (Mufson, 2000). On the other hand, the US fears that Seoul will move too far, too fast with Pyongyang without addressing the nuclear and missile matters that preoccupy Washington.

The task of dismantling the Cold-War structure on the Korean Peninsula will require much energy and endurance. No one argues that the Sunshine Policy is so flawed in its long-term implications that it should be abandoned. Positive outcomes from the engagement policy may require incurring political costs. The breakthrough in achieving the summit meeting can be attributed to President Kim's wisdom and long-term vision. The bottom line is that there is no alternative to the engagement policy toward the North. In fact, something akin to the Sunshine Policy has been in place since the 1970s. South Korea has always had moments of sunshine and rain.

This open-ended policy has no benchmark to gauge success and garner political support, let alone provisions for a possible collapse of North Korea and therefore any crisis management mechanisms. If the South Korean government really intends to accomplish peaceful coexistence and *de facto* reunification of the Korean Peninsula, a situation where the two Koreas allow exchanges and support each other while maintaining their respective identities, the South Korean government should not over-advertise the Sunshine Policy. The key tenets of the engagement policy should be separation from domestic politics and focus on long-term benefits. The evaluation of the policy should be in the hands of the future generation. Unless the Kim Dae-Jung government adopts a future-oriented and far-sighted perspective on this policy, engagement will lose momentum despite the epoch-making effort for peaceful coexistence and eventual reunification on the Korean Peninsula.

PROSPECTS

So far, security developments in Northeast Asia have been positive, at least superficially. But it is important to remember that seemingly independent incidents can interact and cascade to produce disproportionately large consequences. The fundamental variables that define peace and security in the region remain largely unchanged (Kanter, 2000). The key variable is North Korea's own policies and domestic development. The progress of the Four Party Talks and the high-level US–DPRK talks, as well as any government-level talks between the two Koreas, are fully dependent on the attitude and behavior of North Korea. North Korea will maintain its unique regime by all means for a considerable amount of time. There is no alternative to comprehensive engagement toward the North not because it can lead the North to change, as South Korea wishes, but because it is the most realistic option of all.

No one can predict with complete success the future scenario of North Korea. Although the Berlin Agreement on the missile issue and the Perry initiative are the right steps to take for the stability of the Peninsula, the progress of US–DPRK improvements in relations will proceed slowly, particularly with the advent of the Bush Administration. The possibility of a positive inter-Korean relationship is not fully guaranteed. There is every reason to be skeptical about the implementation of the summit agreement, considering the volatility of the North Korean regime itself. There is no telling how North Korea would respond if it gets too much sunshine too soon. Policymakers should follow principles of reciprocity and caution. The trilateral policy consultation among the US, South Korea and Japan is a success so far, but some observers worry that the interests of the three countries are far from identical, just overlapping in some respects. Somehow, we will face the more uncertain and unpredictable, if not totally pessimistic, future regarding the Korean Peninsula.

The regional security environment will also play a role as a parameter. Regarding the international relations surrounding the Korean Peninsula, the year 2001 will be a turning point. The possibility of Chinese–Taiwanese conflict, whether diplomatic or military, and the consequent involvement of the US in this affair will be another factor concerning South Korea because of its spill-over effect. If there emerges a major power conflict such as US–Chinese tension, North Korea will try to take advantage of it. A strategic coalition between China and Russia against the US–Japanese security reinforcement is also possible, if unlikely, and would adversely affect the stability and prosperity of Northeast Asia. General cooperation among the major powers on the issue of the Korean Peninsula will create a convergence of interests. It is our best chance for a peaceful and prosperous area. It requires increased consultations, discussions, and coordination among all the countries in this area.

NOTES

[1] Executive Summary of the Report of the Commission to Assess the Ballistic Missile Threat to the United States, Pursuant to Public Law 201 104th Congress.

[2] In December 2000, South Korea and the US reached full agreement on terms for revising SOFA, if not satisfactorily, including the provision on criminal jurisdiction over US soldiers accused of serious crimes, and on environmental protection which was strongly emphasized by Korean civic groups.

[3] "Kim Sees Progress in North Korea," *The Washington Times*, Oct. 19, 1999.

[4] Scott Snyder, "US–ROK Relations: Trends at the Opening of the 21st Century," Paper prepared for conference entitled "East Asia and the United States – Current Status and 5-year Outlook" February 17, 2000 Library of Congress, Washington, DC.

[5] Robert A. Scalapino, "Korea – the Options and Perimeters," prepared for the Monterey Institute's international conference on Korea held on February 20–21, 1998.

[6] The ties between the South and Shandong province represent a NET (Natural Economic Territory) of great significance, and one now spreading to adjacent regions of China.

[7] South Korea became the fourth largest exporter to China and the fifth largest importer of Chinese goods. In turn, China became the third largest market and exporter to Korea. In 1997, South Korea became the fourth largest investor country in China with total investment of $4.5 billion.

[8] "Seoul confirms Kim Jong Il's Secret Visit to China," *The Korea Herald*, June 2, 2000.

[9] Kiyoshi Sugawa, "The Changing Nature of Japan's North Korea Policy and Its Implications for Policy Makers," Paper presented at the 14th annual conference: The Council on US–Korean Security Studies, October 27–30, 1999, Arlington, Virginia.

[10] "World Gets Wise to Pyongyang's Nuclear Blackmail–Part Two," *JanesIntelligence Review*, Oct. 1999, p. 36.

[11] The drill, involving 1,200 ROK and Japanese sailors, was one of SAR (search-and-rescue), which began with the arrival and deployment of Japanese frigates in South Korean waters.

[12] Scott Snyder, Testimony Before the Asia Pacific Subcommittee, House Committee on International Relations Hearing on "North Korea: Leveraging Uncertainty," March 16, 2000.

[13] In the eight-point joint statement summarizing his talks with President Kim, Yeltsin expressed support for Kim's policy to promote inter-Korean contacts and productive dialogue. In the meanwhile, North Korea blasted President Kim for seeking to win support from foreign countries, characterizing this effort as proof of his subordination to external forces.

[14] Russia has been deeply offended by NATO's eastward expansion. Emphasizing security concerns, including those caused by NATO's activities in Europe, is becoming a major card for both pro-government and opposition political forces in Russia in their struggle for public support.

[15] Ending the war before the reinforcement of the allied forces arrives, the North would try to justify its actions by calling it a civil war started to solve problems within the Peninsula, thus attempting to distort international opinion and prevent UN and allied intervention.

[16] Since 1993, the North has reinforced its artillery capability in the forward area; now it has finished deploying 170mm self-propelled artillery with a range of over 50km and 240mm MRLS in the central and western areas, and is in the process of increasing deployment of these two weapons systems in the eastern area.

[17] This was North Korean defector Hwang Jang-Yop's remark. (See Chung, 1999, p. 35).

[18] Report, Office of the North Korea Policy Coordinator, United States Department of State, "Review of United States Policy Toward North Korea: Findings and Recommendations," Dr William J. Perry, Special Advisor to the President and the Secretary of State, October 12, 1999.

[19] This overture was harshly criticized by the opposition, which claimed that the government is abandoning the existing principle of reciprocity in dealing with the Communist North.

REFERENCES

Abramowitz, Morton I. and James T. Laney (1999), *US Policy Toward North Korea: Next Step,* Report of an Independent Task Force

Sponsored by the Council on Foreign Relations, Washington, DC: Council on Foreign Relations.

Chung, Oknim (1998), *The Origins and Evolution of the Japanese–American Alliance: A Korean Perspective*, Stanford: IIS, Stanford University.

Chung, Oknim (1999), "The North Korea Factor and ROK–US Relationship," *Korea and World Affairs*, 23 (1), 26–44.

Chung, Oknim (2000), "The Sunshine Policy: An Interim Assessment," *Korea and World Affairs*, 24 (1), Spring.

Gertz, Bill (2000), "Russia Sells Missile Technology to North Korea," *The Washington Times*, June 30.

Han, Sung-Joo (2000), "North-South Korea Summit Reflections," *PacNet* 25, June 23.

Harrison, Selig S. (1999), "Sunshine Policy Braves N.K.'s Provocative Tactics," *The Korea Herald*, March 26.

Kanter, Arnold (2000), "Strengthening Security and Stability: Prospects, Problems, and Opportunities," Nautilus Institute, Northeast Asia Peace and Security Network, Special Report.

Manning, Robert A. (1999), "The Enigma of the North," *The Wilson Quarterly,* 23 (3), Summer.

Manning, Robert A. (2000), "The Korean Summit – A Test of Both Kims," Northeast Asia Peace and Security Network, Special Report, May 23.

Ministry of Defense, Republic of Korea (1999), *The Defense White Paper.*

Ministry of Unification, Republic of Korea (1999*), Policy towards North Korea for Peace, Reconciliation and Cooperation.*

Mufson, Steven (2000), "Korean Summit Seen as Election Ploy," *The Washington Post*, April 11.

Snyder, Scott (2000), "US–ROK Relations: Trends at the Opening of the 21st Century," Paper Presented at the Conference Entitled, "East Asia and the United States: Current Status and Five-Year Outlook," the library of Congress, Washington, DC, Feb.17.

Struck, Doug (2000), "Two Koreas Agree To Let Families Visit Relatives," *The Washington Post*, July 1.

Zhebin, Alexander Z. (1997), " The Future of North Korea and Russia's North Korea Policy," *Sasang Quarterly*, Fall, 238–252 (Translated in Korean).

LIST OF ABBREVIATIONS

TMD: Theater Missile Defense
ARF: ASEAN Regional Forum
MIA: Missing in Action
KEDO: the Korean Peninsula Energy Development Organization
NEASD: the Northeast Asian Security Dialogue
ASEAN: Association of Southeast Asian Nations
WMD: Weapons of Mass Destruction
NMD: National Missile Defense
DPRK: the Democratic People's Republic of Korea
WFP: World Food Program
ROK: the Republic of Korea
SOFA: Status of Forces Agreement
R & D: Research and Development
ADB: the Asian Development Bank
TCOG: the Trilateral Coordination and Oversight Group
USSR: the Union of Soviet Socialist Republics
NGO: Non-Governmental Organization

2 Politics, Economics, and the Agreed Framework

Leon V. Sigal

When it comes to the North Korean economy, politics is in the saddle not only in Pyongyang, but also in Seoul and in Washington. What drives the politics of the North Korean issue in Washington is security, not economics. Economic reform will not stand in the way of security interests in dealing with North Korea, nor should it.

The US and South Korea have four main interests in dealing with North Korea at this time: first, they want to ensure that, whatever happens internally in North Korea, the artillery it has placed within range of Seoul is never fired in anger; second, they want to prevent North Korea from acquiring nuclear arms; third, they want to keep North Korea from testing, deploying, and selling any more medium- or longer-range ballistic missiles; and fourth, we seek reconciliation between the two Koreas and the *peaceful* reunification of the peninsula.

The only way of achieving these aims is to test whether or not North Korea is willing to cooperate with the US and South Korea. Coercion will not work. It will only ensure that North Korea deploys more artillery near the DMZ; seeks more aggressively to acquire nuclear arms; and tests, deploys, and sells more missiles.

Some people think it is in the interest of the US and South Korea to encourage the collapse of North Korea. That course is far too risky, especially if the first three aims have not been achieved. Others want to condition aid on reform in North Korea. Yet it would be dangerously doctrinaire to put free market ideology ahead of security. Conditioning economic engagement on North Korean reform is also counter-productive. Change will come to the North when it lets in more outsiders from non-government organization (NGOs) and the international community. Such easing of access is possible only if Pyongyang is willing to cooperate. Again, coercion will not work.

Similarly, South Korea will succeed in its efforts at reconciliation only if it is willing to court North Korea on the North's terms. Kim Dae Jung understands the necessity of such engagement. Others in Seoul see the "sunshine policy" as the way either to remake the North in the South's image or to kill North Korea with kindness. They think Pyongyang is so desperate that it will do what Seoul dictates. They are wrong. Their approach only arouses antagonism in Pyongyang and shuts the door to engagement.

Testing North Korea's willingness to cooperate by diplomatic probe is the only policy with any chance of promoting the national interests of the US and South Korea.

COOPERATION OR CONFRONTATION?

The good news is that, contrary to conventional wisdom around Washington, there is significant evidence that Pyongyang is trying to cooperate with South Korea and the US.

If North Korea had been determined to acquire nuclear arms in the early 1990s, as most experts in Washington believed at the time, it could have shut down its nuclear reactor anytime between 1991 and 1994, removed the spent fuel, and quickly reprocessed it to extract plutonium, the explosive ingredient in nuclear weapons. Yet North Korea did not reprocess any spent fuel after 1991; nor did it shut down its reactor until May of 1994, long after it was expected to do so, and it allowed inspectors from the International Atomic Energy Agency (IAEA) to verify this from mid-1992 on. These actions were a strange way to acquire nuclear arms. North Korea's actions suggest that, starting in 1991, it was restraining itself somewhat in the hopes of concluding a nuclear deal with the US. On November 11, 1993, the North said as much in public.

Similarly, if, as most experts now believe, North Korea is determined to develop, deploy and export longer-range ballistic missiles, it should have been testing and perfecting its No Dong, Taepo Dong-I and Taepo Dong-II missile for the past several years. Yet the North conducted just two tests of ballistic missiles in the past decade – one on May 29, 1993 and the other on August 31, 1998 – and both of them were failures. Again, this pattern of behavior is a strange way to develop new missiles. It suggests instead that North Korea is restraining itself somewhat in the interest of concluding a missile deal with the US. Pyongyang has been expressing such an interest since 1992, both in unofficial discussions with Americans and in its direct talks with US officials. On June 16, 1998, North Korea made this public when it offered to negotiate an end not only to its missile exports but also to its development of missiles. Without more missile tests, it will not have new missiles worth selling or deploying. It coupled that offer with a threat to resume missile tests, a threat it carried out on August 31, 1998, when it launched a three-stage rocket in an unsuccessful attempt to put a satellite into orbit. It threatened to try again in the summer of 1999.

Why is North Korea cooperating? There is no way to know for certain, but probably because North Korea sees that the only way to ensure its security is to change its political relationship with the US, South Korea, and Japan from one of hostility to one of reconciliation. Militarily, South Korea is stronger than its neighbor to the north, even without US help. North Korea fears the growing military might of Japan and, until recently, Japanese diplomacy has done little to dispel that fear. Russia is no longer the North's ally, and it can count on China only if attacked. What better way to restrain South Korea and Japan and provide a counterweight to China than to engage with the US?

Although security considerations are foremost in the minds of the North Koreans, economic matters are also a consideration. The collapse of communism in the Soviet Union and Eastern Europe and the economic transformation of China make North Korea dependent on South Korea and Japan for aid, investment, and trade. Pyongyang began reaching out to Washington, Seoul, and Tokyo in the late 1980s, well before the current economic crisis deepened. When the US tried to impede closer South Korean and Japanese ties to North Korea between 1988 and 1992, Pyongyang learned that Washington holds the key to opening the doors to the World Bank, Asian Development Bank, and economic engagement with the West.

TIT-FOR-TAT

If Pyongyang wants engagement with Washington, then why dig holes and test missiles? Unfortunately, the North Koreans have learned that threats are the only way to get Washington to pay attention and take them seriously – a lesson Washington keeps reinforcing by its own inaction in the absence of such threats. Neglect will only lead to more trouble-making by Pyongyang.

Although the North has held open its nuclear option as leverage for cooperation, it has been punctilious in observing the letter of the Agreed Framework, as demonstrated, for instance, in canning the fuel rods at Yongbyon. Classified intelligence no doubt shows North Korea engaging in activities that concern watchers, but they have to distinguish between threatening to break the Agreed Framework and actually breaking it. North Korea may be deliberately causing alarm by manipulating what the intelligence community is seeing and hearing in order to get the United States to negotiate in earnest.

Why? In Pyongyang's view, Washington has been unwilling to extend cooperation beyond the Agreed Framework, or even to keep its end of the nuclear bargain. The Clinton administration initially understated the funding needed to pay for the heavy fuel oil that it pledged to provide North Korea under the accord in order to get other countries to made up the difference. When it did not, it was slow to seek additional funding from Congress. As a result of Congress's refusal to authorize more funds, fuel deliveries fell behind schedule, and by the end of 1997 the US was not in compliance with the Agreed Framework.

Moreover, construction of the first of two light-water reactors (LWRs), replacements for the reactors that are to be dismantled under the terms of the Agreed Framework, was delayed when previous governments in South Korea and Japan balked at providing the necessary funding. Consistent with the Agreed Framework, this slow start pushed back the removal of up to six bombs' worth of plutonium in the spent nuclear fuel now in North Korea, as well as Pyongyang's obligation to clear up anomalies in the initial material declaration it made to the IAEA. Both of these steps, once regarded as urgent, especially by critics of the Agreed Framework in Washington and Seoul, are now delayed by allied inaction.

Washington has also been hesitant to move beyond the 1994 accord to greater political and economic engagement. To Pyongyang, this reluctance was even worse than the delay in reactor construction. After all, Pyongyang reasoned, if Washington were willing to supply nuclear reactors, improved diplomatic, trade and other ties would surely follow. Yet, until September 1999, the United States had not even taken the modest steps to ease sanctions that the North was led to expect since February 1995 – unfreezing assets seized in the Korean War, allowing commercial loans from American banks, and licensing private investment projects in mining and agriculture.

Absent these steps, North Korea, believing it was adhering to the letter of the Agreed Framework and not getting much in return, began warning in January of 1998 that it might abandon the accord unless Washington proceeded with implementation, including shipping heavy fuel oil in a more timely fashion, speeding up construction of the replacement reactor, and easing economic sanctions. In late April of 1998, the North stopped canning the plutonium-laden spent fuel at Yongbyon, but only after all the 8,000 or so intact fuel rods were put in casks and nothing but nuclear sludge from a few disintegrating rods remained. On May 7 Pyongyang said that maintenance requirements prompted it to "open and adjust" other nuclear facilities, including the reactor, but that it would do so in the presence of IAEA inspectors. The North also hinted it might end its freeze on reprocessing.

The spurt of activity at the suspect underground site at Kumchangni in 1997–98 should be understood in this context. Had North Korea wanted to break the nuclear accord, it could have thrown out the international inspectors, opened the casks, and removed the spent fuel for reprocessing. Instead, the North resumed excavation at the site, which US intelligence has been observing for over a decade and reassessed last spring to be nuclear-related. Even if that assessment had been correct, such an installation would have taken years to build – hardly a sign of Pyongyang's eagerness to break the Agreed Framework.

After talks in New York in early September of 1998, Pyongyang allowed the canning of the spent fuel to resume. It granted American inspectors access to the underground site in return for additional food it may have been led to expect for more than two years. The inspectors found nothing nuclear amiss at Kumchangni. Granting them access also established a precedent for dealing with other suspect sites in the future.

In short, North Korea has been threatening to break the October 1994 accord without actually violating it. Pyongyang appears to have been cooperating when the US cooperates and retaliating when it reneges in the hope of getting Washington to negotiate in earnest.

Pyongyang may have been playing tit-for-tat, not blackmail, on missiles as well when it began preparations for another missile test in the summer of 1999, then agreed in Berlin to suspend testing in September. The only way to determine North Korea's intentions is to pursue diplomatic probes to see whether or not Pyongyang is willing to negotiate an end to its medium- and longer-range missile program.

What might North Korea want in return? Above all, it seeks a new political relationship with the US that puts an end to enmity. Investment in agriculture, including better seed, fertilizer, and technical assistance through the UN Development Plan would enable it to grow more of its own food. Investment in mining and other sectors might permit it to sell some products to the world for hard currency, enabling it to buy much-needed food and other necessities. Investment in its infrastructure, perhaps through the Asian Development Bank, would help it upgrade its electrical power grid and provide electricity in the interim. The North Korean economy is now at such a low level of activity that many forms of investment would help, even in the absence of economic reform.

The best way to ensure peace and security in Northeast Asia is to move beyond the October 1994 Agreed Framework and seek a deal to end North Korea's missile program. To do so, we need to abandon the crime-and-punishment approach to nonproliferation – acting in the belief that the way to get states not to acquire weapons of mass destruction is to demonize them as outlaws and make threats to compel them to disarm. This approach is unlikely to succeed anywhere, especially in North Korea. It also obstructs diplomatic give-and-take with North Korea, which has some chance of success.

The US must do more than just demand that North Korea stop digging tunnels, testing new missiles and exporting missile technology. Pyongyang is unwilling to give away something for nothing. As demonstrated by the Agreed Framework, however, North Korea does not set an unreasonable price, and it is prepared to live up to its end of the bargain so long as the US does as well.

Dealing with North Korea will also require us to suspend our economic beliefs for now, however convinced we are of their correctness. Pyongyang will not play if we dogmatically insist on our rules. South Koreans should readily understand this point, having resisted IMF efforts to impose its economic doctrines on their economy.

3 Putting an Edge on Post-Perry Policy

Katy Oh

The topic of this conference is a very serious one: where do we go from here – "here" being the release of former Secretary William Perry's review of US policy toward North Korea. Apart from what one may think of the content of Perry's report, which at least in its unclassified version seems to provide continuity with the previous US policy of cautious engagement, the fact that the report was mandated by dissatisfied members of the US Congress signifies that the Clinton administration's policy toward North Korea is in trouble.

Framing a post-Perry policy, or commenting on the implementation of the policy he has presented, requires considering both short-term and long-term plans to deal with North Korea, plans that simultaneously address global nonproliferation issues, peacekeeping on the Korean peninsula, humanitarian aid, and human rights. Current policy on North Korea, as embodied in former Ambassador Robert Gallucci's Agreed Framework, was formulated in the relatively forgiving context of assumptions by some people (including Gallucci) that the DPRK would soon collapse (in this instance, soon after the collapse of communism in Eastern Europe). If indeed one expects an imminent North Korean collapse, policy on North Korea needs to be adequate only for the short term. On the contrary, however, one of the conclusions the Perry Report reaches is that the current policy is unsustainable because North Korea is not likely to collapse in the near term.

Kim Il Sung's son, Kim Jong Il, seems to have consolidated his leadership position, even in the face of almost unimaginable economic hardship in North Korea, so US policy must take the long term into account. The debate over whether North Korea will collapse, reform or continue muddling along has been summarized by an article Ralph Hassig

28

and I co-authored for the March–April 1999 issue of *Asian Survey*, based on a report I wrote for the Council on Foreign Relations North Korea Task Force. The article summarizes the problems that have brought the DPRK so low, and presents the opinions of several dozen specialists about North Korea's future. The consensus is that the Kim Jong Il regime will continue to muddle through, doing just enough to keep the ruling elite in power and the country from collapsing from within.

In order to inform my predictions, I interviewed some two dozen North Korean defectors, including former Secretary Hwang Jang Yop, asking what future they saw for North Korea. Not one of them predicted a substantial economic reform – not even as much as the gradual Chinese economic reform underway since 1978. Nor did any of them foresee a collapse of North Korean society or any sort of revolt against the regime. And only a few (including initially Hwang Jang Yop) saw any real danger of North Korea striking out at South Korea in a desperate bid to end its troubles. The consensus was that continuity rather than change is what we should expect from North Korea. Yet, the nature of the current North Korea regime is so "repulsive" (to quote a US AID official) that continuity presents numerous challenges to the US and to North Korea's neighbors, most especially South Korea and Japan.

Supplementing the testimony of defectors and the opinions of specialists on North Korea are the personal views of four foreigners who have had first-hand experience in North Korea. Quite varied in nature, they are a Swiss government official who visited North Korea, an Italian businessman with sympathetic leanings toward North Korea, a Korean-American businessman interested in doing business in North Korea from his base in New York, and a Korean-American woman with relatives in North Korea.

The Swiss told me very simply, "I saw *1984* as it actually exists today." North Korea in his eyes was an authoritarian and arid society.

The Italian businessman, whose impressions were relayed to me through a mutual friend, gives us a glimpse of the nature of North Korea's dictator, Kim Jong Il. Kim invited the businessman for lunch on a North Korean pleasure fishing boat. "Kim was a very articulate speaker, interested in art, fashion and food. He was the chubbiest person on board, and the only one who spoke freely without looking around." From this brief encounter with the reclusive Kim, one might infer that Kim is a man apart from everyone else in North Korea, confident of his power, and able to present a charming face, just as his father did.

The Korean-American businessman had good connections with North Korean officials as well as large American companies, and was accordingly welcomed warmly in North Korea. One day, outside his Pyongyang hotel, he watched as security guards chased off some onlookers with kicks and shoves. Perhaps they were friends or relatives of hotel staff, or maybe just curious citizens, but they were treated like criminals. At dinner that evening, a 15-course feast that included duck and sashimi, the businessman raised the unpleasant issue with one of his hosts, who casually responded that no concern should be given to such people, because in the face of economic hardship North Korea could afford to lose as many as five million of its citizens.

A final telling episode occurred in 1992 at a conference I attended in the United States. Two North Koreans had been invited to the conference to present their propagandistic views on the DPRK. During a question-and-answer session, a Korean-American woman related her frustration over a recent visit she had paid to North Korea. She told the audience how she had for so long dreamed of returning to visit her hometown in North Korea. Going into Korea, she filled her suitcase with items she knew her relatives would appreciate, including food and chocolates, but she was not prepared for the level of poverty she found. After giving away all her presents, she gave away everything else she had brought with her. Her North Korean twin sister looked like an aged aunt, with a frail body and a wrinkled face. Recalling this heart-rending experience, the woman at the conference addressed a question to the North Korean delegates: "How can you claim that things are so good in North Korea? Why do you stand here and lie to the world? Why won't you let foreigners help your people?"

At first the head North Korean delegate avoided her gaze, looking down at the table. Then he suddenly lifted his head and shot back at her: "We are not here to debate and answer questions, but to present our views. We don't have any responsibility to debate." But in his face and trembling body I could read not only anger but pain, for he could not tell the truth. The audience was silent, and the master of ceremonies soon moved on to another topic, closing the window on a glimpse of the horror of life in North Korea – for both the masses and the cadres.

This last incident occurred ten years ago. Over the years, despite hints of change and periodic peaceful overtures from the North Koreans, little has changed. It is naive to expect substantial reform to originate from the Kim Jong Il regime, which has had six years since the death of Kim Il Sung to adopt new policies. The announced premise of the 1994 Agreed Framework, and the hope of the Perry Report, is that engagement on the part of the US, South Korea and Japan will open up and change the North. This engagement is presented in the form of a "comprehensive agreement" or "package deal," in which short-term inducements are intended to build up the confidence and reduce the distrust of the North Koreans, who will finally shed their authoritarian "coats" in the warming rays of the sun. This I believe will not happen.

A comprehensive agreement is too optimistic. It gives the North Korean leaders time to benefit from the short-term inducements to strengthen their regime while postponing changes that will alleviate the suffering of the North Korean people. It freezes but does not eliminate weapons programs. Time is at first on the side of the Kim Jong Il regime, which can delay and renege on agreements for decades with little fear of adverse consequences on the security of their regime. If foreign aid does not come this year, it will come next year. If more North Koreans die in the meantime, their loss is of little consequence to their leaders.

Rather than enter into long-term, gradual engagement agreements with the DPRK, the United States should be negotiating tough, limited agreements to achieve short-term goals. At the same time, we should pursue a more aggressive game plan to unseat the Kim Jong Il regime. Four specific recommendations follow, and conclude my remarks.

First, negotiations over a freeze on North Korea's nuclear and missile programs (presumably followed by chemical and biological weapons freezes) have been conducted in an atmosphere of unnecessary panic. The Kim regime is often seen as so crazy that if it had even one nuclear weapon, the country might actually deploy it. Ballistic missiles with highly questionable accuracy are seen as threatening US territory. If Washington insists on paying North Korea to freeze these programs, the effect of these payments on prolonging the hostile Kim regime must be carefully weighed against the rather limited danger these weapons actually pose to the US or its allies.

Second, while we should be prepared to do all we can to alleviate the suffering of the North Koreans, we should not be intimidated by their government into providing donations that never reach the people. Provisions for humanitarian aid must be negotiated just as toughly as negotiations over weapons freezes.

Third, while negotiations are proceeding, without any expectation of effecting significant change in North Korea, parallel efforts must be made to reach out with information (perhaps tied to foreign aid) to the North Korean people, so they can learn about the reality of their government and the outside world, and develop the desire and the ideas to change their lives.

Finally, and most importantly, with a policy of humanitarian aid and enlightenment underway, we should be confident that the threat posed by the hostility of the North Korean government is being adequately, if patiently, addressed, and resist the temptation to engage in the kind of saber-rattling (suggested as a fall-back policy in the Perry Report) that might trap the United States and North Korea in a spiraling conflict. In any such conflict, it is the South and North Korean people who will suffer most from war, not the Americans. Military confrontation is not a moral option.

4 Vietnam and Korea: Challenges of Opening Up for Development

Bradley O. Babson

This chapter examines whether or not the experiences of Vietnam, as it has opened up to the international community over the past decade, are of any value in predicting the probable course of North Korea, which is now at the point where opening up to the rest of the world seems imminent. After years of isolation and economic distress, both countries now seek improved relations with the international community. It seems timely to examine the dynamics of similarities and differences in the experiences of these two countries from a number of historical and cultural perspectives, and to reflect on how best to engage them as they enter a new phase of relations with the outside world.

HISTORICAL CONTEXT

The isolation of both North Korea and Vietnam is rooted in nationalistic civil wars that emerged after World War II both from colonial experiences with the Japanese and the French and from interventions of large powers engaged in the geo-political struggle of the Free World and communism. Following the Korean and Vietnam wars, both countries slid into protracted isolation from the Western World and developed throughout the Cold War dependencies on political and economic relations with the Soviet Union and China. The latter decided to break its own isolation from the West in the early 1980s and to pursue new economic policies more open to market forces. This decision provided the context for accepting the possibility of change, but did not itself trigger a similar response in either Vietnam or North Korea. The incentive to ease away from isolation has been driven for both countries primarily by economic distress triggered by the loss of

Soviet aid on top of economic policies that failed to deliver basic economic welfare for the people.

Both Vietnam in the late 1980s and North Korea in the early 1990s thus arrived at a situation where survival of their regimes depended upon finding ways to deal with potential economic collapse. However similar the economic causes, the leaders of these countries have responded quite differently, with important implications for strategies to encourage them to make changes that would alleviate the hardships faced by their own people and become more normal members of the international community.

NATIONALISM

Both Ho Chi Minh and Kim Il Sung were fierce nationalists. They were attracted to communism in large part because it gave them the political framework and external support they needed to make credible claims to national leadership in the aftermath of World War II and the collapse of Japanese occupation of both countries. The game after World War II was the assertion of new national leadership after decades of colonial rule in both countries. However, the cloaking of nationalism under communist affiliations reduced natural American sympathies for self-determination in post-colonial Asia. While both the Korean war and the Vietnam war are portrayed as battlegrounds for the struggle between the forces of communism and the Free World, they both also have roots in the struggle to assert national identity against the historical forces of occupation and oppression. Indeed, the leadership of both countries has historically been more focused on the nationalistic aspects of their struggle than on the advancement of global communism.

In today's dialogue on economic reform and integration of Vietnam and North Korea with the international economic community – in the areas of foreign investment, expanded trade relations, humanitarian aid, and official development assistance, these nationalistic aspects are strong factors affecting the language and behavior of the leadership. In the case of Vietnam, the economic reform program has entered a new stage, where domestic savings and investment rates must be raised for sustainable long-term growth, external debt must be controlled to maintain sustainable external account balances and avoid the risks of financial crisis like the one that has just swept Asia, and the capability to manage modern government institutions and commercial enterprises must be improved to increase the efficiency of public and private management. All of these goals receive strong support from the upper levels of the Communist Party – not because the members are born-again capitalists, but because these themes play strongly on their concern for national strength based on self-reliance, discipline, and independence from the excessive influence of foreigners. It is important to understand these motivations when dealing with the Vietnamese.

In the case of North Korea, a strong sense of nationalistic independence has been inculcated in the Juche philosophy of self-reliance, and is more at the root of North Korean self-understanding than communist principles of economic organization and participation in the broader international communist movements. Some would argue that the legitimacy of the regime rests on its ability to sustain the belief that North Korea can be intrinsically self-reliant and not dependent on relationships with foreign powers. The economic reality is that this independence has not been the case historically and cannot be the case in the future. For well over a decade, the North Korean economy has been dependent on subsidies from abroad – first in the counter-trade with Russia and China, and more recently in the KEDO agreements to provide fuel oil and international humanitarian assistance for food and medical supplies. Accepting the necessity for economic interdependence with market economies is essential if North Korea is to break out of its present predicament. However, for the current regime, control over national sovereignty and identity is the key issue for survival of the North Korean State, and is more important than the principle of economic socialism per se. For this reason, I believe that the Government will increasingly come to accept the necessity of adopting market economic principles if they can be introduced in a way that is consistent with these nationalistic imperatives.

CULTURE

Despite a common Confucian value system derived from historical relations with China, a striking difference between Vietnam and North Korea is the impact of culture on the policies of the Party and the behavior of the leadership. Vietnamese culture is rooted in the value placed on consensus over personality. While Ho Chi Minh is an important figure for the modern Vietnamese national identity, the upper echelons of the Party – notably the Politburo, Standing Committee, and National Assembly – are carefully balanced to represent all the major interest groups: North, Central, South; rural, urban; reformers, conservatives; ethnic Kinh, minorities, and so on. The role of individual personalities is far less important than the interests represented. Every group has a voice, and decisions are often delayed until a genuine consensus can be formed. Lack of consensus can lead to inaction, which has proved very frustrating to foreign partners, for whom "time is money." The Vietnamese are also blessed with a future-oriented pragmatism and are willing to admit errors; when proven wrong they are capable of adopting practical solutions and finding the ideological rationale later. These cultural factors are extremely important in understanding how major decisions are made in Vietnam.

North Korea, on the other hand, values leading personalities, authoritarian rule, and compliance among the population to the dictates from above. A holdover from five centuries of stable rule under a single dynasty, these values reflect how deeply ingrained is the idea of the Divine King, who represents Heaven on Earth. With the succession of the Dear Leader to the Great Leader, North Korea is the only Communist State to have embraced a father-to-son succession – not very Communist, but very traditionally Korean. Economic policies cannot be challenged on their performance or logic, but only with the blessing of the Leader. The options of the technocrats struggling to save the failing economy are accordingly severely limited, and a solution to the political threats to the regime must be found before we see more rational economic policies supported by the leadership.

COLONIAL EXPERIENCE

Both the Communist regimes of Vietnam and North Korea were the successors to colonial regimes – France and Japan, respectively. But their experiences under colonialism and the implications for future economic policy are radically different. Both counties received capital investment, new technologies, and new ways of organizing economic activities. In Vietnam, these were primarily in agriculture, for example in the establishment of rubber plantations, in order to feed the markets of Europe. While the Vietnamese were exploited, they also learned new skills, especially in the operations of market economies, and many received education in Europe, where they assimilated Western intellectual history and rationality. In North Korea, by contrast, the Japanese occupation was designed mainly to extract raw materials and labor contributions to feed the build-up of Japanese industry. While the Japanese made significant capital investments and imported their educational methods, North Koreans were not exposed to commercial practices to any great extent. As a result, they received very little education and practical experience in the precepts of market economies. As a result of these different colonial experiences, the Vietnamese were much better equipped to design economic reforms and adapt to new economic policies than the North Koreans, who are terribly handicapped by a widespread ignorance of even the most fundamental concepts of market economics and finance.

CIVIL WAR

It is sometimes easy to forget that both the Korean war and the Vietnam war were civil wars marked by massive foreign intervention. A key difference in the two wars is that in the Korean war the intervention was massive on both sides – with the UN/US for the South, and China for the North. In the Vietnam war, the US intervention for the South was not matched by manpower from China or Russia, although both were major arms suppliers and political supporters. One consequence of this history is the self-assurance the Vietnamese exhibit as the decisive victors. This has allowed them to deal with the process of opening the economy to join the international community in a mature way. The donor group meetings that the World Bank has chaired in recent years have been characterized by a substantive dialogue between the Vietnamese authorities and the donor community on the economic problems and the policies and efforts needed to address them. These have been widely viewed as open and constructive exchanges, made possible by the willingness of the Government to engage on substantive issues without defensiveness. On the other hand, the Party in Vietnam has been unwilling to permit open internal discussion of the meaning of civil conflict and its impact on Vietnamese society as a result of the war and subsequent reunification policies. The ability of the society to heal its wounds is limited, and there remains a major piece of unfinished homework in the process of nation-building after reunification.

For North Korea, the civil war is still not over. To some extent, the legitimacy of the regime rests on its claim to succeed eventually in reuniting Korea on its own terms – a dim prospect given the economic collapse and international commitment to the security of South Korea. While North Korea professes self-reliance as its central virtue, it has in fact been anchored in dependence on China for military support during the war and for political and economic support ever since; thus, unlike the Vietnamese, the North Koreans are in fact much less self-assured in their dealings with the international community, often resorting to belligerent and unproductive positions that reveal their fundamental insecurities. Resolving the civil war on the Korean peninsula is a long-term process. There now seems to be an emerging consensus that such resolution requires accepting a two-state framework and building economic and social relations between the two countries over time. This is the essence of Kim Dae Jung's

"Sunshine Policy," and the foundation for the new thinking in the US government that is reshaping American policy towards the peninsula.

CRISIS

Crisis has played a key role in the economic life of both Vietnam and North Korea since the late 1980s, yet the response to crisis and the use of crisis to advance reforms have also been very different in the two cases.

For Vietnam, economic crisis in the mid to late 1980s threatened the legitimacy of the Party. Facing a decline in Soviet economic assistance, an economic embargo imposed by the West, and no recourse to the resources of the international financial institutions, Vietnam was forced to consider the option of embarking on an economic reform policy without significant international support. The Doi Moi or Renovation policy that was forged under these conditions gave the reformers a chance to prove their ideas. The success of this policy has been well documented, but by 1996 Vietnam was no longer in crisis, and the issue facing the 8th Party Congress was: "If we are no longer in crisis, why continue to reform?" The slow-down in reform actions ever since has been a matter of considerable concern to the international community.

The crisis in North Korea has been even more dramatic than that of Vietnam, but with completely different characteristics. The economic crisis of North Korea is a free-fall decline in GDP since the late 1980s and continuing to the present with no signs of abatement. Rather than making this crisis an opportunity to initiate reforms, the North Korean leadership used it to reassert the legitimacy of their policy of self-reliance, defending their system in the face of the collapse of their trade relations with the Soviet Union, hardening of terms of trade with China, and a succession of natural calamities that undermined agricultural production. The North Korean response to these external contributions to their economic crisis was to deny that their own economic policies were at fault and to create new crises to obtain new forms of international economic assistance. The nuclear crisis of 1994 can been seen through economists' eyes as a way of replacing the lost subsidies on fuel oil from the Russian trade with new subsidies resulting from the KEDO agreements. The appeals for international food aid can likewise be seen as a means of replacing agricultural subsidies from China, the terms of which were hardened after China normalized relations with South Korea in 1992, with food aid from the wider international community, of which the US is the largest donor. The bottom line is that while Vietnam has used crisis to advance economic reforms, North Korea has used crisis to avoid them.

WHERE WE ARE TODAY AND PROSPECTS FOR THE FUTURE

Vietnam has been reforming for ten years. By the mid 1990s, the success of these reforms was widely acclaimed in the international community, and Vietnam had re-established credibility as a country that was engaging internationally and changing internally in ways that could receive widespread support. Relations with the IMF and World Bank were normalized in 1993, and official aid and foreign investment was flowing into the country. Relations with the US as well as Europe were well on the path to normalization, and there was an atmosphere of almost unrealistic optimism about the success of opening up. At the time of the 8th Party Congress in 1996, there was also a shift taking place, with the motivation for reform no longer driven by the economic distress of the late 1980s but increasingly by a vision of a future that could be served by growth and liberalization of both economic and social policy. External observers noted a slow-down in the pace of reform, but not in the direction of change. By this time, foreign investors and aid donors were also getting a taste of what it meant to work with Vietnamese in their own country. Issues of management control and corruption were beginning to emerge as major problems, but these were seen as manageable with a leadership committed to finding ways to improve the climate for investors and willing to tackle difficult problems within the civil service and Party apparatus. By 1997, Vietnam was maturing as a destination for aid and investment, even as the optimism that accompanied the early years of opening up was beginning to fade, and the long-term challenges facing the development of the country were beginning to be recognized and understood.

The Asia financial crisis of late 1997 and 1998 took the wind out of Vietnam's sails. Capital flight from the region affected Vietnam as well as the crisis countries of Thailand, Indonesia, Malaysia, the Philippines and Korea. While Vietnam was not vulnerable to currency devaluation and stock market collapse because of its rudimentary financial system, it was still not immune from the effect of the regional crisis. The sharp depreciation of exchange rates in these crisis countries all of a sudden made Vietnam less attractive as a destination for investment. The official aid community trained their sights on responding to the crisis with massive assistance programs for the countries in the limelight. And regional investors in Vietnam, such as Korea, Singapore and Malaysia, withdrew almost overnight. All of a sudden, the darling of Asia of the 1990s was out of the limelight. The Vietnamese response to these developments was to slow down reform and lower the sights on ambitious development objectives, attend to domestic problems in the rural areas that had become politically sensitive, and amend macroeconomic policies to ride out the storm. These responses have maintained social and economic stability, and at the same time brought to the fore new debates about the best path for future security and prosperity. Political relations with the international community have continued to expand, and Vietnam has become an active participant in ASEAN gatherings, many of which now take place in Hanoi. The prognosis is for continued reform and efforts to deepen international involvement, but at a deliberate pace and with a close eye on potential downside risks.

While North Korea experimented with some half-hearted efforts to introduce Chinese-style economic reforms in the mid 1980s, the appetite for reform disappeared with the collapse of political regimes in Eastern Europe especially in Poland and Romania and the shock of Tienamen Square in China. 1992–93 saw the collapse of the Soviet Union and the loss of Soviet aid and trade. To add insult to injury, China gave diplomatic recognition to South Korea and hardened the terms of its bilateral assistance. These shocks to North Korea's political and economic patronage relationships triggered both a rapid decrease in economic output that had in fact already been declining quietly for some years, and a desperate search for new sources of external subsidies to replace the losses from Russia and China. From a political and economic perspective, the nuclear crisis of 1994 was in reality an effort to forge a new relationship with the United States and to seek new forms of external financial assistance. The Agreed Framework that was negotiated at that time did indeed provide for funding of fuel oil and construction of two light-water nuclear reactors in exchange for North Korea's agreement to shut down a heavy-water nuclear program capable of producing weapons-grade plutonium. The food crisis that emerged in 1995–96 also gave North Korea an opportunity to seek from the US, Japan and Europe new forms of humanitarian assistance that were also in effect new sources of external subsidy for the agriculture sector. These developments, however, did not stem the economic collapse, and by 1999 the economy had shrunk to half its 1994 level, leaving State industries stagnant and rusting, and North Korea's State socialism in shambles. The large infusion of humanitarian assistance, originally in food but now expanded to cover dire health needs, has led to major changes in the ways that North Korea interacts with foreigners. The UN presence has grown significantly, as have the number and variety of NGOs working in different parts of the country. A slow but steady relaxation of the constraints placed on activities and movement of foreigners in the country has also taken place.

North Korea stands today at the brink of a potentially historic shift in its relations with the US and the rest of the international community. Following a careful process of consultation within the US government and with South Korea and Japan, a major new deal has been crafted by former Secretary of Defense William Perry in his special assignment to review North Korean policy. If this new deal succeeds, North Korea will reduce its threats to the security of other countries through curtailment of its missile and nuclear programs, and in exchange the US and others will help North Korea begin to establish normal political and economic relations with the international community and a foundation for permanent peace on the Korean peninsula. Fragile as this moment may seem, it needs to be supported and nurtured by coordinated efforts of the international community. The period ahead will be exciting but extremely challenging. Any more comprehensive engagement must address the tremendous needs for education and training of North Koreans who may be dealing more directly with foreigners and free market practices in the future. The systemic economic collapse must be addressed in ways more fundamental than providing humanitarian aid, however generous, and support for economic reconstruction should be linked to credible progress on the front of political and security concerns of the international community.

5 North Korea's Economic Opening

William Newcomb and John Merrill[*]

When we wrote this paper in mid-1996, views on the DPRK's prospects were polarized. Kim Il Sung had died two years before; his son had not stepped forward publicly but ruled from the shadows; and following widespread flooding, famine and disease afflicted military and civilian alike. Many were predicting the country's collapse; a few were looking for signs of recovery. In Seoul, increasing attention was being paid to a September UNDP-sponsored investment conference in the Najin-Sonbong Free Trade Zone. Optimism about potential investment opportunities in the FTZ was rising. This was perhaps understandable as it was one of the few things that people could point to as the start of a positive trend. In the end, however, the Blue House decided not to have major South Korean companies involved. The highly touted potential of the zone has never been realized.

The only project that has survived the crash in expectations is a hotel-casino built by a Hong Kong business group. Nonetheless – and possibly to everyone's surprise – in the years since, foreign presence in the DPRK has grown considerably. Pyongyang took an unprecedented step by asking for assistance to help it deal with a crippling food crisis. Food aid to stricken areas and humanitarian assistance to hospitals and orphanages probably has helped to soften DPRK attitudes towards the western world in general. While suspicions of western government motives remain high in Pyongyang, the regime's success in managing these contacts in such difficult circumstances has probably bolstered its confidence enough for it

[*] The views in this paper are our own. They do not reflect those of the Department of State or the US Government. We prepared this paper for a conference in Seoul in August 1996, organized by the Federation of Korean Industries and the Korean Economic Research Institute. The theme was the Globalization of the North Korean Economy. Though four years have passed, we think its analysis is still relevant. The text is unchanged.

to seek to broaden spheres of engagement.

Otherwise, internal economic policies have been slow to shift. The collapse of the industrial economy put any plans for economic restructuring the regime might have had on hold. Despite urgings to follow China's lead in economic reform, the leadership has shown a great reluctance to adopt systemic change that could expose it to social unrest – though it has allowed some incentive-type programs to cope with the immediate crisis. The few changes made in economic policy have been attempts to find substitutes for a planning apparatus that had broken down. For example, in farming there has been further devolution of decision making to local authorities, adoption of a small work-team system, and crop diversification. Officials seem to recognize but cannot admit the mistakes the government made in agricultural policy, such as excessive emphasis on grain cultivation. With the economy still mired in a deep depression, a wholesale rebuilding and restructuring beyond Pyongyang's own means will be required to pull it out. No less today than when we wrote this paper, Pyongyang's challenge is to attract sizable foreign government assistance and business investment. This presupposes reducing tensions on the peninsula and expanding and reorienting Pyongyang's diplomatic relations. This has begun.

An article in a leading North Korean economic journal last fall singled out reviving the economy as the nation's top priority, claiming that the ideological and military revolutions had already been carried out. Kim Jong Il also appears to be publicly identifying himself with management of the economy. He has personally been involved in several rounds of negotiations with the South Korean Chaebol Hyundai and has stepped up public appearances related to the economy. Following the June 12–15 summit between South Korean President Kim Dae Jung and North Korean leader Kim Jong Il, the North has approved a number of big projects that signify its intent to let the South play a major role in its long-anticipated, and over-due, economic opening and restructuring.

INTRODUCTION

For some observers, the deepening economic crisis gripping North Korea has put that country on a one-way road to collapse. The only question for them is how the collapse takes place: the North could lash out in desperation, the "Kim system" could suddenly collapse, or the regime's capacity to govern could simply wither away. By its very choice of topic, this symposium on the "Globalization of the North Korean Economy" explicitly rejects such overly deterministic assessments of the North's future. More than forty years ago, the British economist G.L.S. Shackle, who engaged in pathbreaking methodological explorations into the roles of time and expectation in economic decisions, deplored a growing tendency in the economic profession to adopt analytical approaches that took human action out of the equation.

> From the birth of economics there have been those who believed in economic physics and those who believed in economic psychics, and these two kinds of economists are still to be found. Economics is a branch of the study of man, and is essentially concerned with the nature and process of his mind. Theories which bypass the psychological link are surely dangerous. (Shackle, 1958, p. 92)

Predictions of collapse generally extrapolate from longer-term economic trends and, in particular, rest heavily on current circumstances, especially the North's severe shortages of food and fuel, which appear to have scant prospect of being relieved anytime soon. It is a country of deepening hardship, and many reckon there is a limit to how much longer it can continue its struggles. None here would deny the extent and severity of North Korea's economic problems or the difficulties the country faces in trying to resolve them; nor, we believe, would any here rule out the possibility that the North could fail in the attempt. Our topic for today essentially is an exploration of the likely nature of that attempt – for, of the options the leadership has, the opening of the economy offers the richest set of possibilities.

In considering how the North might proceed with this task, it is important to keep in mind its current economic circumstance, but perhaps without lending this as much weight as it receives in the construction of collapse scenarios. Consider the musings of another respected economist – and musing is something economists do less and less, at least in print, so this reference too is a little dated. Writing about the theory of the firm in economics, Neil Chamberlain provides as an analogy a "ship's company embarked on a voyage on an unexplored river with many branches and tributaries, movement along which is a function of time."

Expanding on the time dimension, Chamberlain writes,

> In the firm's voyage, the present is simply a moving front, a transitory position which is the consequence, on the one hand, of its past movements – its history – which have brought it to this present momentary position, and on the other hand, of its future objectives, the point at which it is aiming, toward which it is directing its movement. It is the firm's actual past and its intended future which thus jointly define its actions in the present. In the point of time, *the present is analytically the least consequential aspect of the firm's operations;* it is a

moving pinpoint on a constantly extending line. (Chamberlain, 1968, pp. 5–6, emphasis added)

This presentation will follow that advice and focus more on past movements and how they may relate to efforts to attain future objectives than on the current tribulations.

UNCERTAINTY

Life is uncertain. Just as there is enough uncertainty about what may happen to the North to justify this conference, the DPRK's leaders confront uncertainty in determining how best to deal with the problems that plague their economy. Beyond that lies the uncertainty about how to fashion a new development strategy and the elements it should contain.

For market economies, uncertainty is a tonic; it gives scope for human action. For planned economies, uncertainty is a poison. One of the prime reasons for engaging in national planning is to limit uncertainty, or so planners presume. Centrally planned economies lack equilibrating mechanisms that come automatically into play in response to unexpected shocks. (These shocks are of a particular kind. Foreigners do not have command over goods and services, so an unanticipated increase in the demand for an export will generally result in a foregone opportunity for increased sales though it should raise earnings. The plan defines demand (*ex ante*), and once it is formulated there is little chance of an increase in domestic demand. Similarly, unexpected productivity would result in greater than expected inventory accumulation or possibly exports – neither a "shock." Shocks to the command economy for the most part result either from the failure of output of a major commodity to expand as planned or from an actual decrease in supply of such a commodity.) Shocks instead must be managed; they require bureaucrats to make decisions. Shocks throw the plan out of kilter. Carefully struck material balances become unstuck, and bureaucrats are in conflict over how to revise the allocation of now scarcer commodities. Conflict can only be referred upward for settlement and ultimately is resolved by setting a hierarchy of priorities. Further shocks, for the nature of the economic environment is that they will keep occurring, upset this ordering of priorities, and super-priorities need to be established. Finally, as Janos Kornai observes about supply-driven systems, as one constraint is removed, another automatically takes its place.

The effect of major shocks on the command economy is analogous to price inflation in the market economy – and just as paralyzing. Like money during the period of rapid inflation, orders become worth less and less, must be given by increasingly higher authority, and consequently are "spent" quickly. Goods, likewise, tend to be hoarded for precautionary reasons and as a store of value.

Operationally, economic managers try to get around the uncertainty of shocks by shortening their decision horizon. Planners and managers, for example, have more confidence in the annual plan than in the five-year plan since they recognize that the longer the term, the greater the number of factors that vary. This is why a twenty-year plan is not called a "plan" but a perspective, from the Russian *perspectivnaya*.

In a crisis, taking temporizing, short-term actions offers managers a higher comfort level. Because fewer variables are in play, they are more confident in projecting near-term outcomes. This behavioral response to crises is often called a strategy of muddling through.

STOCHASTIC REFORMS

Given the North's dire economic situation, muddling through is clearly no longer a sufficient policy response. Pyongyang is pragmatic enough to know this, and crisis management does not have to meet a test of economic orthodoxy. But should one be needed, *juche* is sufficiently flexible and encompassing to offer justification for extraordinary measures. One way Pyongyang is coping with its present crisis, for example, is by pushing economic responsibility and decision making to lower levels. This relieves pressure on the center and gives play to local and individual initiatives.

When planners operate with a shortened time horizon, longer-term goals lose importance relative to near-term objectives. Policy inconsistencies are not as apparent, nor is the direction of policy traceable with as much clarity. Because of necessities of the moment, in the North new economic relations and procedures are gradually supplanting old ways of doing things. The cumulative effect of these short-term measures is edging Pyongyang away from total dependence on a central planning and distribution system that in many areas has ceased to work.

For several years, local industry has been responsible for obtaining inputs and marketing its product domestically. More recently, shortages of hard currency and foodstuffs have prompted Pyongyang to encourage local industry to engage directly in foreign trade as well, bypassing state trade organizations. Cutting loose local authorities, factories, and farms from rigid central direction and oversight stimulates individual initiative, gives room for adoption of worker incentives, and through the process of exchange promotes the development of markets. More dramatically, over the last decade Pyongyang has fostered the establishment of permanent urban markets where agricultural products, prepared foods, and consumer goods are available for barter or cash. Although the North took this step partly to make up for insufficient stocks of goods in the formal distribution system, its effect has been to create opportunities outside the state sector. Visitors report that early morning trains to Pyongyang are packed with people coming to the capital with goods to sell or trade in the markets. And, urban residents now travel to rural areas to make purchases in farmers' markets and even directly from farms.

THIRD TIME A CHARM?

North Korea is a small economy with a limited resource base. The collapse of other socialist economies on which it depended for economic assistance, and with them the system of bilateral trade that permitted Pyangyong also to extract unintended economic loans, was the major factor that threw the DPRK's economy into its current downward spiral. The North not only lost access to food, fuel, and raw materials that fed its industry, it also was deprived of the main foreign markets for much of its manufactures.

Socialist aid, however, was just keeping the wolf from the door. The North for years has been in the grip of a system-wide downturn; the capital–output ratio was on the rise; and labor participation rates had seemingly peaked, with women more fully incorporated into the labor force there than in most other countries. These trends are the kiss of death for an economic system dependent on extensive growth techniques. Moreover, development aid, which provided much of the North's industrial base, also saddled it for the most part with dated technologies and older-vintage capital equipment.

With few exceptions, North Korean manufacturers have never been competitive in hard-currency markets, except at deep discount. It is likely that the North was no better and probably worse in terms of manufacturing efficiencies than countries in Eastern Europe, where post-mortem examinations suggest that manufacturing in some sectors contributed negative value-added. (See Jan Prybla's comments in the July 1996 issue of the World Bank's monthly, *Transitions*.) Recent developments in the DPRK, including the loss of access to spares, the deferring of maintenance to keep operating rates as high as possible, and numerous and pernicious bottlenecks surely have driven up unit costs of production even more as total output has fallen.

Ask a North Korean official what his country needs to stage a recovery (as we have not yet had the opportunity to do, this is a conjecture), and it is likely he would answer: "(1) new and refurbished plant and equipment that embodies more advanced technologies and (2) access to concessionary finance to improve and enlarge the nation's infrastructure." North Koreans realize they need outside help to recover (a point clearly evident in appeals for aid but more broadly and tellingly in the increased number of economic delegations Pyongyang sends abroad), but probably most officials would see that help in terms of technical and dollar fixes. They know their economy must open to the industrial nations, but so far appear to have spent more time trying to figure out how to guard themselves from contamination by capitalist thought than how to accommodate this circumstance and help industry extract maximum gain from increased exposure to international market forces.

In fact, for reasons very similar to today's motivation, North Korea has tried to open at least twice before (some make it three times by counting North–South talks in the early 1990s) only to come to grief. The legacy of these efforts will complicate the next attempt to open, but Pyongyang may have learned enough from prior attempts to raise its chances of succeeding.

Numbering and dating these openings is mainly an analytic convenience and involves some subjective evaluations. Openings actually are difficult to date exactly: they are more like waves. It is relatively easy to detect periods of high and low interest and activity, but it is difficult to put an exact date on a beginning or ending of a policy cycle. These waves have a momentum of their own, but they are strongly influenced by outside forces acting on North Korea's economic policy, and it would be a serious omission not to note that the supremacy of political objectives in Pyongyang's hierarchy of goals often gives outside political forces more weight than outside economic changes.

In the late 1960s the North's seven-year plan was on the ropes, due in large part first to the Sino–Soviet split, and later to the Great Cultural Revolution. Finding itself in this fix, North Korea became one of the two centrally planned economies to try to open. (Bulgaria was the other; it too ran into problems.) Pyongyang moved to improve economic relations with Japan and Europe to gain access to the plant and equipment it needed to continue with its industrialization programs. By the early 1970s, the North was ready to make a big push. Unfortunately for it, the North's eyes were bigger than its stomach – and Pyongyang's acquisitions of plant and equipment exceeded the DPRK's absorption capacity.

The development scheme counted on plants being self-financing; the increased production would be exported to pay off the debt acquired in the plants' purchase. Pyongyang did not have access to concessional sources of hard-currency loans, so the debt was on commercial terms – higher interest rates and shorter periods. Furthermore, Pyongyang was inexperienced and untutored in how best to broker and manage these projects. The pace of construction fell off sharply, machinery rusted in open storage at docks and in dirt fields, and many important plants were not up and running until the close of the decade.

The first attempt to open also was doomed by bad timing. The oil shock of the early 1970s slowed growth in industrial countries and softened prices of the North's primary hard-currency exports. Consecutive weather-reduced agricultural harvests that required an extraordinary increase in grain imports depleted the North's cash. By the mid 1970s, the DPRK was in arrears on most of its newly acquired hard-currency debt. The economy plunged into a steep recession, and the effort at export-led growth was abandoned in favor of a return to a more self-reliant scheme that featured import substitution.

North Korea's second attempt at opening came in the mid 1980s. It was a more restrained effort. The impetus again was economic necessity born largely from the failure to resolve problems caused by its prior attempt to open. This new attempt came in the wake of the 1980 party congress, as relations between new administrations in Washington and Seoul began to solidify, and on the eve of new overtures toward the South. The import-substitution strategy had been succeeded by the notion of making a big push in infrastructure, much of which Pyongyang calculated it could construct on its own. But the effort would leave little for modernization and industrial expansion. The USSR in the early 1980s had not offered much in the way of new assistance, limiting its commitments mostly to completing work on projects underway. Pyongyang actively sought debt rescheduling to get some breathing room as pressure from its creditors mounted, and learned early that commercial lenders would demand very tough terms, if they would even agree to lend at all.

The North's second opening featured two interesting developments. First, Pyongyang promulgated a joint venture law. Second, it pushed to become a major supplier of military weapons.

The focus on joint ventures set an important precedent, led to some new financing mechanisms, and spurred limited institutional and legal changes. Some Korean-owned and Japanese firms did invest in a few projects, and as a result direct intra-Korean trade began in 1988.

This initiative could have made more progress if groundwork had been laid first and if, at its earliest stage, there had been less tension on the peninsula. The joint venture initiative came less than a year after the Rangoon bombing. By the end of the decade, South Korean chaebols were beginning to make contact with the DPRK. Hyundai chairman Chung Ju Young visited North Korea in 1989 to discuss tourism development and other deals. Samsung, Daewoo, Lucky Goldstar and other companies soon began to discuss projects of their own and to trade with the North.

The timing of North Korea's second opening suggests that it may have been influenced by the early reform experience of China. By the mid 1980s, foreign investors were beginning to show keen interest in China, and Beijing's newly established special economic zones were attracting international attention. Kim Il Sung visited China twice in the early 1980s. (At this time, however, SEZs were far from posting a "profit.") North Korea's press gave evidence of a wide-ranging discussion on the DPRK's need for economic reform. Steps under debate called for substantial changes that exceeded significantly any actions Pyongyang actually took. Conservatives in the DPRK had grown increasingly distrustful of Beijing once it began to improve relations with the United States and had became even more suspicious of the socialist credentials of the post-Mao leadership once Deng Xiaoping announced that the color of the cat did not matter, only that it caught mice.

The second aspect of the North's 1980s opening was less benign: it pushed to become a major supplier of military weapons. The Iran–Iraq war gave Pyongyang a sellers' market and a long-sought chance to solidify political relations with a major oil-exporting nation. These strange bedfellows were further united by their joint, aggressive opposition to the US. Pyongyang's miscalculation of how the arms market would develop in coming years and how much market share it could win led it to over-invest in military industry, to the detriment of the capital-starved consumer-goods industry. Furthermore, Pyongyang made a critical error by not applying some of its sizable arms earnings to satisfying its creditors. The government's failure to use a portion of these hard-currency receipts to reduce debt demonstrates the depth of the rift even then between the military and civil sectors in the economy.

Along with its second attempt at opening (and maybe at the urging of conservatives who wanted to close the door to reform talk), Pyongyang moved to repair relations with the Soviet Union. In May 1984, Kim Il Sung made an extended trip to Moscow and East Europe to seek military and economic aid. Pyongyang was more successful in bringing about a rapprochement with Moscow than in opening to the West. Kim got a commitment to equip the North Korean air force with more modern combat aircraft and the promise of a substantial increase in trade and project assistance. By the end of the 1980s, the USSR accounted for above 70 percent of DPRK trade. It was this unbalanced success that set up the North for such a hard fall in the 1990s.

The late stages of this second attempted opening featured an effort to normalize relations with Seoul. Five rounds of high-level meetings between the two sides culminated in the December 1991 Agreement on Reconciliation, Non-Aggression, and Cooperation. Implementation of this agreement was stymied, and the second attempt to open ground to a halt, because of the growing controversy over the North's nuclear program.

NORTH KOREA'S CURRENT OPENING

Since the conclusion of the Framework Agreement, the DPRK has redoubled its effort to normalize relations with the US and end economic sanctions, which it believes have hamstrung its economy. Pyongyang also has held some lower-level talks with Japanese officials.

North Korea has made the development of a free-trade zone in the Najin-Sonbong area the focal point of its current economic opening. The zone has a potential tie-in with the Tumen River Development Program, and even incorporation into it, if sovereignty issues can be ever resolved. The DPRK has also benefited significantly from the planning and funding of the UNDP.

Najin-Sonbong is a frail reed, but even throughout the nuclear crisis, North Korea never wavered in its commitment to the FTZ. Most recently, DPRK delegations have traveled widely to offer "sales seminars" designed to boost attendance at the conferences in Najin-Sonbong and eventually attract significant amounts of investment. Nonetheless, conditions in the FTZ remain primitive, especially for business that needs modern communications, reliable power supplies, rapid transport, etc. Military construction troops are hard at work making infrastructure improvements, financial services are being established (ING bank, Perigrene, for example), and officials are promising that the zone will operate along market lines.

Pyongyang's tentativeness in pursuing a broadened opening, moving more aggressively to improve ties with other regional actors, particularly with the US, South Korea, and Japan, likely stems from the high stakes. The North cannot afford another policy setback: it will likely not have another chance to open. The leadership may prefer no action and continued reliance on coping measures to slow the economy's decline to leaping blindly into negotiations as the weaker party.

This is the primary reason that Pyongyang seems to prefer "buffered engagement" with the South, such as that provided by KEDO and the Najin-Songbong FTZ. The leadership is most concerned about opening on terms it can handle. Conservatives must be brought along and involved in the decision. The new regime cannot afford any major missteps. For now, it can lay much of the blame for economic problems at the feet of others: the failure of the USSR and East Europe to stay true to socialism, the economic embargo of the US, the conspiring of South Korea, and the incapacity of Japan to repent past wrongs.

But too much caution can also be fatal. A key determinant in framing an opening policy will be whether or not the leadership tries to hedge its bets. Given the strength of conservative forces in the North, an opening strong enough to succeed cannot be blamed on a fall guy if it fails. The choice for top leaders is essentially between a restrained opening with a modest chance of succeeding and little chance of their being held responsible for its failure and a bolder opening with a better chance for success on which they stake all their political capital. The choice facing Washington, Seoul, Tokyo, and Beijing is whether to try to raise the potential payoff of opening to induce Pyongyang to commit to the bolder course.

OPENING IS NOT ENOUGH

There are many recent examples of how difficult it is for command economies to open. In a planned economy, the center can neither give foreigners command over goods and services, nor tolerate firms deciding on their own to ship abroad lest they mess up the plan. Trade channels thus are restricted, even monopolized, and currency is non-convertible. State traders are buffers, accumulating extraordinary profits or dependent on large subsidies from the state budget. If the North opens in a small way, or very gradually, it can use buffers to ease the transition to new trade relations, but what Pyongyang seeks to protect is the very thing that must change – industry must be exposed to the competition of the market to spur improved efficiency. Business must be able to receive and react to market signals. The North cannot open and succeed without also committing itself to beginning economic reform.

The spur for change is crisis. Reforms are only born of adversity, and no leadership undertakes a reform program without exhausting its other alternatives. For years, Pyongyang has tinkered with and tweaked its planning system, trying to improve the economy's performance. These efforts may have bought Pyongyang a little time, but they could not stave off the inevitable decline as tightening input constraints began to pinch off growth. And the delay in recognizing the need for system changes has proved to be very expensive.

There is no "theory" of economic reform. But, there are types. One type could be labeled the "big bang" approach. In this, the leadership acts as if it would bet all on a cut of cards. This approach is favored by a number of economists. Milton Friedman, for example, counseled Chinese premier Zhao Ziyang to do just that in the mid 1980s when asked for his advice.

Leaderships that want to retain power, however, are unattracted by this high-stakes gamble and prefer to move slowly, step-by-step. But piecemeal reform is troublesome in its own right. It does not pay off early and those who sacrifice may not be those who gain from reform. Each step on the reform path brings into view other necessary changes. Some reforms actually worsen their problems in unanticipated ways. One of the major drawbacks to this approach is the time it permits for opposition to mobilize.

There is an iterative, experimental quality to gradual reform. World Bank economists have explored the appropriate sequencing of reforms. There is no theoretical reason to prefer one ordering to another, however, except perhaps if the criteria are able to account for a reform measure's practicality. Both Vietnam and China approach reform in this way. The Chinese aptly capture the nature of piecemeal reform with their expression for it, "crossing the river while feeding the stones beneath your feet."

EARLIER ATTEMPTS AT ECONOMIC REFORMS

Over the years, Pyongyang has experimented with several reform initiatives, so it is not without some experience. The extent and nature of these "halting" efforts have been explored more fully by one of the authors of this chapter in an earlier article (Merrill, 1991). They thus will be only briefly surveyed here.

Prior efforts at reform were aimed at improving the operation of the planning system. Acceptable measures might augment planning, but the leadership never considered taking steps to replace it. In industry, the first opening in the 1970s was accompanied by a shift to local budgeting. The priority afforded heavy industry had sacrificed consumer well-being. Local budgeting was instituted to lessen the tension between these sectors by making provincial authorities responsible for all economic and social activities not directly funded by the state. This responsibility would include the operation of stores, schools, and hospitals as well as local light industries. Attempts to raise production of consumer goods also was a feature of the second opening in the early 1980s. Kim Il Sung endorsed provision of material incentives to workers as a reward which is not out of place in a system in transition. But incentives were to cut two ways: wages were linked to fulfillment of production norms, and workers had their pay docked if factory goals were not met.

In agriculture, limited experiments in reform along Chinese lines were conducted in the mid 1980s – under Kim Jong Il's patronage. This effort was halted when Kim Il Sung learned of it. The official directing it was fired, and the elder Kim publicly pushed to move ahead with the shift from collective to state farming. Though agricultural reforms are among the most sensitive, current severe food shortages have put them high on the list of need changes. In a recent North Korean press article, attributed to an official in the Agricultural Commission, the need for material incentives was reservedly highlighted. To spur higher grain output, the portion of production in excess of the planned target is to be distributed to the relevant sub-work team.

In most economic sectors there has been a decentralization of decision making. Managers and farmers now have a greater say in setting goals and determining how best to meet them. This shift in control is a display of pragmatism. Pyongyang knows it can do better. Leaders saw a glimmer of manufacturing's potential – if it had more up-to-date machinery and marketing know-how – in the successful efforts of factories that export clothing and musical instruments to Japan. They now appear prepared to pin their hopes on the attracting an educated, disciplined workforce prepared to labor for low wages and on their location at the center of the three strongest economies in Asia. But if this initiative is to work, Pyongyang's pragmatism must embrace the necessity of thorough, systemic, economic reform.

PROSPECTS

Most of us would consider the North's chances of managing successful reform and staging an economic recovery as a long shot. Its chances could be improved, depending on the objectives Pyongyang sets. What are the leaders' objectives? Do they want simply to ensure survival of the country and the regime, or, like China, do they seek to raise the North's influence and voice on regional and global matters? Does opening mean abandonment of reunification on the North's own terms? Foreign investors, after all, want security and would be put off by a new round of saber-rattling. Could the North's leadership be content with being just a partner on the peninsula rather than the managing partner? And, if by chance the North does make progress in opening, where will the gains go? Will an unreformed military sector feed off the opening and continue to starve the civil sector of investment capital? Will the people, the workers, see any of the gain in terms of improved living standards?

In figuring the odds for the North, however, it is worth recalling that China was not given much of a chance when it launched reforms in the late 1970s. Beijing's economic goals were thought to be out of reach, and those who sold China short felt even more confident in their prediction when Beijing was forced to retrench in the early 1980s, so that they were more surprised when China achieved its objectives early, including a record grain harvest that allowed the PRC to become a net exporter. Who gave reform in Vietnam much chance in the early 1980s? For that matter, how many outside observers in the 1960s thought South Korea had much of an economic future? The point is to remain aware of what Shackle labeled the "potential for surprise."

Any new opening, to succeed, must resolve problems left from past efforts to open. The main legacy is debt. We do not know how big the debt is and neither do Pyongyang's creditors. To a great extent the debt is composed of penalties and penalty-interest accumulated during the years of being in arrears. To reckon the debt could take accountants several years; they must reconcile accounts of the debtor with accounts of creditors. Only then can Paris Club or, more likely, London Club negotiations on debt restructuring begin in earnest.

A prerequisite to a successful opening is regaining access to credit markets, and debt rescheduling is only one of several major obstacles Pyongyang must maneuver around. Commercial credit terms are too stiff to support development programs, as Pyongyang learned long ago. North Korea's poor credit rating and record of not always honoring business commitments will make it tough to improve access to suppliers and buyers credits. The only way for the North to regain confidence and creditworthiness is to begin acting responsibly – making sure all newly contracted bills are paid on time and in full. This will be a slow process.

To obtain concessional terms, Pyongyang can seek government-to-government loans or look to the international financial institutions (IFIs). In actuality, North Korea must do both because of the extent of its financial needs. The attraction of bilateral funds is that the agreement is negotiated and subject to renegotiation, a process where Pyongyang has confidence in its skills. These are the days of tight budgets, however, and, except for the possibility of reparation payments by Tokyo, no single government is likely to offer sufficiently large loans.

To get development loans from the IFIs, Pyongyang must join them. Membership of the IMF, World Bank, and Asian Development Bank will require Pyongyang to accept a much higher degree of economic transparency than it has provided at any time since the late 1950s. Moreover, the current members must vote the North in. Membership criteria are not subject to negotiation other than possibly on timing. And, as members, the North's economic conduct must conform with the rules – if Pyongyang goes into arrears on IFI loans, its membership would be suspended. Even if North Korea today decided to seek membership of the IMF and World Bank and would do whatever it took, including opening its economic accounts to outsiders, it would take years to gain entry. The North is in such a financial fix that it cannot afford the delay.

It seems that creativity is needed and that maybe there is scope for action by various UN agencies. UNICEF, for example, has undertaken debt swaps for children's programs. Other kinds of debt swaps might have possibilities

– for example, pollution clean-up, reforestation, and education and training. The North could use a group of patrons which "co-sign" its notes in exchange for an advisory or managerial role in making sure the funded project is properly undertaken. This type of cooperative help will not be volunteered, but could arise from on-going talks in a number of venues.

We all have a stake in this process. Economics is about alternatives, and the alternatives to the North's opening are not pleasant to contemplate. In the worst case there is war, with Pyongyang seeing no way out of an increasingly desperate situation and willing to roll the dice. In this context, economic engagement with North Korea would help create an external environment conducive to a successful opening and reinforce our own joint security. As US Ambassador Laney recently remarked, deterrence is essential but no longer enough.

There are also grim alternatives short of war. Survival policies could lead to creating by default in the FTZ a haven for criminal activities. IPR violators, for example, would be quick to set up shop in a region where they could be unregulated.

Even if the North adopts a solidly conceived opening policy coupled with a strong effect at reform, Pyongyang's chance of success is very low if it does not get outside help. The North left it too long; its timing is not good; it missed the "bull market" for Asian exporters. It even missed the opportunities offered by China's economic boom. In deciding on how much help to extend, the South and others must make some "uncertainty" calculations of their own. They must balance the risk and cost of a North Korean collapse with the cost of bolstering an opening that might not succeed.

Deciding to engage the North economically will be complicated by the military question. The successful opening and reform programs of China and Vietnam followed from a decision that their borders were secure – the risk of war was slight. China's Four Modernizations put the military last. Deng made the historic bargain to forgo current military spending to build up the nation's economic strength. North Korea's leaders cannot make that decision and cannot strike that bargain.

North Korea's economy is not one, but many. The civilian economy is split between national and local, and there are a few small separate offshoots serving the Kim family, the elite, and the party that provide them an independent financial base. The military economy over the years increasingly has become vertically integrated so that it could pursue its objectives without having to rely heavily on the civilian sector. It is a command system with overtones of feudalism. While reform might be launched for the civil sectors, it is unlikely to penetrate the military economy.

The North cannot afford its military, but should an attempt to open fail, the military would be the last card the leadership would have to play. Even in the absence of conflict, tension would likely be kept high by Pyongyang to give this card its greatest potential value.

To sum up, for now we do not believe collapse is likely. North Korea for some time can continue taking damage-control measures to cope with severe economic problems. The North's leadership also is aware that once again it has an opportunity and a pressing need to open. It is pursuing this option in a limited way. The attempt to open is directed at reviving the economy, but this effort will require in addition a concurrent economic reform program. North Korea's leaders, however, are unlikely to put their regime at risk by embracing reform unless they are confident of staging an economic recovery. And they likely have concluded that an opening that does not receive extensive international support will fail. Forging international consensus on what to do about aiding North Korea will be difficult because of differing national policy agendas. But it is time to shift thinking in the North and West from a view of negotiations as a zero-sum confrontation to seeing engagement as a way to obtain a win–win outcome. A start in this direction was made by the Framework Agreement and establishment of KEDO. This agreement provides a base on which to build confidence and trust, and exemplifies the type of creative solution needed to foster an opening that is in everyone's best interest.

REFERENCES

Chamberlain, N. (1968), *Enterprise and Environment: The Firm in Time and Place*, New York: McGraw-Hill.

Merrill, J. (1991), "North Korea's Halting Efforts at Economic Reform," in Chong-Sik Lee and Se-Hee Yoo (eds), *North Korea in Transition,* Institute of East Asian Studies, University of California at Berkeley.

Shackle, G.L.S. (1958), *Time in Economics,* Amsterdam: North-Holland.

6 Economic Cooperation between the Two Koreas: An Historical Analysis

Youn-Suk Kim

INTRODUCTION

The zeal with which South Korean businesses approached investing in North Korea beginning in 1992 produced its own economic bubble. By 1997 the bubble had deflated substantially and it was expected to disappear completely due largely to the South's economic squeeze. It has become increasingly difficult for the South's companies to invest in the North without incurring short-term losses. Small companies have pursued investment opportunities in the North as part of their survival strategy, and under the 1997–98 economic crisis such investment has grown all the more important for small companies. The wage differential between the two Koreas is substantial, pushing the South's small companies to shift their production facilities to the North in search of lower labor costs.

With economic cooperation the two Koreas could increasingly shave production costs by combining the North's relatively inexpensive labor power and mineral resources with the South's capital and technological assets. These economic transactions would create a synergy effect derived from production efficiency, economies of scale, low transaction costs of trade, and effective resource allocation.

The world is changing at a dazzling rate. The two Koreas are at an historical crossroad of inter-Korean cooperation towards economic integration. Inter-Korean trade and investment have great potential to help the two Koreas and to realize economic integration, and the economic engagement would lead to peaceful coexistence with increased economic gains and mutual trust through economic exchange.

The South seeks gradual transformation together with the North's economy. This chapter analyzes the historical path of the two Koreas' economic relationship with the recognition that the integration of the two economies would make a united Korea a formidable regional economic power.

HISTORICAL ANALYSIS OF THE TWO KOREAS' ECONOMIC COOPERATION

Japan's defeat in World War II liberated Korea after 36 years as a colony, but Korea emerged as a divided country. The division of the Korean Peninsula in 1945, enforced by the United States and Soviet Union, resulted in an unbalanced separation of natural and human resources, with disadvantages for each part of the divided country.

Economic Systems of the Two Koreas[1]

The North's task after liberation from Japanese rule was to reform the colonial economic structure into a socialist system. From 1953 on, the North had struggled with rapid economic development, assisted in these efforts by large amounts of aid from other communist countries. This aid was effective in the years immediately following the end of the Korean War, and a remarkable amount of economic rehabilitation was achieved. Although the North's economic system was originally inspired by the Soviet model, the North has attempted to combine the economic foundation of a modern socialist state with its own economic development plans, stressing minimum reliance on external sources of capital, investment and technology.

Consequently, the North possesses a unique type of command economy based on *juche* ideology, that is, a system of self-reliance. The North's pricing mechanism is based on the value of socially needed labor. The prices of goods and services are derived from labor cost, not through the pricing mechanism of supply and demand interactions. But the North's central economy has run into trouble as it has grown more complex. It has had difficulties in controlling the many intertwined variables of the economic system in the absence of a market mechanism for allocating resources and distribution. The North's commercial management system is made up of wholesale commerce, which has been controlled by the central government, and retail commerce, which is controlled by the regional governments. The government is therefore the North's sole source for the entire distribution of goods.[2]

In contrast, the South's economic system has relied on the market mechanism, though the government assumed a vital developmental role in deciding major projects, allocating financial resources, and offering tax incentives to those who undertook production and export in strategic industries. The South adopted a policy of export-oriented industrialization in 1961. This policy extended preferences to exporters regarding import licenses, duty-free imports for manufacture of exports, and generous capital depreciation allowances. Domestic savings were promoted through higher interest rates on deposits. Such measures eventually resulted in reduced inflation rates and lower rates of real interest, which in turn further promoted export-led industrial growth.

In order to import scarce resources, the export-led strategy, based on comparative advantage, expanded industries that used the South's abundant labor supply. Labor-intensive manufactured goods were exported. To facilitate an open economy, the South gradually reduced its protectionist policy by encouraging domestic industries to compete at home and abroad. When the US announced troop reductions in the 1970s, the South perceived this action as foreshadowing the necessity for a greater industrial base for its own military purposes and began to promote development of chemical and heavy industries. The South also saw Japan's pattern of industrialization as one that its own export industries should pursue. The government considered conglomerates, or chaebol, as suitable institutions to implement industrialization in chemical and heavy industries, shipbuilding, steel, non-ferrous metals, machinery, petrochemicals, and automobiles.

Overview of Inter-Korean Trade

A major turning point came in 1984 as the North's proposal to provide aid for flood victims in the South was accepted. Shortly thereafter, the North for the first time proposed tripartite talks with the US and the South, a change from its previous insistence on bilateral talks with the US only. Talks between the North and the South continued on several different levels. Inter-parliamentary discussions failed to get off the ground due to a lack of agreed agenda, and economic talks were terminated prematurely due to procedural differences. Nevertheless, Red Cross negotiations bore fruit dramatically in September 1985 when family reunion exchange visits between the South and the North took place. Although eventually unsuccessful, attempts were also made to organize a joint Korean team for the 1988 Seoul Olympics.

With the rapidly changing international environment, President Roh Tae-Woo unveiled a new foreign policy initiative towards the North and other communist countries on July 7, 1988. Subsequently, Roh called for a summit meeting between himself and President Kim Il-Sung. President

Kim, who was certainly aware of and sensitive to such new developments as detente between the East and the West as well as the South's application for admission to the UN in autumn 1990, countered in his 1990 New Year address by proposing talks between the prime ministers.[3]

The first inter-Korean exchange of goods occurred in 1988. This development had the potential significantly to alter both North Korea's future economic development and its foreign economic relations. Trade began modestly with the November 21, 1988 arrival of 40 kilograms of North Korean clams at the South Korean port of Pusan. A second transaction, in January 1989, involved South Korean imports of the North's art, including paintings, pottery, woodwork, and industrial artworks.

Yet, the North still tried to avoid direct trade with the South. Thus, small-scale trade was carried on through third countries, with country-of-origin labels removed. The South has traded through agents in Hong Kong, Singapore, Japan, and China, and has increasingly imported raw materials from the North via foreign intermediaries since 1988, when a ban on the North's imports was lifted. While rejecting direct trade, the North has increasingly engaged in indirect trade. Even more significant is that the North's trade officials have busily contacted the South's businessmen inside China to explore possible investment projects in the North. In July 1990, North Korea accepted direct delivery of some 800 tons of South Korean rice collected by Christians through a "rice of love" campaign for the poor.

Trade has been transacted through counter-product arrangements by clearing other countries' cash accounts, and evolving gradually toward countertrade, in which the South's chaebol have dominated, while its small and medium-sized firms have participated only marginally. The North's economy became more responsive to outside market signals in order to implement its plan of a foreign-trade zone. Moreover, the North's economy has gone through a slow transformation since 1993, starting with agriculture and foreign trade. The operation of trading companies and the relaxation of the agricultural collectives are considered signs of reforms towards market orientation. The changes involved increasing use of markets and the profit incentive to increase both foreign-exchange earnings and output.

The North opened direct trade with the South's trading companies in 1991. Moving toward direct trade makes it possible to reduce the usual transport costs of foreign trade in transshipment, warehousing, and insurance. If inter-Korean direct trade were fully realized,[4] the mineral resources of the North would be shared with the South, and the South's labor shortage would be relieved by employing the North's labor. Both domestic markets would be expanded, and the competitiveness of both Koreas in the world market would be greatly enhanced.

The North's Kumgangsan Company imported 5,000 tons of rice from the South, and its state-run trading company, Yongman Chemical, imported $4 million worth of the South's Lucky Goldstar TVs in 1991.[5] The South's imports from the North amounted to $176.29 million, down just over 1 percent from $178.16 million a year earlier, as a result of the political chill in 1994. But the North's imports of steel, electronics, and other manufactured products from the South rose significantly to $18.25 million in 1994, more than double the previous year's $8.42 million. The North's exports to the South included zinc ingots, gold ore, thermal coil, steel billets, anthracite coal, and copper. The North imported capital goods (sock-weaving and vacuum-packaging machinery), consumer goods (rice, televisions, and clothes), semi-raw materials (plasticizer), petrochemical products, and polyester textiles.

The North's government-sanctioned trading companies have implemented the foreign trade portion of the economic plan, negotiated with foreign counterparts, executed contracts, and held final responsibility for actual transactions. As long as implementation is within the authority of the economic plan, the trading companies set their own terms of export and import as independent units.[6] In other words, the North's trading companies have an exclusive right as agents representing powerful authorities such as the party's central committee and army headquarters to earn foreign exchange so as to import much needed merchandise.

Trading companies have in the past dealt in specialized commodities, whether mineral products or marine merchandise. However, the North has in recent years adopted an independent accounting unit practice for each trading company, thereby causing drastic changes in transactions. Exports and imports are handled more like those of the general trading company. Granted the erratic nature of trade volume due to political factors, the general trend is positive. Trade between the South and the North has been intermittently expanding as shown in Table 6.1. Inter-Korean trade in 1997 has increased a sizeable 20.7 percent over 1996.[7]

Steel and metal items accounted for more than 50 percent of the South's imports from the North in recent years. Gold and zinc ingots comprised the lion's share of these imports, with gold ingots representing fully 25 percent of all the North's exports to the South. Due to the IMF crisis, however, imports of gold ingots from the North have been declining sharply. In the first 10 months of 1997, an average of $4.36 million worth of gold ingots was imported every month from the North. This figure plunged to $2.64 million in November 1997. Zinc ingots suffered a corresponding drop: in the following January–October period, imports averaged $3.07 million each month, falling to $1.41 million in November. Imports of the North's steel and metal items were likely to have declined as well in 1998–99 because of

Table 6.1 Trade between North Korea and South Korea (on a custom clearance basis)

Year	North to South		South to North	
	Number of items	Value (US$ 1,000)	Number of items	Value (US$ 1,000)
1988	4	1,037	–	–
1989	24	18,655	1	69
1990	21	12,278	3	1,187
1991	50	105,722	17	5,547
1992	81	162,863	24	10,563
1993	77	178,166	21	8,425
1994	83	176,298	42	18,248
1995	99	222,855	90	64,435
1996	125	193,069	102	69,638
1997	145	193,069	129	115,269
Total		1,252,305		293,381

Note: The South's exports to the North in 1995 excluded $237 million of rice assistance.
Source: S. Korea National Unification Board 1998.

the ongoing gold-collection campaign and sluggish production activity in the South.[8]

Three factors contribute to dramatic changes in the North's policies. First, the rapid demise of the Soviet Union and other communist Eastern European governments was one of the most traumatic political difficulties the North has ever experienced. Second, the agreement between the former Soviet Union and the North, signed in November 1990 and establishing trade in hard currency exchange at world prices, was a crushing blow to the North's economy: the North must now settle its bilateral trade account with convertible hard currency instead of acting on the old, long-term barter basis. The gravity of this change can better be understood by recalling that the North imported from the Soviet Union about a third of its crude oil and petroleum products, coking coal, and machinery and equipment parts. Third, the North's only choice in responding this matter was to turn to China as an alternative source. It has imported from China crude oil, raw materials, and food items, and from Japan and South Korea capital goods and consumer products.

Analysis of Inter-Korean Investment

After the enactment of the Joint Venture Law in September 1984, the North has displayed a hitherto unseen flexibility in its external policies relating to Western countries. North Korea had high hopes of this law. Not only could joint ventures bring about an economic modernization program with foreign capital and technology, but they were integrated into the economic plan, solving bottlenecks in necessary inputs, and would blend the North's management and production with foreign inputs so as to upgrade the North's products and international marketing.

The North denies that it has followed the People's Republic of China in drafting a Joint Venture Law intended to attract foreign investment.[9] However, it is hard to overlook similarities to the Chinese law, which was giving greater priority to increase exports in order to earn foreign exchange. North Korea desperately needs foreign exchange and has been making concerted efforts to attract foreign investment and to expand the variety of policy options for foreign investors. A total of 35 joint venture projects were set up in the North from the promulgation of the North's Joint Venture Law in September of 1984 until May 1989.

The high expectations for its Joint Venture Law not having been met, the North adopted a new processing-on-commission trade (PCT) law and a foreign-investment law in October 1992. Unlike the 1984 joint-venture law, these laws contain a special provision implicitly encouraging the South's investment. The North recognizes that foreign companies are less willing than the South to invest in the North due to its heavy foreign debt and to risk in general.[10] These changes increase market and profit incentives in an attempt to earn foreign exchange and to increase output. Contractual joint ventures give the North authority over production and management; and the South's partners are compensated according to the provisions of the joint venture contract so as to accord with the principle of *juche*.[11] The South provides intermediate materials and equipment in kind, with PCT investors sending processed materials, product designs, equipment, and technical personnel to the North. In return, the South's investors receive finished products at prices compensating for the risk and costs incurred in supplying those inputs. The rationale of this arrangement is that the South has involved world markets by getting foreign buyers and help in marketing, financing, and technology. In order to compete in the global market, the South has imported both capital goods and product designs to sell its products at internationally competitive prices, to deliver on time, to meet quality standards, and to realize economies of scale. And the North has benefited from the South's investments and technology, increasing foreign trade, and undertaking the PCT with both the South and foreign countries.

The South's investment in the North has largely taken the form of the PCT (see Table 6.2); and, as economic contacts progress, a commercial relationship based on mutual trust should develop, accompanied by appropriate laws, regulations, and financial clearing systems.[12] The North's PCT seeks benefits from the flow of capital, technology, management, and other factors of production from the South, Japan, Germany, and other industrial countries (see Table 6.3).

Table 6.2 Inter-Korean Processing-on-Commission Trade (PCT) (on a custom clearance basis, unit US$ 1,000)

Year	North to South PCT	South to North PCT
1992	638	200
1993	2,985	4,023
1994	14,321	11,342
1995	21,174	24,718
1996	36,238	38,164
1997	42,894	36,175
Total	118,250	114,622

Source: S. Korea National Unification Board, (1998).

It is reported that the North's average wage is about $40 a month, while workers for a joint-venture firm receive an average of $150 a month. Though the South, due to its high wage level, has been investing in Southeast Asian countries, its business prefers to invest in the North because of no language barriers and transportation cost advantages. The two Koreas' business transactions provide the North with on-the-job training along with the market system. Table 6.4 demonstrates how the two Koreas' business transactions work through the processing-on-commission trade with the South.

The North has quietly welcomed a group of 13 technicians and engineers from Daewoo Corporation, the general trading arm of Daewoo, one of the South's big industrial groups. The team has helped train North Korean workers to make garments and bags for export. Under an agreement reached in May 1995, the North provides land, building and manpower at an industrial complex in the port city of Nampo, 50 kilometers southwest of the North's capital city, Pyongyang. This is the first time since the end of the Korean War in 1953 that North Korea has allowed South to remain in

Table 6.3 Processing-on-Commission Trade (1992) with Foreign Countries (Unit: US$ 1,000)

Country	Imports of Fabrics & Semi-Raw Textiles	Exports of Clothing
Japan	52,236	63,855
Hong Kong	9,392	15,596
Germany	1,784	69,488
Italy	800	100
France	–	6,700
Ireland	–	1,000
Switzerland	–	500
China	58,157	–
Singapore	9,500	–
India	1,000	–
Total	132,209	157,239

Source: KOTRA, (1993, p. 115).

the country for an extended period. The arrangement is also striking because it allows the South Koreans to have day-to-day contact with the North's factory workers, though the North has technically forbidden private contacts between its citizens and foreign visitors.

On December 30, 1991, the North formally permitted the unofficial economy to operate when it announced the creation of economic and free trade zones in Sonbong, Rajin, and Chongjin, south of the Tumen River. These zones offer foreign investors customs reduction, tax incentives, and capital protection. The North specifically established the free-trade zone in the Rajin-Sonbong area as an alternative to China's Tumen River Development Plan, and is advertising worldwide to induce foreign investment.

The Rajin-Sonbong region is a web of obsolete port facilities proclaimed a free-trade zone in 1991. Here North Korea hopes to incubate its economic turnaround. The North has engaged to develop this region by leasing out Chongjin Harbor to China and solidifying its position in shaping Northeast Asian economic cooperation around the Tumen River. The zone occupies a strategic transshipment point for cargo between Japan and China, and it is

Table 6.4 Consigned Processing Trade with South Korea's Business Sector
(based on permits, unit US$ 1,000)

Firm	1991	1992	1993	1994	Total (by firm)
Kolong	23	183			206
Seyoung Corporation		33			33
Ssangyong		94			94
Ssangbangwol			16		16
Yangji Enterprising			23		23
Hunt Corporation			100		100
Kukjae Trading			10	58	68
Samsung		218	1,879	4,461	6,558
Lucky Goldstar			660	5,967	6,627
Daewoo			1,460	2,666	4,126
Kohap			169	406	575
Hanil		28	67	605	700
Hyosung				19	19
Shinwon				48	48
Jindo Fashion				41	41
Total	23	558	4,384	14,271	19,234

Source: Federation of Korean Industries (1994, p. 13).

sufficiently remote to keep foreign ideas from infiltrating North Korean cities. The North is developing the Shinuiju and Nampo regions, since these are closer to China's economic centers and have better social overhead capital. As the Tumen River Project develops, it also serves for inter-Korean business transactions. The Tumen River Project could also be a model for attracting international business ventures, since it offers a framework for multilateral cooperation, but financing will be crucial to its success and may not be forthcoming (see Greg, 1994).

Once the North has carried out economic reform and attempts economic development, the South's business community should share management skills, information and experience with the North, and undertake any required training. Through these efforts, a new economic system is likely to take root in the Koreas. Its significance lies in a possible blending of the

North's labor and the South's capital and technology for a worldwide market. Hyundai's chairman Chung visited the North in 1989, at which time he reached a general agreement with the North to develop Kumkang Mountain into a world-famous tourist resort and to establish a joint venture locomotive plant and various other projects with the North. Hyundai Precision and Industry Co. and Inchon Iron and Steel Co., both affiliates of the Hyundai Group, have also promoted a joint-venture project with the North, to dismantle old ships. Two other Hyundai subsidiaries, Kumkang Development Industrial Co. and Hyundai Mipo Dockyard Co., plan to establish jacket manufacturing and ship-repair businesses, respectively, in the North.

Other large industrial firms of the South including Samsung, LG, and Daewoo, have also taken steps to initiate joint-venture projects with the North. Samsung has been trying to obtain permission from the North to set up and operate a telecommunications center in the Rajin-Sonbong free-trade zone. At the same time, Samsung would like to engage in the electronic business in the North in the form of processing-on-commission trade. LG, which has been already involved in a TV assembly plant in the North, plans to set up a color TV plant and scallop farms there. Daewoo is establishing a home appliance assembly plant in the North's Nampo industrial estate, while negotiating to establish hotels in the Rajin-Sonbong free-trade zone.

In a related development, Park Sang-hee, president of The Korea Federation of Small Business, visited the North, along with about 30 heads of Korea's small and medium-sized companies, to promote bilateral business transactions. Since the economic crisis, the need for a major breakthrough, like investment in the North, is growing more important for small companies, as the government's policy on imported foreign workers will almost certainly become less accommodating in the face of sizeable unemployment. In February 1998, the South raised the cap on direct investment in the North from $5 million to $10 million and planned for a complete relaxation of controls on nonstrategic investment. The South has also moved to change its export control rules *vis-à-vis* the North from a limited list of items that can be exported to a limited list of items that cannot be exported (see Task Force Report, 1998).

PROSPECTS FOR THE TWO KOREAS' ECONOMIC INTEGRATION

This historical overview of the two Koreas' economic transactions has revealed buoyant opportunities for reconciliation with erratic ups and downs. Despite concerted efforts of inter-Korean economic negotiations and transactions, the outcomes have been short-lived, truncated by political and security considerations. In contrast, the two Koreas now face a unique opportunity, not only because of global implications but also because they both seem so willing. The four powers – the US, China, Japan and Russia – provide an extra stimulus for them to resolve critical issues of nuclear, missile, and food. Specifically, the US–North Korea Agreement Framework of 1994 obligates the US to construct two light-water generators involving both South Korea and Japan.

The light-water reactor project may thus become the most important spark to further inter-Korean economic cooperation. Ground was broken for the construction of light-water nuclear reactors in the Kumho area of Sinpo, North Korea, in August 1997. Preceding the event, agreements were reached through the Korean Peninsula Energy Development Organization (KEDO) on such technical issues as entry and exit procedures, customs clearance, labor, and postal and medical service, contributing to the institutionalization of inter-Korean relations.

The agreements have enabled a number of procedural measures to be worked out, including the navigation of barges through the North's waters, the permanent presence of the South's technicians and government officials at the project site, the opening of a bank branch, the establishment of a direct telephone link, and the exchange of postal services.

The KEDO's implementing mechanism may be one of the bright spots in US–South Korean–Japanese cooperation with the North, establishing precedents for forthcoming foreign direct investment.

In another development Ralph Cossa, the Executive Director of Pacific Forum, proposed a Korean Peninsular Agricultural Development Organization, as initiated by the South, in order to resolve the chronic agricultural problems in the North. This organization would administer the future food aid and agricultural assistance programs that will channel the US, Japanese, and other international food aid to the North, with the South in the driver's seat and an emphasis not just on handouts but on agricultural development to address the North's long-term food needs. This approach could depoliticize US and Japanese food aid and provide a meaningful demonstration of actual support for President Dae Jung Kim's engagement policy.

Such a consortium would have distinct merits. First, the South's business would be able to invest in the North without bearing the brunt of the burden. Second, unexpected interference by the North could be prevented through multilateral cooperation. Third, the antagonism and fear of absorption that the North still harbors regarding the South could be diluted in a multilateral framework. Fourth, Japan and other countries could be checked from gaining the upper hand in the North by taking advantage of funds linked to Japan's diplomatic normalization with the North.

The most promising area for multilateral investment in the North seems to be in the tourism sector. One idea is to develop the Kumgang and Paekdu Mountains jointly as tourist attractions and distribute the resulting revenues among the investors. In addition to tourism, joint investments can be made in the development of industrial estates in the North. Hyundai reached an agreement with the North to develop the Kaesong Industrial Complex just north of Inchon, with 200 small and medium-sized businesses in making a variety of consumer products.

Despite the many difficulties and problems on the road towards inter-Korean economic cooperation, the mandate of the cooperation policy seems to be understood by North and South alike. Although the North's system is generally considered to be more vulnerable to alien shocks than that in the South, the North has made prodigious efforts to ensure that it could absorb and digest impacts from China's modernization programs and the Soviet Union's Perestroika policy without a considerable internal shake-up.

CONCLUSION

Understanding the track record of the two Koreas' business exchanges can help us in the critical task of finding a way to accelerate the two Koreas' economic transactions. Increased economic cooperation will lead to peaceful coexistence and economic integration with the concomitants of market extension, economies of scale, learning curve effects, competition, and trade creation.

Although the winds of political change throughout the communist world seem to have touched the North only belatedly, various signs of the two Koreas' economic cooperation seem most encouraging. The two Koreas should promote maximum business contacts toward economic integration. President Dae-Jung Kim urges the US and Japan to exchange liaison offices with the North as a prelude to establishing diplomatic relations and inducing the North to join the world community.

The North's leadership knows that reform should be introduced for economic recovery, and that their economic failure is the result of their long-practiced socialist economic principles and self-reliance. They also know that introducing reform creates the so-called reform dilemma and endangers their regime unless improvements are forthcoming at accelerating rate. The South should engage in business transactions with the North for realizing economic integration through trade promotion and dynamic international division of inputs. The leadership is at a crossroad.

South Korea must do all in its power to insure that North Korea takes the path toward the mutual prosperity and Korean unification.

NOTES

[1] Economic systems are compared by examining differences in economic ideology and political institutions. Capitalism is an economic-cultural system, organized around the institutions of private property and the production of goods for profit, and based culturally on the idea that the individual is the center of society. In a socialist system, the agents of production are, to varying degrees, owned by the state and operated not with a primary view to profit, but for the service of the population as a whole.

[2] The North's economic system is discussed in Kim (1991); see also the Bank of Korea (1993).

[3] This proposal was accommodated in due course by the South, and the historic four-day inter-Korean prime ministers' talks began on September 4 in Seoul, with a 90-member delegation from Pyongyang visiting via the "truce" village of Pamunjom.

[4] Though the inter-Korea trade has increased since 1988, the South's total foreign trade is much higher – $158.4 billion to the North, $2.7 billion in 1992 (Koo and Jo, 1995).

[5] New approaches toward economic integration have occurred through inter-Korean business talks, cultural contacts, sports events, and movements of businessmen between the two Koreas (Kim and Chang, 1998).

[6] The North's trading companies are discussed in Kim 1995; the Bank of Korea 1993.

[7] The South's exports in 1997 included $2.9 million in fuel oil and $1.7 million in materials for building light-water nuclear reactors, both provided under the 1994 Geneva Accord.

[8] Inter-Korean trade was analyzed in the IMF era (Park, 1998).

[9] There is, however, an important difference between the North's open-door policies and China's opening up to the outside world. The Chinese stance has been backed by policies designed to boost the domestic economy by expanding the market price system. In general, Chinese economic reform policies, including the agricultural contract system and industrial sector autonomy, have been developed gradually in a form that supports external liberalization policies.

[10] Hwang discusses North Korean laws applicable to foreign capital and practical approaches to foreign investment in North Korea (Hwang, 1994); foreign investments in North Korea expect to follow the model of South Korean companies already making advance there (*The New York Times*, 1999).

[11] Inter-Korean PCTs were relatively balanced because the PCTs, trade involved essentially the same items (Flake, 1998).

[12] See Lee (1995) for a discussion on North's processing-on-commission trade.

REFERENCES

Bank of Korea (1993), "The Estimation of North Korean GNP in 1992," Seoul: the Bank of Korea.

Federation of Korean Industries (1994), *South-North Economic Cooperation in Action: Facts & Interpretation (*in Korean), November.

Flake, L. Gordon (1998), "Inter-Korean Economic Relations", *Korea's Economy1998*, 14, 131–5.

Greg, Harold (1994), "A Regional Development Strategy for the Tumen River Economic Development Area," Preliminary Draft Report for the UNDP, April 22.

Hwang, Eui-gak (1994), "North Korean Laws for the Induction of Foreign Capital and Practical Approaches to Foreign Investment in North Korea," *Vantage Point*, XVII, (3), March, 1–10.

Kim, Samuel S. (1995), "North Korea in 1994," *Asian Survey*, XXX (1), January, 23–26.

Kim,Youn-Suk (1991), "Prospects for the Two Koreas' Economic Cooperation," *The Journal of East and West Studies,* 20 (2), October, 1–12.

Kim, Youn-Suk and Semoon Chang (1998), "Inter-Korean Business Economics," *Asian Profile,* **26** (3), June, 207– 214.

Koo, Bon Ho and Dongho Jo, (1995) "Comparative Analysis of the North and South Korean Economies," in Lee-Jay Cho and Yoon Hyung Kim (eds), *Economic Systems in South and North Korea: The Agenda for Economic Integration,* Seoul: Korea Development Institute, May, 21–57.

KOTRA (1993), *Investment in North Korea* (in Korean), June.

Lee, Young-Sun (1995), "North Korean Economy, Inter-Korean Cooperation," *Korea Focus,* 3 (2), Seoul: Korea Foundation, March–April 1995, 41–55.

Park, Jin (1998), "Inter-Korean Economic Relations in the IMF Era," *Korea Focus*, **6** (2), March–April, 69–71.

S. Korea National Unification Board, (1998), *Monthly Report on North -South Trade & Cooperation.*

The New York Times, November 21, 1999, 7.

Task Force Report (1998), *Managing Change on the Korean Peninsula.*

The Wall Street Journal, November 23, 1999, A19

7 Can Reindustrialization of North Korea Support A Sustainable Food Supply?*

Xinshen Diao, John Dyck, Chinkook Lee, and Agapi Somwaru

NORTH KOREA'S FOOD DILEMMA

North Korea has been facing food shortages at least since the early 1990s, and the shortages have led to widespread malnutrition and even deaths (see Chang (1999) and the reports of the World Food Program for detailed analysis during the 1990s). While in the short term food donations may help North Korea to overcome this shortage, in the medium to long term the country will have to pay for imported foodstuffs. It is far from clear at this moment how these payments can be accomplished.

North Korea was reportedly a grain-deficit region throughout the period of the Japanese Occupation (which ended in 1945). Prior to the partition of the Korean peninsula in 1948, the colder and more industrialized North imported food from the more fertile South. While it has abundant water and some fertile plains, North Korea's weather is treacherous: the growing season is rather short, and cold snaps occur during the season. Widespread

* This paper was presented at the Korea–America Economic Association, Washington, DC, October 4–5, 1999. The authors acknowledge the help of Birgit Meade in developing a foodgrain deficit estimate for North Korea, and are grateful to Joy Harwood, Praveen Dixit, Bill Kost and the conference participants for their critical comments and suggestions. The views expressed in this paper are those of the authors and do not reflect the official position of the Economic Research Service, the US Department of Agriculture and International Food Policy Research Institute.

crop failure for rice is therefore a distinct possibility every year. The short season also makes production of corn, the other main crop, quite volatile. After the partition, North Korea sought food security through self-sufficiency, encouraging the production of rice in the southernmost provinces, while corn, potatoes and other staples were grown in the northern provinces. However, even if North Korea has surplus labor and uses inputs like fertilizer and fungicide generously, natural conditions will prevent its annual harvest from satisfying domestic needs so often that it should not consider self-sufficiency in grains as a realistic goal (see Dyck, 1997). Table 7.1 presents recent estimates of North Korea's production, trade, and consumption of food grains, the staple food of North Korea.

Table 7.1 Total Grain Situation in North Korea

Production/ Use	Area (hectare)	Yield (ton/hectare)	Production	Imports (1000 tons)	Consumption	Food aid	Population (million)
1995/1996	1233	2.04	2509	931	3440	400	23.2
1996/1997	1205	2.38	2874	1345	4377	323	23.5
1997/1998	1289	2.20	2838	1219	4057	814	23.8
1998/1999	1279	2.66	3400	—	—	—	—

Note: Area, yield, and production refer to the earlier year, and trade and consumption to the later year, because the fall harvest is used in the following calendar year.
Source: World Food Program, with adjustments by the authors. Not official USDA estimates.

North Korea's shortage of food is also a symptom of its sharp economic decline and rising population. In the late 1980s, North Korea was able to import large amounts of grain (see Dyck, 1994). After the breakup of the Soviet Union, the end of central planning in the Soviet Union and East European countries, and changes in the economic philosophy of China, North Korea's economy imploded. Its key export markets vanished, and its ability to trade for inputs, such as petroleum, disappeared.

Given a better economic performance, North Korea could buy from the world market the food it lacks. This shortfall is significant. A recent estimate of North Korea's minimum grain needs, based on population data and grain consumption per person needed to maintain a minimum level of health, indicates that North Korea's grain import needs could be 1.55 million tons in 2000, rising as high as 1.64 million tons in 2007.[1] Such estimates have a large margin of error, both because historical data are estimated based on partial information and because assumptions about future levels of production in North Korea may be far off the mark. With an estimate of $253 per ton for the average value of North Korea's grain imports for 1995–97 as a proxy for the price of grain imports in the future, the cost of covering this food gap would be $350 million in 2000, rising to $415 million in 2007. The composition and pricing of future grain imports are likely to be different from the past, introducing even more uncertainty into this estimate. However, it may represent the correct order of magnitude for the potential costs of grain imports.

Export strategies for North Korea may exist that can fund this level of commercial food imports and close the grain gap. North Korea's chief resource today is its population. Because much of North Korea's industry has shut down or reduced output, a potential pool of labor is available at wages considerably lower than in the rest of Northeast Asia. From such a base North Korea can develop export-oriented light industry that is intensive in the use of labor. Recent history suggests that industries in the textile and footwear sectors meet these criteria. Given trade opportunities and foreign capital investment that will supply machinery and intermediate inputs (like fabric or leather), North Korea can earn foreign exchange and pay for food imports. But the North's government must permit firms to operate efficient commercial undertakings inside the country and afford them the necessary foreign linkages so that inputs can be imported and outputs exported (Lee, 1994).

A significant "processing on commission" ("*Jia-gong Cheng-bao*") trade of the sort outlined above already exists in North Korea. Organized by firms in South Korea and elsewhere, shops in North Korea provide the labor for sewing imported fabric into wearing apparel for export. The North Korean operations receive commissions in return for processing the fabric, and the output (chiefly wearing apparel) is then exported. North Korea does not publish trade data, so judging the size of the trade is difficult. The largest market with detailed data on the export flow out of North Korea is Japan. During 1994–96, Japanese imports of textile/footwear products from North Korea ranged between 9 and 14 billion yen (or $90–$130 million). Of this, about 90 percent was in the category of woven textile products, such as suits, pants, and shirts.

Figure 7.1 shows the imports of woven textile products by Japan from both North and South Korea. South Korea, once a principal exporter of finished textile, footwear, and leather goods, has seen its global exports of these products slump since the end of the 1980s. More than any other factor, rising labor costs in South Korea have caused labor-intensive activities to leave the country. Sewing cloth into garments is labor-intensive, while spinning yarn from raw fibers, and weaving and knitting fabric from yarn can be mechanized. Similarly, tanning leather is easier to mechanize than sewing shoes, purses, and so on, from leather. As is evident in Figure 7.1, Japan's imports from South Korea fell in the early 1990s,

Figure 7.1 Woven Apparel Imports of Japan from South and North Korea

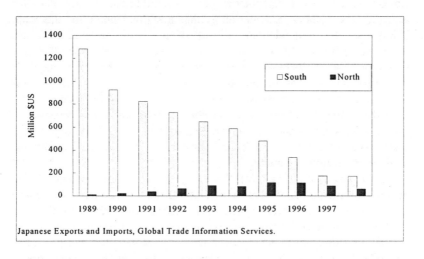

Japanese Exports and Imports, Global Trade Information Services.

while imports from North Korea rose, at least for a few years. Presumably, the imports from North Korea were largely organized by South Korean firms, which shifted labor-intensive portions of garment assembly from South Korea (or possibly third countries) into North Korea.

Inspired by this evidence of actual trade activity, our analysis probes the rationale behind the "processing on commission" trade and the potential revenues that it can generate. Some explanations of the activity of South Korean firms in North Korea may be strategic or political. Perhaps such firms have been intent on establishing an early relationship with the North Korean market for strategic reasons, rather than to make money in the short term. Possibly the investments were made out of humanitarian concerns or to please South Korea's government. Our study seeks confirmation of a solid economic rationale for such investments, separate from the motives just suggested. The study also seeks plausible scenarios in which the size of the expansion of South Korea's textile industry into the North would be sufficient to generate returns that could pay for food imports of the amount estimated above.

METHOD FOR THE STUDY

The information about North Korea's economic structure and trade is fragmentary. Any standard empirical method, whether using time-series or cross-section data or a set of data from a social accounting matrix, is hard to apply to the case of North Korea due to the information limitations. Noland et al. (1999a and 1999b) use data from a pre-reform (1979) Chinese input–output table to create a Social Accounting Matrix (SAM) for North Korea and conduct a computable general equilibrium (CGE) modeling analysis. The authors' assumption is that a starting point for the inter-industry input–output relations in North Korea is performance in China, reflecting common links to 1970's-vintage Soviet manufacturing technology. While the cross-entropy technique used in that study may help in constructing a SAM for North Korean economy, the reliability of the underlying Chinese data set is still questionable. However, the conclusions from the studies by Noland et al. (1999a, 1999b) are quite interesting. It finds that only trade- and reform-centered strategies are likely to provide a sustainable solution to North Korea's problems. This finding supports the intuition motivating our study.

As in Noland et al. (1999a), this study employs a general equilibrium model. However, unlike Noland et al. (1999a), we do not attempt to create a CGE model for North Korean economy. Instead, we create a CGE model for South Korea, and artificially extend the South Korean economy, by simulating a situation in which it can tap North Korean labor in just a few textile/leather sectors. Using this model, we try to assess how much foreign exchange North Korea earns through its exports of textile/footwear products. Because the possibility of such an increase in North Korean exports relies on South Korea's investing in the North's textile/footwear industry or shifting its own industry up there, a general equilibrium model for South Korea is more crucial for the study.

Textile, footwear, and leather industries have been major export sectors in South Korea; the shift of these labor-intensive activities out of the country started at the end of the 1980s. Our study is based on data from the 1990 Social Accounting Matrix (SAM) of South Korea (constructed by the Bank of Korea, 1991), which contains relatively detailed textile sectors. A SAM is a data set that includes production activities like inputs and output; intermediate and final demand, imports and exports of each sector's goods; factor endowments and their allocation across sectors; and trade policy (tariffs and export subsidies/taxes) by sector. The data in a SAM are for one year and are organized to obtain a balanced outcome. In the SAM, for example, the output of fabric production becomes the input for producing wearing apparel. Total demand for apparel equals total domestic production minus exports and plus imports, while demand includes consumption, intermediate use, investment, and increase in inventory. The cost of apparel includes the value of fabric as a part of intermediate costs and production factor costs like wages and returns to capital. Since textile sectors were larger in 1990 than in 1999 in South Korea, the study may overestimate the potential for South Korea to shift its textile sectors out of the country and to the North.

There are 29 textile, footwear and leather product sectors in the 1990 SAM of South Korea (see Table 7.A1 in Appendix). We identify 5 of them as labor-intensive, with the potential for relocation to the North, and aggregate the other 24 into nine sectors that can be mechanized or are mainly upstream or relatively capital-intensive. In addition to textile/footwear, the model contains nine aggregated sectors for agriculture, other manufacturing, and services. These sectors also compete for inputs of economy-wide resources like labor and capital. The model follows the traditional neoclassical economic theory, assuming that a representative firm for each sector maximizes profits in its choice of primary and intermediate inputs. The derived final demand for each commodity is also included in the model in a manner consistent with the utility maximization theory. In the representation of trade, domestic and foreign goods are specified as imperfect substitutes, following an Armington specification. A detailed model description can be found in Diao et al. (1999).

The economic motivation for the firms in South Korean textile industry to relocate production capacities into the North is modeled to utilize North Korea's low-cost labor supply. To simplify the model, we assume that there are no capital adjustment, training, relocation, or transactions costs when capital facilities are shipped to and established in North Korea. With such simplification, the analysis can focus on what level of textile/footwear export activity is needed for North Korea to pay for its food shortfall through its input–output relationship with the South Korean economy.

SCENARIOS AND RESULTS

As in any CGE model, the study employs counterfactual simulations to assess the magnitude of foreign exchange earning by North Korea stemming from the extension of South Korean textile and footwear sectors into the North. Specifically, we assume that firms in South Korea's textile and footwear sectors can pay a lower wage rate to North Korean workers, that the supply of North Korean labor is perfectly elastic at this price, and that North Korean workers are not allowed to emigrate to the South. A lower wage rate also applies to South Korean labor in the textile/footwear sectors (The Bank of Korea, 1995), but we separate the labor market for textiles/footwear from that for all other sectors in South Korea's economy, disallowing North Korean labor to be used by the other sectors. Thus, the pool of lower-cost North Korean labor in the textile/footwear sectors can depress wages among South Korea's textile/footwear workers, but not among workers in other sectors. Due to a lower wage rate, South Korean textile/footwear firms' demand for labor increases, and is met by North Korean workers, so that workplaces relocate to North Korea.

The sectors assumed to employ North Korean workers are the five labor-intensive textile/footwear sectors in the SAM. They are wearing apparel, leatherwear articles, other leather products, leather footwear, and non-leather footwear. Two scenarios are conducted for two different levels of wage rates. In the first scenario, the wage rate that workers face is arbitrarily assumed to be 15 percent lower than that for South Korean workers as a whole, while in the second scenario, this wage gap increases to 25 percent. If South Korean firms can pay a low wage rate for North Korean workers, the wage rate for South Korean workers who are employed in a similar sector would be pushed down. In addition to this hardship for the existing South Korean workforce in these specific sectors, South Korean labor unions would respond with concern that South Korea might lose all employment within the country in the textile/leather industry as such jobs moved outside the country. Some of these costs of dislocation would be alleviated as South Korea moved ahead with economic expansion: increased domestic demand for more skilled labor and outsourcing for unskilled labor might benefit the economy over time (Lee and Schluter, 1999). Structural adjustment issues like these are beyond the purview of this paper (but expressed well in, for example, Lee, 1994).

The purpose of these two scenarios is to assess the range of income generated at different wage levels. Accordingly, we concentrate on the model results regarding the effects of a lower wage rate on production, exports, and additional labor demand in the five labor-intensive textile/footwear sectors.

The input structure of the five sectors, as portrayed by the South Korean SAM of 1990, is presented in Table 7.2. Labor costs accounted for more than 80 percent of total value added all of the sectors, but the other leather products. They use intermediate inputs so intensively that these inputs accounted for 65 percent of the total value of sectoral output for the non-leather footwear sector, and more than 70 percent in all the rest. The last three columns in Table 7.2 show shares of output, exports, and sectors are clear in the table. Each accounts for more than 30 percent of the total output

Table 7.2 Shares of Input Costs and Output in the Selected Five Sectors (percentage)

	Share of intermediate inputs in sector output	Share of labor costs in sector value added	Output[a]	Exports[b]	Labor demand[c]
Wearing apparel	78.1	80.4	37.9	33.0	28.9
Non-leather footwear	64.8	79.5	34.7	36.8	46.3
Leatherwear articles	80.1	83.7	12.8	16.1	9.7
Other leather products	71.6	67.0	9.5	11.3	10.2
Leather footwear	77.0	86.9	5.1	2.8	4.9

Notes

[a] Total % output of the five sectors included in the table is 100.

[b] Total % exports of the five sectors are 100.

[c] Total % labor demand by the five sectors is 100.

here. While the share of wearing apparel is the largest in total output, the largest share of labor employment is in non-leather footwear, which implies that the non-leather footwear is more competitive for low-cost labor. The non-leather footwear sector also accounts for the largest export share in the five sectors. Thus, if this sector employs more North Korean labor than other sectors, the foreign exchange generated from exports would be larger.

Non-leather footwear in the 1990 data is quite a large employer of labor due to its highly labor-intensive character. However, in recent years this sector has shrunk significantly. Data from South Korean statistics show that its share in total textile wage costs was only about 20 percent in 1995, down from more than 30 percent in 1990. Thus, the simulation results may overestimate the current ability of South Korea's footwear sector to shift to the North.

Since the major purpose of the simulations is to see the aggregate impacts of lowering the wage rate on output, exports, and labor demand, we first report these aggregate results in Table 7.3. The simulation results show that demand for labor in the highly labor-intensive sectors is elastic with respect to changes in the wage rate. Thus, with a low wage rate, these

Table 7.3 Impacts of Lowering Wage Rates on Five Sectors' Production
and Labor Demand (compared to the base year in the SAM)

	Lowering wage rate by	
	15 percent	25 percent
Increase in total output (%)	50	113
Increase in total labor demand (%)	81	205
Increase in total labor income (billion won)	1423	3161

sectors' demand for labor dramatically increases. For example, with the
Cobb–Douglas technology used in the model's production function, if the
wage rate falls by 15 percent, holding output price constant, demand for
labor increases by more than 75 percent, while output surges 50 percent. Of
course, if the supply elasticity of input is more (less) than unitary, that is,
the production function is not Cobb–Douglas in nature, the input demand
response will be smaller (larger) than the case we discuss here. Moreover, if
the output price faced by the producers changes due to the general
equilibrium linkages between demand and supply, the response of labor
demand will also be different. Thus, the numbers presented in Table 7.3
merely suggest the magnitude of increases in income, output, and labor
demand when wage rates are reduced.

Given that the effect on total labor demand of lowering the wage rate in
the five sectors is significant, we examine which sectors would hire more
labor. This analysis provides an indication of which sectors would be more
attractive for South Korean firms if they could take advantage of a lower
wage rate in the North. Table 7.4 shows that more than 90 percent of low-
cost labor would be hired by the non-leather footwear sector, while the
capacity for the other four sectors to hire new low-cost labor is much
smaller. Moreover, the lower the wage rate, the more labor would be hired
in the non-leather footwear sector.

This is an intriguing result. It is true that the non-leather footwear
industry was a large sector in terms of the value of its total output, as
it accounted for 35 percent of production in the total five sectors (Table
7.2). However, the wearing apparel sector is even larger, accounting for
38 percent of the five sectors' total output (Table 7.2), but does not generate
a large demand for low-cost labor in this scenario, with its labor demand
rising only about 6 percent. Thus, the size of the sector is not the main

reason. There must an explanation related to the production structure of these sectors. For this, we look further at the labor employed by per unit of output for each sector (Table 7.5).

The implication of the non-leather footwear sector's employing more labor in terms of per unit of output is that it is most labor-intensive if the intermediate inputs are taken into account in the production function. This characteristic, together with the size of the sector, causes the sector to hire more labor when labor becomes less expensive, as predicted by the Stolper–Samuelson theory.

Table 7.4 Share of Increased Demand for Labor by Sector (total increased demand is 100)

| | Lowering wage rate by | |
	15 percent	25 percent
Wearing apparel	5.6	3.7
Non-leather footwear	92.5	94.9
Leatherwear articles	7.4	4.2
Leather footwear	0.9	0.7
Other leather products	-6.3	-3.4

Table 7.5 Labor Employed by Per 100 Unit of Output in 1990s SAM

Wearing apparel	15.16
Non-leather footwear	26.51
Leatherwear articles	14.93
Leather footwear	17.33
Other leather products	22.67

A priori, we guessed that the wearing apparel sector should be more elastic in response to a low wage rate and hence have the highest opportunity to hire more low-cost labor among the five sectors. The simulation results do not bear out our expectation (see Table 7.4). We must ask more questions. It turns out that wearing apparel uses more intermediate inputs in its production process. The share of intermediate input costs accounted for more than 78 percent of the wearing apparel sector's revenue in 1990 (Table 7.2). When the wage rate is lowered and demand for labor increases, so does production. More output needs more intermediate inputs. In the general equilibrium model, such additional demand for intermediates pushes up the price for these commodities so that producers of intermediate goods can respond with supply. At a higher level of prices for the intermediate goods, costs for any sector using them more intensively will increase more. The result will be a more modest response to a low-cost labor supply. The change in output of the five sectors due to the low wage rate (Table 7.6) is consistent with this analysis. That is, wearing apparel sector's output rises by only 4.0 and 2.4 percent, respectively, in the two scenarios, while the output of non-leather footwear sector rises by 135 and 320 percent, respectively.

Table 7.6 Changes in Output by Sector in the Simulations (percent from the 1990s data)

| | Lowering wage rate by | |
	15 percent	25 percent
Wearing apparel	4.14	2.43
Non-leather footwear	134.95	318.81
Leatherwear articles	48.40	59.88
Leather footwear	7.01	11.31
Other leather products	-52.82	-76.87

In the data of the 1990 SAM, the other leather product sector is the least labor-intensive among the five sectors, with the labor cost accounting for less than 70 percent of value added in the sector (Table 7.2). Accordingly, even though the other leather products industry does not use intermediate input more intensively than the other three sectors (except for non-leather footwear), it still cannot compete with other sectors for low-cost labor. Following a typical general equilibrium outcome, the output of this sector falls due to increased capital costs driven by production expansion in the other sectors.

Increasing North Korea's exports is the goal for our simulations. The five sectors are quite export-oriented in the 1990 South Korean SAM. Except for the sector of Leather Footwear, exports accounted for 60 to 90 percent of output for the other four sectors (Table 7.2). This pattern makes it reasonable to believe that the expansion of production due to the supply of low-cost labor from North Korea would stimulate exports. Table 7.7 does show such results.

From Table 7.7 we see that the export response to low-cost labor supply is larger than the supply response (in Table 7.6) for most sectors, except for other leather products. These results imply that these sectors become more dependent on the world market while South Korea's domestic consumption may fall when the wage rate is lowered in the light industry sectors. This further shows that the fear by South Korean workers, especially the unskilled ones, that shifting labor-intensive textile sectors to North Korea may hurt their direct interest is reasonable. If the unskilled workers who used to work in those labor-intensive sectors can be partially compensated or re-employed by other sectors through necessary training, the negative consequences may be reduced.

Table 7.7 Increases in Exports by Sector due to Lowering Wage Rate (percent from the 1990s data)

| | Lowering wage rate by | |
	15 percent	25 percent
Wearing apparel	5.44	2.35
Non-leather footwear	160.10	379.00
Leatherwear articles	53.76	66.40
Leather footwear	14.39	22.48
Other leather products	-63.17	-83.46

The results from the two scenarios indicate the potential of expanding the textile/footwear industries into North Korea. Lowering wage rates (tantamount to adding labor) by relatively modest proportions generates increased production, exports, and labor income. The result in both scenarios is largely dependent on expansion in the non-leather footwear sector, because of the high dependence on primary labor inputs of that sub-sector. However, as we have seen in the real case, woven apparel (part of the wearing apparel sector in the model) dominates the key trade between North Korea and Japan, and there are no indications that any actual shift of the non-leather footwear sector into North Korea has occurred.

Does our result of expanded production still hold if, for some reason, transfer of the labor-intensive parts of non-leather footwear production into North Korea is infeasible? To address this question, we add a third scenario, in which the non-leather footwear is excluded from the sectors in which wage rates are lowered. When the model is run again, but with four disaggregated textile/footwear sectors rather than five, the results show a shift into another leather category, the Leatherwear Articles. Further restricting the sectors by excluding the leatherwear articles sector, the model finally generates a large increase in the production and exports of the wearing apparel. In this case, the total increase in labor income is 515 billion won ($368 million) in the scenario of 15 percent wage reduction, rising to 1,300 billion won ($929 million) in the 25 percent wage reduction. It appears that shifting labor-intensive light industries into a lower-wage setting affects the industries' expansion differently. From the final scenario, it appears that extra income accruing to the wearing apparel sector alone can generate enough income to accommodate for food grain demand.

In reality, the woven apparel industry constituted the main North Korean "processing for commission" sector in the early 1990s. The footwear and leather goods industries of South Korea, which our analysis suggests would be the ones with the most to gain from a lower wage rate, did not do so. The woven apparel industry had already experienced a significant shift out of South Korea by 1990, our base year, and perhaps the parts of that industry remaining in South Korea had limited potential for expansion. The absence of a shift of footwear production to a North Korean platform may reflect rigidities due to the difficulty of capital transfer. The results are sensitive to *which* textile or footwear industry is considered, since the industries differ in capital and labor needs as well as in profitability.

SUMMARY AND CONCLUSION

Using scenarios that lower wage rates in the textile/footwear industry in South Korea, we have examined a limited reindustrialization of North Korean light industry to generate income sufficient to import food and alleviate hunger in North Korea. Our results indicate that if North Korea had been willing to open up its economy in 1990 it could have used low-wage surplus labor to produce output in selected sectors of the textile, footwear, and leather industries. Our scenarios have shown in a counterfactual fashion that enough income could be generated to buy grain on the international market and close North Korea's foodgrain deficit. Even the Wearing Apparel sector by itself can generate enough income. This was the subsector in which industry actually did shift to the North in the early 1990s. Our analysis suggests that if shifting footwear and leather-goods industries to the North had occurred, much greater gains could have been obtained. Further analysis should continue to explore such a limited, or sectoral, reindustrialization as a means for making North Korea's food supply secure.

A partial shift in the structure of light industry in North Korea is easier to outline in scenarios on paper than to implement in reality. We can show that a significant expansion in industrial activity is possible if North Korean labor were available to South Korean companies. We can measure the extra output and the putative wage bill. However, how the division of earnings is to be effected among participating North Korean workers, North Korea's government, and South Korean firms is obviously problematic, and the risk of mistreating workers is not to be treated idly. The ability of commercial enterprises to survive in a society like North Korea that is not organized to support the activities of a firm is another matter worth questioning. Presumably, some of these issues have arisen among the actual enterprises that have been involved in the "processing on commission" and other kinds of commercial activity in the North in recent years. Case studies of these enterprises would be useful to assess the likelihood that partial re-industrialization can succeed. The problems it would help solve are so serious that the incentive is large indeed.

NOTES

[1] The estimate uses grain balance data maintained by the Food and Agriculture Organization (FAO) in the Food Security Assessment framework used at ERS. See USDA/ERS (1998) for this methodology.

REFERENCES

The Bank of Korea (1995), *Economic Statistics Yearbook.*

Chang, Namsoo (1999), "Status of Food Shortage and Malnutrition in North Korea," *Korea Focus,* **7** (1) (January–February), 47–62.

Diao, Xinshen, John Dyck, Chinkook Lee, David Skully, and Agapi Somwaru (1999), "Structural Change and Agricultural Protection: The Costs of Korean Agricultural Policy, 1975 and 1990," a paper presented at the American Agricultural Economics Association, Nashville, Tennessee, August 8–11.

Dyck, John (1994), "The Agricultural Situation in North Korea," *Asia and Pacific Rim,* Economic Research Service report WRS-94-6, Oct. 1994, 47–50.

Dyck, John (1997), "Korean Agriculture in the 1990s and beyond," paper presented at the Food and Security on the Korean Peninsula Conference, University of Maryland, College Park, MD.

Global Trade Information Services, *World Trade Atlas, Japan Edition* (cd

-rom).

Lee, Chinkook and Gerald Schluter (1999), "Effects of Trade on the Demand for Skilled and Unskilled workers," *Economic Systems Research*, Journal of International Input–Output Association, 11 (1), 49–65.

Lee, Hy Sang (1994), "Economic Factors in Korean Reunification," in Young Whan Kihl, (ed.), *Korea and the World: Beyond the Cold* War, Boulder, Colorado: Westview.

Lee, Young Sun (1994), "Economic Integration of the Korean Peninsular: A Scenario Approach to the Cost of Unification," in Seung Yeung Kwack, (ed.), *The Korean Economy at a Crossroad*, Westport, Connecticut: Praeger.

Noland, Marcus, Sherman Robinson, and Tao Wang (1999a), "Famine in North Korea: Causes and Cures," Working paper Series Number 99-1, Institute for International Economics.

Noland, Marcus, Sherman Robinson, and Tao Wang (1999b), "Rigorous Speculation: The Collapse and Revival of the North Korean Economy," Working paper Series Number 99-1, Institute for International Economics.

United States Department of Agriculture, Economic Research Service (1998), *Food Security Assessment*, December.

APPENDIX

Table 7.A1 Textile, Footwear, and Related Sectors in South Korea's
1990 Social Accounting Matrix

---

1. Raw silk and silk yarn
2. Cotton yarn
3. Woolen yarn
4. Hempen yarn
5. Rayon yarn
6. Synthetic fiber yarn
7. Thread and other fiber yarns
8. Silk fabrics
9. Cotton fabrics
10. Woolen fabrics
11. Hempen fabrics
12. Rayon fabrics
13. Other synthetic fiber fabrics
14. Other fiber fabrics
15. Knitted underwear
16. Knitted outwear
17. Other knitted products
18. Cordage, rope and fishing nets
19. Textile products
20. Other textile products
21. **Wearing apparel and apparel accessories**
22. Leather
23. **Leather apparel**
24. Luggage and handbags
25. **Miscellaneous leather products**
26. **Leather footwear**
27. **Tennis footwear and other shoes**
28. Fur
29. Fur products

Note: The sectors in bold are the focus of this study

8 North–South Korean Economic Cooperation in Telecommunications

Sang Taek Kim

INTRODUCTION

North–South Korean economic cooperation in information and telecommunications has been promoted in a very limited fashion because the North Korean government feared the consequences for its political regime. However, the telecommunications network is one of the most important infrastructures in any national economy. Economic cooperation in information and telecommunications plays a critical role in determining the degree and speed of any other cooperation in economic, social and cultural fields.

By enabling both North and South Korea to communicate and cooperate with each other without any physical contact even in a situation where political mistrust still prevails, it can also be a very effective tool to speed up reunification and to restore the national homogeneity that has been lost for more than half a century. Economic cooperation in telecommunications should continuously be promoted to ease the burden of reunification, given the enormous social cost of overcoming social and cultural divergence between the North and the South.

Preventative measures must also be considered to minimize the social disorder caused by a lack of telecommunications infrastructures in the North. As presented in Figure 8.1, the request for improving telecommunications infrastructures was much higher than for any other fields of the social overhead capital after the German reunification. Rapidly establishing telecommunications network in the North and integrating it with the network of the South will clearly be critical for Korea as well.

This study presents measures to promote cooperative projects in telecommunications before achieving reunification between South and North Korea, and provides guidance on telecommunication business policies after reunification (see Figure 8.2). The current telecommunications industry and services in North Korea are outlined in the beginning, along with the objectives and functions of telecommunications. Examples of cooperative projects in information and telecommunications are then presented in five different classifications: business, academic, socio-cultural, geographic and international approaches. These are designed to help the reader understand the current projects between the two Koreas, and are also combined to deduce and develop concrete economic cooperative projects. Within a framework built to analyze the policy issues after reunification, possible national objectives are stated, with policy measures presented and discussed to accomplish them. Discussion of the framework focuses on regulatory subjects like entry regulation, price regulation, fair competition and relations with foreign firms.

Figure 8.1 Request for SOC Improvement after the German Reunification

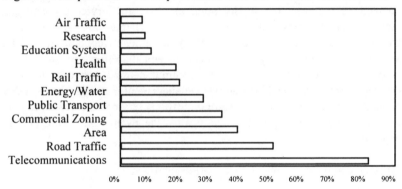

Source: Deutsche Telekom.

Figure 8.2 Objectives of Study

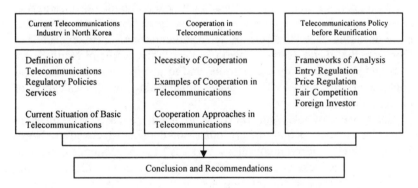

TELECOMMUNICATIONS SERVICES IN NORTH KOREA

Understanding the telecommunications industry is difficult because only a few statistics have been disclosed so far from North Korea. North Korea itself barely reports its statistics, so most of the information has been obtained from international organizations or from the Third World nations with diplomatic ties with the North. Based on this limited amount of information, it is possible only to estimate the underdeveloped state of the telecommunications industries in North Korea.

A basic understanding of the institutional structures, laws and facilities that constitute the divergent North and South Koreas is necessary to promote economic cooperation in telecommunications between the two sides. Required statistics can be conceptually divided into supply and demand. First, from the supply point of view, are service capacity and facility characteristics. Capabilities of personnel must also be evaluated based on specialties in organization management, regulations, special knowledge, the possibility of re-education, and the effects of training, as well as on the quality of the telecommunications network, network capacity, technical levels, and network management methods. On the other hand, demand estimation of telecommunications services is essential to plan the construction of required capacity after the evaluation of the current capacity.

Objective and Functions of Telecommunications

Telecommunications in North Korea are designed for the propagation of information using such media as newspapers, broadcasting stations and magazines. North Korean leaders regard telecommunications services as a tool to support the communist party and national economic organizations in supervising and guiding economic activities. In addition, North Korea has been declaring that "the role of telecommunications is to explain and propagate the '*juche*' (self-reliance) ideology to the people of North Korea and foreign revolutionary compatriots, and to justify the political line and policies of the party." They place broadcasting in the category of telecommunications as well.

The concept of telecommunications in North Korea is very different from that in South Korea or any other non-communist countries. North Korea defines "telecommunications services" as an economic field that facilitates the process of social production and serves as a lifeline for the residents by means of transmitting and receiving utility services such as electricity, telephone and mail. Hence its role is to satisfy the administrative demand of the party, the government, and the armed forces. Nevertheless, the way telecommunications services are classified in North Korea is not significantly different from other countries, as shown in Figure 8.3.

Figure 8.3 Classification of Telecommunications Services in North Korea

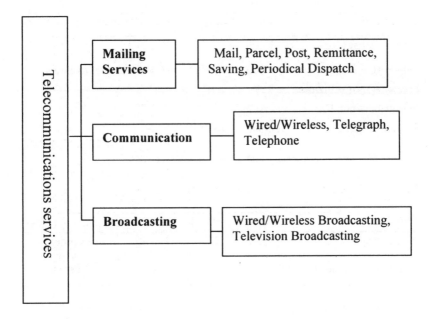

Basic Telecommunications Facilities

Because the purpose of telecommunications services in North Korea is to satisfy public administrative demand, meeting private demand is not considered urgent. Telecommunications facilities in the North are therefore grossly inadequate for the population as a whole.

Since raw data are scanty, the precise number of local service subscribers and lines can only be estimated. The World's Telecommunications Index issued by TTA in 1995 shows that the number of subscriber lines in the North was 1,307,200 in 1993, 1/15 the number in South Korea. The number of subscriber lines per 100 persons was 4.82 in the North, 1/8 the 37.75 level in the South. In 1993 16,640 people were officially waiting for services.

In general, only high-class officials such as Communist Party executives can subscribe to telecommunications services. Other private citizens can only use pay phones or public phones installed in factories and collective farms. The number of pay phones installed in North Korea was 2,720 in

1996, 1/125 of the South. The number of lines per 1,000 persons was 7.45 in South Korea, while the North Korea's level was 0.12, 1/62 of the South.

Table 8.1 Comparison of Subscribers

Classification	Unit	North(A)	South(B)	Comparison (B/A)
Service capabilities	1,000	1,307.2	20,223.1	15 times
Subscribers	1,000	1,089.3	16,632.6	15 times
Percentage of utilization	%	83	82.2	–
Subscribers per 100	Persons	4.82	37.75	8 times
Service waiters	Persons	16,640	–	–

Source: Korea Telecommunications Technology Association (1995).

Table 8.2 Comparison of Pay Phones (1996)

Classification	Unit	North(A)	South(B)	Comparison (B/A)
Number of Phones	EA	2,720	339,240	125 times
Number of phones per 1000	EA	0.12	7.45	62 times

Source: ITU (1998).

At an early stage of reunification, most of the telephone traffic between North and South Korea is expected to be calls between administrators, businesses, and separated families. Because residential phones are few in number, and constructing more after reunification will take time, public pay phones will be essential in the transition. Rapidly increasing the supply of pay phones should therefore be a priority in the early stages of reunification.

PROPOSALS FOR COOPERATION IN TELECOMMUNICATIONS BEFORE REUNIFICATION

Business Approach

North Korea permits very few types of economic cooperation projects. Three possible forms of businesses for foreign investors and the Korean ("Chosun") compatriots residing outside of North Korea (i.e. in South

Korea) have been defined: joint-management, joint-ownership, and foreign-ownership firms.[1]

Current economic cooperation in the information and telecommunications industry is based entirely on commission processing (in particular, for mid-to-small firms). In the future, these simple transactions and commission processing are expected to become joint-management and joint-ownership firms due to the limits on such simple forms of trading. The following economic cooperation methods can be promoted as business approaches: software and database processing on commission, internet portal site for local specialty products, pay phone business, and the exchange and education of labor forces.

Software and DATABASE processing on commission

North Korea has been emphasizing the development of software rather than hardware that requires more investment. Due to aggressive support by the North Korean government, the software programs developed by such organizations have been highly evaluated. Research, development, and production have been carried out by the General Program Research Center of National Science Institute, Pyungyang Pro-center, Chosun Computer Center, and Kim Il-Sung General University.

Economic cooperation in developing software programs, utilizing the capital of the South and the know-how and the manpower of North Korea, should therefore be considered. One example is processing a database on politically non-sensitive information. Software and database processing can generate economic benefits to both North and South Korea without imposing heavy political burdens on the North Korean government.

Programs for computerizing international trade transactions and local firm operations, processing databases for sightseeing and culture in the North, and creating databases for separated families are just some of the software development projects that can be considered.

Internet portal site for local specialty products

When North and South Korea are reunified in the future, goods and services can be exchanged freely, to the great economic benefit of both sides, but various restrictions now limit this exchange. One of the most critical is the shortage of foreign currency in North Korea. Consequently, barter is the only viable form of trade. Since this system requires much information on the available goods and services, developing an Internet site introducing local specialty products of North Korea would facilitate trade and introduce benefits well before unification.

Collecting all tradeables of North Korean specialties, finished goods, and tourism souvenirs into one Internet homepage would save advertising costs and increase revenues. South Korean firms should also be included in the portal site to advertise the products available for export through the barter system to North Korea.

Pay phone business

As mentioned above, all but high officials and communist party executors in North Korea are limited to grossly inadequate pay phones and public phones installed in factories and on collective farms. Increasing "private" supply should therefore be a priority.

Pay phones have fewer political overtones than residential phones, so perhaps they could be manufactured and supplied through joint ventures with South Korean manufacturers. At North Korea's request, obsolete but functional telephones of South Korea could also be furnished free of charge, especially in connection with projects to reunite separated families. In these ways, the welfare of private citizens could be greatly enhanced.

Exchange and education of labor forces

One of the problems South Korean firms face when considering the North Korean market is the insufficient education and different culture of North Korean labor forces. Thus, exchange and education of labor forces are key to determining ultimate profitability. As success depends eventually on people, exchange and education of technical labor forces seem very important to economic cooperation and reunification, even though they may bring forth no immediate and tangible results.

Because the North Korean government prefers private cooperation to government-level cooperation, exchange and education of labor forces in telecommunications should be promoted by academic circles and private firms in close connection with international organizations such as UNDP, APT (Asia Pacific Telecommunity) and ITU (International Telecommunication Union). Technical training of North Korean labor forces can be carried out in China or Japan rather than within the nation to relieve the burdens for North Korea.

Academic Approach

Half a century after the division of the Korean peninsula, language and culture as well as ideology have greatly diverged between North and South in the absence of meaningful exchange between the two. In particular, the Korean language, terminology, and such applications as keyboard arrangement are very different.

In order to prevent rampant confusion after reunification and to standardize Korean characters in computers, North and South Korea have been holding character standardization conferences in China once a year since 1994. The conference held in 1996 was very successful in the sense that the two sides consented both to adopt agreements on joint translation of computer terminology and on the Korean alphabetical order for the communication code system (Park, 1997, p.6), and to introduce common keyboards.

It has been and will be effective to approach the North academically. If the tension between North and South Korea can be gradually eased during the process of achieving reunification, regional campuses for South Korean universities or North–South joint universities may be established to exchange data and to unify many technical and cultural aspects.

Socio-Cultural Approach

Support of telecommunications for joint international sports and cultural events

International sports and cultural events could jointly be held not only to promote exchange of sports and culture, but also to enhance cooperation in telecommunications. Such socio-cultural events can help restore homogeneity between the two sides, inspire international interest, and increase transactions in telecommunications. They have a precedent in the hosting of the South–North Basketball Game by Hyundai Business Group.

As clearly evidenced in the ping-pong diplomacy between China and the US, sports events can be substantial in easing tensions and achieving cooperation. In particular, if co-hosting of the 2002 World Cup soccer becomes possible, cooperation in telecommunications to prepare for the event will be inevitable. Coherent promotion of such sports events will greatly contribute to the improvement of cooperation in telecommunications and broadcasting.

Utilization of Internet for reunion of separated families

North Korea restricts private citizens from accessing the Internet. The government fears the importation of liberalism and concomitant threats to its regime. Thus, although North Korea has been registered officially under the nation code "kp",[2] no address has been registered with that code. Twenty web sites have, however, been created by foreign pro-North Korean groups, many of which are used to propagate the North Korean political system led by Chung-Il Kim and for operations against the South.

The Internet may also be restricted for communication between separated families. The Ministry of Reunification in the South accordingly established a Separated Family Information Center in September 1998. The center created databases with information on separated families, and started providing services over the Internet. Unfortunately, the data come only from the South and its impact has therefore been limited.

Reaching an agreement between the South–North governments or holding Red Cross conferences would help this most worthy project. In addition, South Korea could consider paying the cost of processing and inter-operating databases with the South Korean database and dispatching supporting personnel to the North.

Geographic Approach

Analyzing previous instances of economic cooperation, the North Korean government prefers geographically restricted free trading zones such as Najin and Sunbong since they appear to bring few risks and threats to its regime in the process of revitalizing its economy. North Korea's decision to build free trade zones can be regarded as a prelude to introducing a market-oriented and open economy, as seen in the case of China before it. Of course, if inter-Korean economic cooperation is further extended, such geographic restriction will be gradually eased and North Korea might even allow the areas of cooperation to be extended to Pyungyang and other major cities in the North.

Najin-Sunbong free trade area
Investment in the Najin-Sunbong area, where the North uniquely allowed free trade with foreigners, seems to be a realistic way to enhance South–North economic cooperation. If the South participates actively in the development of the area, investment in the area would increase significantly, contribute greatly to the development of the area, and vitalize future South–North economic cooperation.

The North Korean government has also taken a positive attitude in amending the foreign investment laws, so as to develop Najin-Sunbong area as a point of strategic importance in connection with TRADP (Tumen River Area Development Programme), which is under the management of UNDP (United Nations Development Projects). As of December 1997, 121 firms – 35 from South Korea and 86 from other countries – had obtained approval for business in the area (Korea Ministry of Reunification, 1998). The South Korean firms operating there communicate with headquarters in the South via a third nation, using the satellite communication center located in Pyungyang. As economic cooperation increases, North Korea must construct additional telecommunications infrastructures and networks in the

Najin-Sunbong area, and South Korean firms may get a big piece of this action.

Extended support of telecommunications in Mt Kumkang Tourist Project

A total of six lines were installed through IDC Japan to support North Korea's Mt Kumkang Tourist Project. The North Korean government has been reluctant to install direct lines connecting the North and the South. However, if the Mt Kumkang Tourist Project extends its scope, the number of communication lines connecting the South and the North should also be extended. In addition, a wireless mobile network may be created around Mt Kumkang to provide tourists with convenient telecommunications services. The direct hot lines between the two sides, utilizing wireless mobile networks, can also be constructed using microwave technology from Kumkang Mountain to Solac Mountain in the South.

Networking with dedicated lines

Establishing public switched telephone networks (PSTN) that enable private citizens to use telephone services will be a heavy economic and political burden to the North Korean government. Not only are the monetary costs high, but increased communication may pose a threat to the communist regime's hold on the country as well. Dedicated lines, on the other hand, are cheaper and easier to control, being "dedicated" to certain uses. In addition to being the most convenient solution at the moment, they can easily be converted to PSTN when necessary. Connecting Najin-Sunbong area, Chungjin, Pyungyang, the Panmunjum truce village and Seoul with a dedicated line can even be accomplished using existing facilities.

International Approach

In May 1997, at one of APT conferences, a telecommunications consultation committee in the Asia-Pacific Region, the North Korean Ministry of Communication requested of the Asia Pacific Telecommunity (APT) that telecommunications and measurement equipment be used mostly for research centers and universities (*The Mail Economic Daily*, May 10, 1997). Approaching the North indirectly, with the help of APT, ITU (International Telecom Union) and UNDP (United Nations Development Project), may be more effective than approaching the country directly.

Step-Wise Approach

Economic cooperation in the information and telecommunications industry may occur with combinations of different approaches. An example of both the geographical and the business approach is to promote the wireless mobile phone business in the Mt Kumkang project. Telecommunications business in the Tumen River area will be promoted by combining geographical, international, and business approaches.

Table 8.3 divides conceptually the period before reunification of North and South Korea into three stages, and specifies the projects that should be implemented in each stage.[3] Conceptually, Stage 1 refers to the period when the current relationship between the South and the North continues without much progress. Stage 2 indicates the period when humanistic, academic, and cultural interchanges as well as direct economic transactions are extended further than in Stage 1. Stage 3 occurs when inter-Korean reunification talks have progressed so much that the two nations are ready to cooperate for reunification.

Table 8.3 Step-Wise Approach

	Step 1	Step 2	Step 3
Geographic approach	Najin-Sunbong, Mt Kumkang Project	Pyungyang, Nampo, West Coast Industrial Area	Other major cities
Business approach	Commission processing, joint management, joint ownership	Joint management, joint ownership, foreign ownership	Joint management, joint ownership, foreign ownership
Academic approach	Character standardization, regional campus establishment	Foundation of joint ownership universities, basic data exchange	Negotiation of government policy after reunification
Socio-cultural approach	2002 World Cup Construction of DATABASE for separated families		
International organization approach	Indirect support through ITU, APT, UNDP Direct support after relations improve between North–South Korea		

TELECOMMUNICATIONS POLICIES AFTER REUNIFICATION: A CONCEPTUAL FRAMEWORK

This section presents a framework of analysis (see Figure 8.4) that may be useful after reunification. Regulatory policies of telecommunications after reunification will progress through procedures like establishing new objectives, deducing measures, evaluating them based on the pre-set objectives, and fulfilling the new objectives.

Establishment of Objective

Rapid development of telecommunications service capacities in North Korea can be set as the first objective. This objective can help restore national homogeneity, and will help satisfy the basic telecommunications demand in North Korea.

Figure 8.4 First Frameworks of Analysis

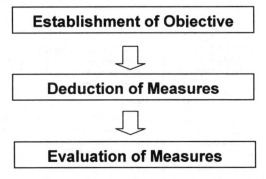

Consider the following comparison of Korea with the experience of Germany. While the number of telephone lines per 100 people in North Korea was about 1/10 that of the South in 1996, the number of East Germany when the nations unified was about 1/4 of the West. To make matters worse, this difference is expected to widen when reunification becomes a reality.

The second objective is to establish a systematic and coherent telecommunications network covering both South and North Korean regions. Such a system promotes efficiency in the long run. The third objective is to provide universal services, while the fourth is to provide various, inexpensive and high quality services. The fifth objective is to observe the principles of efficiency, flexibility, fairness, and independence of regulations; while the sixth is to introduce new services to meet the telecommunications needs of the North Korean residents. The seventh objective is to make telecommunications service providers competitive, and the eighth is to create new demand in North Korea. The ninth objective is to find incentives that would encourage private firms to participate in the telecommunications business. The tenth objective is related to financing.

The order of priority in the abovementioned objectives is currently arbitrary. One should be achieved through consensus and then used to evaluate measures.

Deduction of Measures

Figure 8.5 Second Frameworks of Analysis

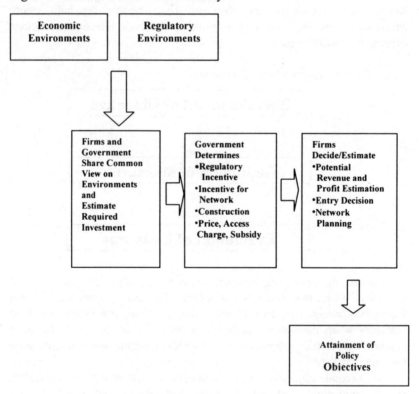

The first step is to consider the environments that affect service providers in determining their profits. Such environments can be divided into the basic economic environment and the regulatory environment (Figure 8.5), the latter limiting the former. While it takes time to improve the economic environment, the regulatory environment may be modified within a rather short period of time.

The basic economic environment consists of the following elements:[4]

- Level of income
- Purchasing power of telecommunications equipment and services
- Preference
- Necessity of telecommunications
- Degree of development of related industries
- Existing telecommunications network
- Distribution of population
- Easiness of fund raising.

The regulatory environment acts on these factors to affect the profit of each service provider, and consists of the following elements: entry, price, and fair-competition regulation. Entry regulation includes:

- Number of current competitors
- Number of potential competitors
- Service areas (for each service)
- Degree of actual competition (price competition, service competition, productivity competition, etc.).

The followings are the elements of price regulation:

- Relative level of each service price
- Level and calculation method of access charge per telecommunications network
- Level of international settlement rate
- Level and method of universal service subsidies.

Finally, the elements of fair-competition regulation include:

- Connection of inter-Korean telecommunications network
- Open network disclosure
- Information disclosure
- Interconnection and interoperability with other telecommunications networks

● Collaboration between service providers.

Each service provider maximizes its profit in the economic and regulatory environment. Regulatory policies should induce each service provider to pursue national objectives.

There are two conflicting views among specialists with regard to entry of potential entrants to the North Korean market. The optimistic view is that many firms will be greatly interested in the North Korean telecommunications market. The pessimistic view is that service providers will not be interested in the North Korean telecommunications market. Figure 8.6 organizes a brief description of these views.

While final decisions regarding these two views are in abeyance, policy measures to determine the entry regulation environment should be considered (Figure 8.7).

Three types of ownership may be considered based on nationalities. They are South Korean, North Korean, and foreign firms. It is possible to create consortia to make combinations of these three forms of ownership, generating both merits and demerits. The balance will depend on the chemistry and power balance of each organization. Analysis of a consortium can only be made, however, after analyzing the three forms in detail.

Figure 8.6 Two Different Opinions among Specialists

Affirmative Opinion	**Negative Opinion**
● In the long run, business in North Korea will be as profitable as in South Korea ● Potential entrants to the North Korean market can anticipate profit and government subsidy ● Example: South Korean PCS license	● Economic environment in North Korea is so poor that profit can not be expected ● South Korean government will face financing problem (no subsidy) ● Firms may want preemption, and network construction will be delayed ● Example : Loaxley group in Najin and Sunbong area

Figure 8.7 Measures for Entry Regulation

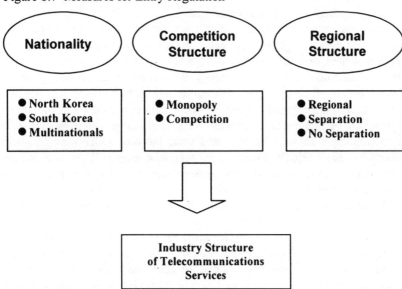

Closing the North Korean market to foreigners is difficult because of the WTO agreement that the South Korean government signed. Because a large proportion of North Korean switches and transmission facilities have been installed by non-Korean manufacturers, entry into the North Korean market seems easier for them than for South Korean firms. Under these circumstances, a consensus must be reached on how to treat foreign service providers in the North Korean region. If foreign firms are treated the same as domestic firms, no preliminary work is needed. On the other hand, if the public consensus is asymmetric unfavorable treatment to foreign firms, preparatory measures must be devised, and the South Korean government may need to stipulate special laws. Diplomatic efforts must also be made before inter-Korean reunification. Before foreign telecommunications equipment and services suppliers dominate North Korean markets and set their own products as the standard, South Korean service providers and equipment vendors must establish a presence. Government-level support would make a difference.

Another question involves the investments that foreign firms have already made in the North Korean region. Should the validity of business licenses given to foreign firms and investment agreements made between them and North Korea be maintained even after inter-Korean reunification?

If such rights and agreements continue in place, no problem will arise. Destroying them is another matter.[5]

The next issue is the competition scheme of service providers. Will monopoly rights be granted to each service provider for a pre-determined period of time, or will competition reign? Competition is in general the best way to maximize economic efficiency, but the enormous amount of initial investment required by the telecommunications industry and the difficulties of financing during early stages of reunification may make a monopoly system the best choice to accomplish the first objective with relative ease. If a monopoly is allowed for a limited time, the monopolist may construct networks more rapidly to enjoy monopolistic power faster and longer. Whether to apply the monopoly system throughout the nation or just in some areas must also be considered.

Another issue is price regulation of service, access, and international settlement rates. Consider service prices first.

It is customary to set the service price based on its cost, as if the market were competitive. However, the various layers of service demand and income levels may make different price systems more effective for a limited time. The income levels of most North Koreans are so low that it may be best to set the service price low at first to achieve universal service and enhance demand. If so, raising funds to support low prices must be considered. Even a monopoly's profits depend on regulation. In its absence, a monopolistic service provider may enjoy high profits, but strict price regulation will reduce or even eliminate them. Hence, depending on the regulation, a monopoly firm will have different incentives for financing, timing the establishment of networks, and providing universal services. Price regulation, in other words, may be used to finance universal services.

Also affecting the financing and productivity of each service provider is how access prices and international settlement rates are determined. Access charges affect the cost of a service provider using other networks, and most calls go through many networks. Access charges are also the revenue of service providers supplying the access service, so the profits of both kinds of service providers can be dramatically affected by their regulation. If access prices are based on cost, a subsidy is basically created for the firms that provide services to North Korea (from the perspective of South Korean firms). Since the cost of network establishment at its initial stage is very high (because, inter alia, of depreciation), the international settlement rate can be considered as a form of access charge, and setting it can also create a subsidy. Because low income regions usually have more incoming than outgoing calls, setting a high international settlement rate can contribute to financing the service providers in the North Korean region.

A final issue is fair competition. It must be based on equal treatment of service providers in the region. Detailed regulatory policies related to fair competition will be devised after the determination of the telecommunications market structure in North Korea.

CONCLUSION

North–South Korean cooperation in information and telecommunications has been promoted in a very limited fashion due to the North Korean government's understanding that it may pose a great threat to its political future. The telecommunications network resembles the nerve system of the human body. Like this system, it is most important to overall well-being. North–South Korean cooperation in information and telecommunications will play a critical role in determining the degree and speed of economic cooperation throughout the Korean economy, society and culture; it can also be a very effective tool to speed up reunification and to restore a national homogeneity that has been lost for more than half a century. North–South cooperation in telecommunications will enable contact and cooperation without any physical contact, even in a situation where mistrust still prevails.

There are two purposes and five sections to this study. The first purpose is to develop and deduce North–South Korean cooperative projects in information and telecommunications before reunification. The second is to present a framework to analyze regulatory problems after reunification. The first section introduces purpose and organization to the reader. The second section picks up and describes the current telecommunications industries in North Korea. The third section presents examples of cooperative projects in information and telecommunications. These examples are presented in five different classifications: the business, academic, socio-cultural, geographic, and international approaches; and, especially in combination, they can help deduce and develop concrete economic cooperative projects. The fourth section presents a framework to analyze policy issues that may occur after reunification. Discussion focuses on regulatory subjects, including entry and price regulation, fair competition, and relations with foreign firms. The fifth and final section, this conclusion, summarizes the discussions.

Due to inadequate statistics, this study could not provide a more precise policy conclusion. Whenever important raw data become available, they should be put to immediate use in programs to help prepare for reunification. Thorough preliminary consensus and consequent measures must be devised in order to avoid unnecessary confusion and possible conflicts with foreign service providers with regard to the WTO requirements and investment guarantee agreements.

NOTES

[1] According to articles 2 and 3 of the North Korean Foreign Investment Act, Joint-Management firms are those in which North Korea and foreign investors invest jointly and divide profits in proportion to the investment of each party. North Korea and foreign entities invest together in Joint-Ownership firms, but only North Korea manages them, and profits are divided according to contracted terms and conditions. Foreign investors invest in Foreign-Ownership that manages them independently.
[2] South Korea uses 'kr'.
[3] Each stage is not strictly delineated and is merely conceptual.
[4] The list is not comprehensive.
[5] As the intention of other service providers' entry into the North Korean market is mostly to dominate the market and to earn profit from South Korean firms, limiting by patent systems the number of South Korean service providers entering the North Korean market will reduce foreign investors' incentive to enter. However, if foreign investors obtain exclusive rights to service or business in certain areas of North Korea, the patent system will not be enough to protect South Korean firms in this market. Cautioning that all investment agreements or guarantees of business rights made with foreign investors in North Korea may be invalid after North and South Korea are reunified and stipulating this condition in agreements are both appropriate.

REFERENCES

ITU (1998), *World Telecommunication Development Report*.
Kim, S.T. and Y.I. Kong (1997), "North-South Economic Cooperation in Telecommunications," *Journal of Informatization*, 4 (4), Republic of Korea: National Computerization Agency.
Korea Development Institute (1997), *Economic Cooperation Strategies in Reunification of the Korean Peninsula*, in conference proceedings, Republic of Korea.
Korea Ministry of Information & Communication (1996), *Annual Report on Telecommunications*, Republic of Korea.
Korea Ministry of Reunification (1998), *Guidelines of Trades between South and North Korea*, Republic of Korea.
Korea Ministry of Reunification (1999a), *Reunification White Paper for 1998*, Republic of Korea.
Korea Ministry of Reunification (1999b), *Guidelines of Economic Cooperation between South and North Korea*. Republic of Korea.
Korea Ministry of Reunification (1999c), *Weekly North Korean Situation*, 430, Republic of Korea.
Korea Telecommunications Technology Association (1995), *World Telecommunications Index*, Republic of Korea.
Korea Trade Association (1996), *Environment of Investment in Najin-Sunbong Free Trade Area*, Republic of Korea.

North Korea Research Institute (1994), *Superintendence of North Korea*, DPRK.

Park, C.M. (1997), *Analysis of North Korean Situation of Computerization*, Republic of Korea: National Computerization Agency.

Whang, D.E. (1997), "Current Situation of North Korean SOC-Telecommunications," in *Reunification Economy*, Republic of Korea: Hyundai Economic Research Institute.

9 Foreign Investment Regulation in North Korea: An Assessment[*]

Haksoo Ko

INTRODUCTION

Since its establishment in 1948, North Korea has maintained one of the most secluded and closed economies in the world. In recent years, however, this country has shown signs of changes. After a long period of withdrawal, in 1992 North Korea began to promulgate various laws and regulations in foreign investment areas. Compared to the past, this profusion of legislation is dramatic and perhaps signals an important change in the direction of North Korea's economic policy.[1] North Korea may finally have realized that inducing foreign investment is necessary for the revival of its shrinking economy.

Moreover, in 1991, North Korea established its first Free Economic and Trade Zone (FETZ), located in the Rajin-Sonbong area, and granted various preferential treatments to those investing in the area.[2] In September 1996, in an effort to lure foreign investors into this area, the North Korean government held a major conference for international investors. Although this was an unusual event in such a reclusive country, the conference did not draw serious interest from investors, while it caught the attention of many foreign reporters.[3] This lack of interest can perhaps in no small part be attributed to the lack of information regarding foreign investment regulation in North Korea, as well as to the risks involved in investing

[*] This is an updated and revised version of the author's "Note: Foreign Investment in North Korea: An Assessment of Recent Laws and Regulations" (1998), *Virginia Journal of International Law,* **38**, 221-41. The author would like to thank editors' helpful comments and suggestions.

there.[1] Outside investors were simply not given enough information properly to weigh the potential risks and benefits of investment. Recent developments in the relationship between the United States and North Korea suggest a possible loosening of the trade and investment restrictions imposed on US corporations that have been prohibited from engaging in serious trade or investment activities with North Korea. To this day, while the US government is moving toward lifting sanctions imposed against North Korea, investment prospects are still murky.

Nevertheless, hopes abound and it may not be long before many foreign investors find themselves doing business in North Korea. A meaningful increase in foreign investments will, however, require well-functioning legal and other infrastructure, which will boost investors' confidence. When it comes to individual laws and regulations, while many provisions still require further clarifications, such ambiguities have been lessened in recent years as more enforcement regulations have been promulgated and more experiences have been accumulated. Table 9.1, which lists the major laws and regulations in the foreign investment area in North Korea, reveals such a trend. The enactments of the early 1990s indicated the general direction of the regulatory regime in foreign investment, and many regulations that were announced in more recent years have closed loopholes and clarified those declaratory provisions. (See T 9.1 at the end of the chapter.)

This chapter reports and analyzes developments during the past decade in laws and regulations governing foreign investment in North Korea.[2] First, it briefly reviews the constitutional and other legal grounds for laws inducing foreign investment in a country where private property is not permitted. Second, the body of the chapter addresses various issues surrounding the operation of foreign-invested corporations. These include: incorporation procedure; regulation of business activities; purchase of materials and sales of products; labor regulation; land regulation; financial and foreign exchange regulation; tax; liquidation procedures; and dispute resolution mechanisms. A separate section describes special laws and regulations applicable to business operations located within the FETZ, which grants preferential treatments for foreign investors. The conclusion summarizes the current state of development in North Korea's efforts to induce investment.

CURRENT LAWS AND REGULATIONS

Constitutional Grounds and Civil Code Provisions

Because North Korea is a socialist country, the "means of production" are owned solely by the state and cooperative organizations (Constitution art. 20), and it may sound contradictory to allow for foreign investments. The North Korean Constitution also asserts, however, that "the state shall encourage joint operation and joint venture enterprise" between North Korean corporations and foreign investors (Constitution art. 37), and guarantees the protection of the "constitutional rights and interests of foreigners" (Constitution art. 16). The provisions for encouraging and protecting foreign investment were in fact inserted in a 1992 amendment, perhaps so that North Korea could demonstrate its willingness to honor foreigners' property rights in their investments and lessen some concerns of foreign investors. The degree to which foreign investors' rights will be acknowledged and protected, however, remains unclear.

Perhaps reflecting the constitutional dilemma between maintaining the socialistic economic structure of collective ownership and encouraging foreign investments, private ownership of land is still not allowed. Rather, the "right to use" land is treated as a permissible property right in the context of foreign investments. Although limited in many respects, market mechanisms and the principle of profit maximization are also permitted to function in some minor sectors of the economy.

While the Constitution does not provide very clear guidance as to permissible property rights, the Civil Code deals with issues in property relationships and other contract matters in greater detail. Provisions on property rights are contained in the Civil Code, Part 2, Chapter 1, where property rights are defined as the rights to "occupy, use, and dispose of" property within the limits proscribed by law. Such property rights may only be owned and exercised by the state, cooperatives, or individuals. Collective ownership is given preference, however, and various restrictions are attached to individual ownership. In general, individual ownership is limited to small items for personal consumption (Civil Code art. 58). State ownership is treated as the principal way of owning properties and the collective ownership of cooperatives is permitted as an alternative ownership structure only during times of transition. The latter is thus limited to land and such other items necessary to carry out production activities of individual cooperatives as animals, agricultural machinery, fishing boats, and plants (Civil Code art. 54). After all, the state is the only entity allowed to exercise property rights without restrictions. Such rights are exercised through government agencies and other operations, and property rights may, in part, be transferred to a third party at the will of the owner of the rights (Civil Code art. 47). When there is transfer of property rights from the state, it is deemed that only a part of the rights are transferred and fundamental ownership rights are considered to remain with the state (Civil Code art. 48).

Categorization of Foreign-Invested Corporations

Under the Foreigners' Investment Law, foreign-invested corporations are categorized into three groups of equity joint ventures, contractual joint ventures, and wholly foreign-owned enterprises (Foreigners' Investment Law art. 2). An equity joint venture is a limited liability corporation in which investors in North Korea and in foreign countries invest jointly, operate the business jointly, and distribute profits according to their investment shares. In a contractual joint venture, North Korean and foreign investors invest jointly and share the profits in accordance with the terms of the contract. Unlike an equity joint venture, however, a contractual joint venture allows only its North Korean party to manage operations, which may work as a great drawback for foreign investors. On the other hand, a contractual joint venture may take a wide variety of organizational and managerial forms, including production sharing, processing on commission, licensing, franchising, and management services. Management is performed by the North Korean hosting party during the lifetime of a contractual joint venture, and the ownership of the venture is transferred to the hosting party when the contract term is over. Thus, under this scheme, once investments are made, foreign investors lose much of their control.

A wholly foreign-owned enterprise, on the other hand, is a corporation owned and operated exclusively by a foreign investor. Since foreign investors are allowed to make their own managerial decisions, they appear to have greater room for maneuver. Because no North Korean parties are involved in the management, however, wholly foreign-owned enterprises are heavily regulated by North Korean authorities. More importantly, while equity joint ventures and contractual joint ventures may be incorporated anywhere in North Korea, wholly foreign-owned enterprises are allowed to be established only in the FETZ (Foreigners' Investment Law art. 3).

Incorporation and Operation

Because a foreign investor may incorporate and operate a joint venture only with a North Korean "institution, enterprise or association" (Equity Joint Venture Law art. 9, Contractual Joint Venture Law art. 6), North Korean individuals may not be party to such a venture. As an exception, "Koreans living outside" North Korea are, however, permitted to invest (Contractual Joint Venture Law art. 5, Equity Joint Venture Law art. 2, Foreign Enterprise Law art. 6). Further, equity joint ventures in which Koreans living outside North Korea participate "shall receive preferential treatment such as reduction and exemption of tax and favorable conditions of land use," similar to equity joint ventures in priority projects or in preferred geographic areas (Equity Joint Venture Law art. 7).[3] One can easily surmise that, with this form of preferential treatments, the North Korean government has been perhaps targeting South Korean investors and Korean investors who are residing in other countries, in particular in Japan, and are eager to invest in North Korea. The absence of provisions to clarify the precise nature of these special treatments should, however, dampen this interest considerably.

When foreign entities invest in North Korea, they are not given complete freedom to choose any industry whatsoever. Rather, pertinent laws and regulations limit their options. These legal provisions often contain only declaratory principles and may not provide clear guidance regarding the permissibility of individual projects. For example, the Foreigners' Investment Law allows investment in "various sectors such as industry, agriculture, construction, transport, telecommunication, science and technology, tourism, commerce and financial business" (Foreigners' Investment Law art. 6), but also states that North Korea "encourages" investments in "sectors that require high and modern technologies, those which produce internationally competitive goods, sectors of natural resource development and infrastructure construction, and scientific research and new technology development sectors" (Foreigners' Investment Law art. 7).[4] While the precise meaning of "encouraging" a project is not clear, the Foreigners' Investment Law provides that foreign-invested corporations operating in such sectors "shall receive preferential treatment including reduction and exemption of income and other taxes, favorable condition of land use, and preferential supply of bank loans" (Foreigners' Investment Law art. 8). The same law, however, "prohibit[s] or restrict[s]" investment in "projects which hinder the development of the national economy and do harm to national security, or which are technically out-dated and harmful to environmental protection" (Foreigners' Investment Law art. 8).[5] The types of investments that are "harmful to the development of the national economy" are subject to a broad range of possible interpretations, and which criteria will determine whether or not to approve an investment project and to grant any preferential treatments are not yet clear.[6]

Before investments are made, an application must be submitted and approved by the external economic department of the administration council as to specific foreign investment projects (Contractual Joint Venture Law art. 7, Equity Joint Venture Law art. 9, Law on Foreign Enterprises art. 7). Once an application is submitted, the committee must decide whether to approve a project within 50 days from the date of the application (Contractual Joint Venture Law art. 7, Equity Joint Venture Law art. 9). In the case of a contractual or equity joint venture, consultation with "relevant bodies" is a prerequisite for processing and approving an application (Contractual Joint Venture Law art. 6, Equity Joint Venture Law art. 9). Once approved, a new corporation must register within 30 days with the administrative and economic committees of the province in which it operates (Contractual Joint Venture Law art. 8, Equity Joint Venture Law art. 10, Law on Foreign Enterprises art. 9). [7]

Once in operation, corporations are discouraged from pursuing any projects other than those listed in their original plans, and the pursuit of a new project must be approved by the external economic department of the administration council or the FETZ authority (Contractual Joint Venture Law art. 9, Equity Joint Venture Law art. 25).[8] Also, if a party to a contractual joint venture intends to transfer its rights and duties to a third party, it must obtain the approval of the administration council in addition to the agreement of the other party to the contract (see Contractual Joint Venture Law art. 10).

The exact amount of capital each party contributes is expected to be determined by the contracting parties through negotiations and "mutual agreement" (Equity Joint Venture Law art. 11). The investment may be made in the form of "cash, property in kind, industrial property right, technical know-how, the right to use land and so on" (Equity Joint Venture Law art. 11). When the investment is made in a form other than cash, valuation of such an investment could easily be a contentious point among contracting parties, and the law strives to solve the problem by providing that the price should be decided through "mutual agreement between the partners on the basis of international market prices prevailing at that time" (Equity Joint Venture Law art. 11).[9] Also, "[t]he registered capital of an equity joint venture enterprise shall be [sic] over 30–70 percent of the amount of total investment," and although investing partners may increase the amount of a registered investment, they cannot reduce the amount of their investments (Equity Joint Venture Law art. 15).[10]

Regulation of Management

An equity joint venture must appoint a board of directors to function as the "top decision-making body" of the venture (Equity Joint Venture Law art. 16), and, separately, it may opt as well to employ "managerial personnel" (Equity Joint Venture Law art. 18). In a contractual joint venture, on the other hand, the hosting North Korean party performs managerial activities, but the parties to the venture may jointly establish a "non-standing body of mutual consultation" to "examine important matters concerning the operation of the venture such as introduction of new technologies, improvement of quality, and reinvestment" (Contractual Joint Venture Law art. 16). Through this body, although indirectly, the foreign party to the venture is, in principle, allowed to participate in the management of the venture.[11]

Employing various regulations, North Korea's socialist planned economy restricts a joint venture's purchase of materials and sale of completed products.[12] Materials are in general encouraged to be procured domestically, and finished products are mostly expected to be exported. If a venture decides to purchase materials in North Korea, it must submit a material purchase plan for the following year within a specified period of time set by relevant authorities (Equity Joint Venture Law art. 23). On the other hand, if the equity joint venture intends to import materials from a foreign country, there are more stringent restrictions and the venture must first obtain prior approval (Equity Joint Venture Law arts. 23–24). This regulation may have been put into place to encourage domestic procurement and domestic production, and thus to help secure foreign exchange that North Korea desperately needs. Depending on the type of individual projects and on the planning and production schedule of the economy as a whole, however, in some sectors it may be difficult for a venture to procure necessary materials on a timely basis.

The sales of completed products are governed by similar restrictions that are geared to promote exports rather than domestic sales.[13] A foreign-invested corporation must submit its export plan to the appropriate provincial administrative and economic committee, and it can sell its products in domestic markets "mainly through the foreign trade agency" (Law on Foreign Enterprises arts. 16–17). Thus, there are additional administrative procedures to be taken before engaging in domestic sales.[14]

Labor Regulation

North Korea does not recognize the principle of employment at will. Instead, the government heavily regulates employment in general and employers must accept stringent limitations in their power to hire and discharge employees. Foreign investors are required to employ North Korean nationals in all fields except "management personnel, technicians and skilled workers of special job classifications" (Labor Regulations for Foreign-Funded Enterprises art. 4). To work in North Korea, a foreign employee must procure an approval from the external economic body of the administration council.[15] Moreover, and more seriously, although a foreign-invested corporation is allowed to determine the total number of the workers needed for its operation, it must employ them through contracts that are entered into, not directly with the workers, but with a labor service agency (Labor Regulations for Foreign-Funded Enterprises art. 11). These contracts must "define the number of workers by industrial classification and technical qualification, the duration of employment, payment, conditions for ensuring working life and the like." The labor service agency is therefore a key player in the labor market, although not much information is available regarding its precise role and its relationship with individual employees. In addition, a corporation is required to conclude a contract with trade unions, specifying "duties of the employees, the amount of production and quality index, working hours and rest, remuneration, insurance and public welfare, labor protection and working conditions, labor discipline, prize and penalty, provision of retirement and so on" (Labor Regulations for Foreign-Funded Enterprises art. 9).

An employer must therefore sign employment contracts both with the labor service agency and with the trade union, and the overall negotiation for employment contracts would involve three distinctive parties of employer, employees, and the labor service agency. The corporation must also employ workers "sent by the labor service agency in the area of its operation," instead of choosing employees through its own selection process (Labor Regulations for Foreign-Funded Enterprises art. 14). When an existing North Korean corporation is a party to a contractual or equity joint venture, the joint venture must employ the workers of the existing "mother body" corporation first (Labor Regulations for Foreign-Funded Enterprises art. 13). Through these regulations, the labor mobility of North Korean employees is heavily restricted, and the labor service agency has a strong influence in the whole process of employment decision making. From the perspective of foreign investors, managers' ability to screen, hire, and fire employees is accordingly severely limited. Also, in the negotiation process for employment contracts, employers may have to consider the will of the agency more seriously than the qualification of individual employees.

Similarly, when dismissing an employee, a corporation must secure an agreement both with the trade union and with the labor service agency, and termination is allowed only under certain circumstances specified in relevant laws (Labor Regulations for Foreign-Funded Enterprises art. 15).[16] Employees, on the other hand, may quit for various reasons, including the situation where there are "unavoidable personal circumstances" (Labor Regulations for Foreign-Funded Enterprises art. 16). Thus, while employees are allowed to leave their jobs fairly easily, employers are not given much discretion in making decisions regarding hiring and dismissing employees, and, in that respect, the working of the labor market is very rigid.

The work schedule for an employee is generally eight hours a day, six days a week, although there is room for flexibility (Constitution art. 30, Labor Regulations for Foreign-Funded Enterprises art. 23). One important provision prohibits the state from mobilizing employees of a foreign-invested corporation for political activities or other purposes except in the event of "irresistible cases such as natural disaster" (Labor Regulations for Foreign-Funded Enterprises art. 5). In a country where labor mobilization occurs with some frequency, this must be considered a considerable concession to foreign-invested corporations. North Korea has set a minimum monthly salary at 220 North Korean won for employees of foreign-invested corporations.[17] In the FETZ, however, in an apparent attempt to give an added incentive for foreign investments, the minimum wage is set at 160 North Korean won per month.

Land Regulation

While private ownership of land is not permitted in North Korea (Constitution art. 20), the government has provided a way for foreign investors to make use of land, by allowing real property to be leased and by granting lessees the "right to use" it (Law on the Leasing of Land arts. 2, 7). Compared to full ownership, however, this right has significant limitations because the leased land must be returned after the term is over and there are various restrictions in transferring the right.[18]

These provisions allow land to be leased, transferred, mortgaged, and otherwise "used," while the ownership of such land remains with the state or cooperatives (Law on the Leasing of Land arts. 9, 15, Constitution art. 20). A leasing contract is signed only after "consultation" is made with North Korean authorities, while, in the FETZ, leasing is also possible through tender or auction (Law on the Leasing of Land art. 9). The right to use land may be granted to either foreign investors or the North Korean party to an equity or contractual joint venture, but it cannot be granted to a domestic party not associated with such a venture (Law on the Leasing of Land arts. 2, 5).[19] Once land is leased, in principle, the lessee may sell, sublease, donate, bequest, or mortgage the right to use the land.[20] Transfer of the right to use land, however, is allowed only with the prior approval of the land administration office (Law on the Leasing of Land arts. 18, 20). Further, when transferring such a right, "the rights and obligations relating to the use of the land, and of the structures and their appurtenances on it" must be transferred at the same time (Law on the Leasing of Land art. 17). Similarly, mortgage contracts must be consistent with the general terms required for leasing (Law on the Leasing of Land art. 22).

Upon the expiration of the lease, the right to use the land automatically reverts back to the state. In addition, any remaining "structures and their appurtenances on the land" become the property of the state without compensation to the lessee (Law on the Leasing of Land art. 34).[21] The lessee, moreover, may be required to "withdraw the structures, facilities and their appurtenances on the land at his own expenses and clear the land" (Law on the Leasing of Land art. 37). Should "unavoidable circumstances" occur prior to the expiration of the lease, the lessor authority may either cancel the lease and offer the lessee other land or pay proper indemnity for any losses (Law on the Leasing of Land art. 38).[22]

Financial Regulation

The Foreign Exchange Control Agency controls and administers foreign exchange transactions and the flow of foreign funds within borders of North Korea (Law on Foreign Exchange Control art. 4). In North Korea, the circulation of foreign currency is prohibited and foreign exchanges must be converted into North Korean won before use (Law on Foreign Exchange Control art. 6). Only authorized banks are allowed to buy or sell foreign currency. The law specifically provides that foreign currency may be used for payments in trade or non-trade transactions, for selling or buying North Korean won, or for capital transactions (Law on Foreign Exchange Control art. 11). The flow of foreign currency is also heavily monitored. Thus, any organization, enterprise, or entity using foreign funds must submit quarterly and annual reports of foreign exchange balances to the Foreign Exchange Control Agency (Law on Foreign Exchange Control art. 21).

Foreign exchanges are scarce in North Korea and they may be brought into the country without limit. Once they are brought into the country, however, their use is heavily restricted (Law on Foreign Exchange Control arts. 22–24). Foreign assets, whether in cash, securities, or precious metals, may be taken out of North Korea only with the permission of the Foreign Exchange Control Agency. The amount may not exceed the amount declared to the customs office upon entry into the country (Law on Foreign Exchange Control arts. 23–24, 26), except for areas designated as the FETZ, where foreign exchanges may be carried out without reference to the customs declaration made upon entry to the country (Law on Foreign Exchange Control art. 25). Income earned through investment in North Korea may be remitted without tax (Law on Foreign Exchange Control art. 27), and a foreign employee may remit up to 60 percent of his/her personal income abroad (Law on Foreign Exchange Control art. 28).

Foreign investors may invest in a bank or choose to incorporate a bank themselves in North Korea in the form of a joint venture bank, a foreign bank, or a branch of a foreign bank (Law on Foreign-Invested Banks art. 2).[23] Foreign-invested banks are required to engage in foreign exchange transactions and are not allowed to execute transactions in North Korean won.[24] While this restriction severely limits the ability of foreign-invested banks to conduct businesses, these banks receive preferential treatments, including exemption from or reduction of the corporate tax, the turnover tax, and the tax on income from offshore banking (Law on Foreign-Invested Banks art. 28).

When it comes to procuring capital needed to establish foreign-invested corporations, the Foreigners' Investment Law provides that "preferential supply of bank loans" will be furnished if the intended foreign investments are for those areas encouraged by the Law (art. 8). Given the general lack of financial resources in North Korea, however, procuring loans from North Korean banks may not be realistic, and provisions in other laws concern borrowings from foreign lenders instead (Equity Joint Venture Law art. 29, Law on Free Economic and Trade Zone art. 32).

Tax Regulation

The Constitution of North Korea declares that "taxes have disappeared" in North Korea (Constitution art. 25). Foreign investors, however, face a separate tax law, the Law on Taxes on Foreign-Invested Enterprises and Foreigners, applicable to foreign individuals, foreign-invested corporations, and Koreans living outside of North Korea who are doing business in North Korea. Taxes on foreign investors are levied based on either the "source principle" or the "residence principle." The source principle applies to the taxation of all Korean citizens irrespective of their place of residence, while the residence principle applies to foreign-invested corporations, requiring them to pay taxes on the revenue from their business activities inside and outside of North Korea, including income earned through their branches, agencies, or subsidiaries (Law on Taxes on Foreign-Invested Enterprises and Foreigners art. 8).

Separately, foreigners residing in North Korea for more than one year are required to pay personal income taxes (Law on Taxes on Foreign-Invested Enterprises and Foreigners art. 17).[25] The government also imposes property taxes on buildings, vessels, or aircraft owned by foreigners (Law on Taxes on Foreign-Invested Enterprises and Foreigners art. 23), and inheritance taxes are imposed, in principle, on property within and without North Korea if inherited by a foreigner residing in North Korea (Law on Taxes on Foreign-Invested Enterprises and Foreigners art. 31).[26]

Certain forms of preferential treatments are extended to foreign-invested corporations operating within the FETZ and to certain types of investments. For example, the corporate income tax rate applicable to the industries officially encouraged by the state, including "high technology, natural resource developments and infrastructure construction, scientific research, and technical developments," is 10 percent, compared to 25 percent for other industries (Law on Taxes on Foreign-Invested Enterprises and

Foreigners art. 12). Corporations may deduct from taxable income interest payments on loans granted by foreign governments, international financial institutions, or foreign banks under favorable terms (Law on Taxes on Foreign-Invested Enterprises and Foreigners art. 15). If in operation for at least ten years, a foreign-invested corporation in the service industry is exempt from corporate income taxes for one year following its first profit-making year, and is granted a tax reduction of up to 50 percent for the following two years (Law on Taxes on Foreign-Invested Enterprises and Foreigners art. 15). If a foreign investor reinvests the profits generated and operates the corporation for more than five years, the government refunds 50 percent of the income tax on the profits that were used in the reinvestment. Further, if the investor reinvests such profits for infrastructure development, the government refunds the full amount of the income tax (Law on Taxes on Foreign-Invested Enterprises and Foreigners art. 16).

Additional taxes include turnover taxes and various local taxes (Law on Taxes on Foreign-Invested Enterprises and Foreigners arts. 37–43). The former are levied on the sale of goods and services. Export goods are, however, exempt from otherwise applicable turnover taxes, and the rate applicable to service industries in the FETZ is reduced by half (Law on Taxes on Foreign-Invested Enterprises and Foreigners art. 40). Local taxes include city management taxes, registration and license taxes, and vehicle taxes (Law on Taxes on Foreign-Invested Enterprises and Foreigners art. 43).

Liquidation

A foreign-invested corporation dissolves upon the expiration of the term specified in the contract establishing the corporation (Contractual Joint Venture Law art. 20, Equity Joint Venture Law art. 43, Law on Foreign Enterprises art. 28). The corporation may, however, choose either to dissolve itself before the expiration of the contract term or to extend its period of operation. Either case requires prior approval (see Contractual Joint Venture Law art. 20, Equity Joint Venture Law arts. 44–45, Law on Foreign Enterprises art. 28).[27] A liquidation committee, initiated by the board of directors or by the court, supervises the dissolution of a venture and the settlement of its outstanding transactions (Equity Joint Venture Law art. 44).[28]

Dispute Resolution

The general principle governing dispute resolution is that "[a]ny disagreement related to foreign investment shall be settled through consultation" (Foreigners' Investment Law art. 22.). While "consultation" is granted priority over other methods, dispute resolution may also be procured through judicial decision or arbitration.[29] Investors clearly want a guarantee of impartial and fair methods of dispute resolution; expectations on how disputes are resolved have a significant impact on their decisions to invest at the outset. Perhaps to alleviate concerns over impartiality of judgments, relevant legal provisions allow arbitration by a dispute resolution body located in a third country, if contracting parties agree to such a solution. This option may not, however, be viable to all possible types of foreign investments because, while the Foreigners' Investment Law and the Equity Joint Venture Law identify it as an acceptable form of dispute resolution (art. 22 and art. 47, respectively), such a provision exists neither in the Contractual Joint Venture Law nor in the Law on Foreign Enterprises. Also, the enforceability of results from adjudication or arbitration in a third country is in no way clear since, among others, enforcing such results in North Korea would inevitably involve North Korea's domestic judicial system, the working of which is not well known to outsiders.

Regulations on the Free Economic and Trade Zone (FETZ)

The FETZ is a zone of "preferential trade, transit transportation, processing of export goods, financing and services" (Law on Free Economic and Trade Zone art. 2).[30] Invested capital, earned income from investments, and other rights of investors are specially protected by law in the FETZ, and investors operating there are given a higher degree of flexibility in choosing the forms of business organization (Law on Free Economic and Trade Zone arts. 4, 5).[31] Business activities within the FETZ face fewer restrictions than in other areas, and free-market mechanisms, albeit limited in many respects, are permitted to operate in this area. Buyers and sellers in the FETZ, for example, are free to negotiate the prices of goods without the intervention of the state (Law on Free Economic and Trade Zone art. 22), although prices of certain "mass consumption goods" remain under state control.

In the FETZ, certain goods are exempt from customs duties. These include goods brought into the FETZ for processing and exporting purposes, materials needed for the operation of enterprises and manufacture of export products, certain quantities of miscellaneous materials for personal needs, materials needed for the infrastructure construction in the FETZ, and foreign cargo passing through the FETZ (Law on Free Economic and Trade Zone art. 26). Additionally, foreigners and foreign-invested corporations are allowed to trade foreign securities within the FETZ (Law on Free Economic and Trade Zone art. 34).

Other preferential treatments available in the FETZ primarily involve taxation. For example, the income tax rate for foreign-invested corporations in the FETZ is 14 percent, compared to the rate of 25 percent in other areas (Law on Taxes art. 12, Law on Free Economic and Trade Zone art. 36). The income tax rate on dividends, interest, rent, and royalties is 10 percent in the FETZ, half of that in other areas (Law on Taxes art. 13). Also, buildings erected in the FETZ are exempt from property tax for five years (Law on Taxes art. 25). As is the case with foreign-invested corporations in the service industry, if a foreign-invested corporation in the "production sectors" of the FETZ in a "preferential sphere," operates for ten years or more, it is then exempt from paying corporate income taxes for a three-year period after the first profit-making year and is entitled to a tax reduction of up to 50 percent for the following two years (Law on Taxes art. 15, Law on Free Economic and Trade Zone art. 37). A foreign-invested corporation investing 60 million won or more in the development of FETZ infrastructure is exempted from paying corporate income taxes for a four-year period after the first profit-making year, and receives a tax reduction of up to 50 percent for the following three years (Law on Taxes art. 15). Also, when production takes place both inside and outside the FETZ, if materials or parts that were processed outside the FETZ comprise less than 40 percent of the total value of a corporation's production, the products are treated as if they are 100 percent produced in the FETZ and are eligible for available privileges and preferential treatments as such (Law on Free Economic and Trade Zone art. 24).

Foreigners may enter North Korea without obtaining visas if they intend to travel directly to the FETZ and to remain within the FETZ (Law on Free Economic and Trade Zone art. 41). While this privilege may reduce the cumbersome administrative procedures that they would otherwise face, such foreigners still need to obtain formal invitations from "a body, an enterprise, an organization or a foreign-invested enterprise in the zone" (Regulations on the Entry and Exit of Foreigners in and from the Free Economic and Trade Zone art. 6). In order to travel any other regions of North Korea outside the FETZ, they must also receive a visa or "certificate of tourism" (Regulations on the Entry and Exit of Foreigners in and from the Free Economic and Trade Zone arts. 7, 10). However, cargo ships and members of their crew, regardless of their nationality, may freely enter into and depart from trade ports in the FETZ (Law on Free Economic and Trade Zone art. 23).

Foreign corporations may establish representative offices in the FETZ, including "missions, agencies, or traveling agencies" (Regulations on Resident Representative Offices of Foreign Business in Free Economic and Trade Zone art. 3). Such offices, after receiving approval, may engage in "service-related activities such as liaison, consultation and dissemination of economic and technical information related to transactions of the foreign business" and in "agent activities by entering into contracts with clients and by making payments and deliveries of goods along the line authorized by the parent business" (Regulations on Resident Representative Offices of Foreign Business in Free Economic and Trade Zone art. 5).

CONCLUSION

Thus far, investors have demonstrated general reluctance to invest in North Korea, even in the FETZ where various preferential treatments are available. Although strategically located to serve northeastern China, South Korea, and Japan, the FETZ infrastructure is still primitive. Its production facilities are outdated, and its wages are not necessarily competitive with those in other competing countries.[32] Also, while it appears that, with a slow opening to the outside world, North Korea is following the Chinese model of "socialism with Chinese characteristics," North Korea's potential as a meaningful market is fairly limited by small domestic markets, which makes it a less attractive place for investments compared to, say, China.[33]

Although liberalization of North Korean trade policies has not yet yielded significant benefits, North Korea appears ready to institute more substantial changes in the future. While progress has been slow, North Korea has shown signs of stepping up its efforts to open its economy to foreign investors, and, in recent years, foreign investment laws have increased significantly in number and sophistication. As shown in Table 9.1, the principal laws enacted in the early 1990s indicate the general direction of future developments, and many administrative regulations promulgated in recent years have provided clearer guidance and therefore have more practical significance to many foreign investors. Also, with the increase in trade and interaction with other economies, it is expected that many precedents will be accumulated which will serve as useful guidance.

Still, critics argue that North Korea may eventually be forced to accelerate the pace of reform dramatically or even to undertake a complete and fundamental overhaul of its economy. By emphasizing opportunities and advantages available to foreign investors, however, North Korea may be able to succeed in attracting enough capital to revive its faltering economy. To that end, North Korea must strive to provide a friendly and favorable atmosphere for investors by making changes that would reduce the risks such investors face in the country where hosting parties have limited experience and where regulatory authorities have ample discretionary power. While it is a significant step forward, enactment of laws alone would not be enough to lure investors. Building proper institutional infrastructure and gaining confidence among investors will prove to be more important and more difficult.[34] In particular, for a country like North Korea, where it appears a strong tradition of the rule of law has not yet been deeply established and many foreign investors have suspicions regarding the enforceability of the contracts signed, gaining investor confidence should be a foremost concern. If the enforceability of a contract is in doubt, the wording of relevant legal provisions, however detailed and well-prepared, may well be meaningless to many investors, and the developments made so far will turn out to be futile.

NOTES

[1] Many laws and regulations have been promulgated since late 1992. Prior to October 1992, the only law addressing foreign investment activities was the Equity Joint Venture Law, first enacted in 1984 and amended in 1994.

[2] The FETZ is often called the Special Economics Zone (SEZ), and term of the SEZ appears to be gaining popularity. To avoid unnecessary confusion, in this chapter, only the term of FETZ is used.

[3] After the conference, the Rajin-Sonbong area reportedly drew investments of $33 million from foreign investors. See Steve Glain, "Opened Door: A North Korean Port, Now Seeking Business, May Play Crucial Role," the *Wall Street Journal*, Sept. 18, 1996, p. A1.

[4] These risks include political instability, uncertainty regarding the country's future, and uncertainty surrounding contract enforceability and general respect for the rule of law. It appears North Korea is likely to maintain its policy of gradual liberalization, which was recently reaffirmed by its bid to join the Asian Development Bank and other international institutions. Political instability appears to be decreasing as well after Kim Jong Il, son of the late Kim Il Sung, was elected as general secretary of the ruling Korean Workers' Party in October 1997. Kim Jong Il is now both general secretary and commander of the armed forces, the two most important posts in North Korea. Although the possibility still exists for a tumultuous end to the present regime, the view that the regime will survive has perhaps gained more popularity in recent years. See Noland (2000).

[5] Academic research on North Korea's foreign investment regulation is meagre. Bryan et al. (1998) and Yoon (1997) are among only a few available in English. While there are more materials written in Korean, Shin and Ahn (1998) appears to be the most comprehensive.

[6] Theoretically speaking, treating Koreans living outside North Korea as investment partners and granting them special treatments may conflict with the North Korean Constitution,which declares that North Korea "represents the interests of all the Korean people," within or without North Korea, (art. 1) and may provide an avenue for disputes and conflicting claims in the future when investment activities become more active involving different categories of Korean investors.

[7] Similar "encouraged" projects are also listed in the Contractual Joint Venture Law (arts. 3, 4), the Equity Joint Venture Law (art. 3), and the Law on Foreign Enterprises (art. 3).

[8] In like vein, the Law on Foreign Enterprises states that "[t]hose enterprises which would harm [North Korea's] national security or which are technically backward shall not be established" (art. 3).

[9] Ambiguity, for instance, still surrounds whether an investment project in computer technology or in telecommunications will be encouraged as high technology investment or be discourged as harmful to national security. Such ambiguity would leave much room for discretionary judgment to North Korean authorities.

[10] A wholly foreign-owned enterprise is given 80 days during which the enterprise must register (Law on Foreign Enterprises art. 8).

[11] A similar provision can be found in the Law on Foreign Enterprises (art. 14).

[12] This "solution" may fall apart when parties cannot agree on "international market prices" or when such prices do not even exist. In particular, it may be extremely difficult to assess the value of buildings, land, and other real estate because there is no market for real property in North Korea.

[13] The permission of relevant authorities is required even to increase the amout of investments.

[14] Functions that can be carried out by this "non-standing body" are not clear, however. As explained above, management decisions are made solely by the North Korean party to the venture.

[15] See Equity Joint Venture Law arts. 23–24 for the requirements for filing procurement plans. Similar provisions can be found in article 12 of the Contractual Joint Venture Law and articles 16 and 17 of the Law on Foreign Enterprises.

[16] See Contractual Joint Venture Law art. 12, Equity Joint Venture Law art. 24, Law on Foreign Enterprises arts. 16–17.

[17] Therefore, for most industries, targetting North Korean markets may not be a viable option available to foreign investors, even if production takes place within North Korea. For instance, "processing on commission" might be a better investment strategy if securing an export market is not a big concern. There are, however, legal restrictions regarding the import of goods produced in North Korea into other countries, most noticeably into the US, and these restrictions may have discouraged potential investors from investing in North Korea. See, e.g., Trading With the Enemy Act, 50 U.S.C. app. §§ 1-44 (1994); Foreign Assets Control Regulation, 31 C.F.R. § 500 (1996). There are signs showing that these regulations may change.

Goods manufactured in North Korea may, however, encounter fewer obstacles if exported to South Korea. In addition to the advantage of geographic proximity, common language and common culture, South Korea may treat imports from the North as domestic goods that are exempt from tariffs. In fact, for statistical purposes, inter-Korea trade is not included in the category of foreign or international trade in South Korea.

[18] Labor Regulations for Foreign-Funded Enterprises art. 4, Equity Joint Venture Law art. 26. Other laws allow the employment of foreigners if an agreement is

reached with an agency with relevant authority (see Contractual Joint Venture Law art. 11).

[19] A venture may dismiss an employee who cannot work due to a non-work-related illness or injury; when there are "extra employees"; when the venture is bankrupt or otherwise has to reduce its workforce; or, when the employee has caused a significant loss to the venture. The Labor Regulations also specify circumstances in which a corporation is not allowed to dismiss an employee (Labor Regulations for Foreign-Funded Enterprises arts. 15, 17).

[20] According to the official exchange rate, 220 North Korean won is approximately equivalent to US$102, although the market rate would show a much lower dollar amount.

[21] Also, there is no provision regarding the appraisal of buildings or structures that may be built on land or other investments that can be made. Without provisions on ownership or valuation methods of such investments, inventors' incentive to invest in buildings, fixtures and other equipmnet may be hindered.

[22] Further, since North Korean individuals are not allowed to participate in a joint venture as a contracting party, the right to use land may be granted only to institutional or corporate entities.

[23] When selling the right to use land, parties with "lessor authority" have the "preferential right to buy," which appears to mean the right of first refusal (Law on the Leasing of Land art. 19).

[24] When land is leased for more than 40 years and buildings are constructed within 10 years before the expiration of the lease, however, compensation is granted for the residual value of the buildings (Law on the Leasing of Land art. 34). There is no provision regarding the method of appraisal or the form of such compensation, however.

[25] There is indication neither as to what constitutes an "unavoidable circumstance" that would justify the cancellation of a lease contract nor as to how the losses incurred by cancelling such a contract would be evaluated.

[26] Foreign banks and their branches are allowed only in the FETZ (Law on Foreign-Invested Banks art. 2). The incorporation procedure for foreign-invested banks is similar to that for non-bank corporations, except that prior approval from the Central Bank of North Korea is required to incorporate a foreign-invested banks (Law on Foreign-Invested Banks arts. 8–17).

[27] Further, laws specifically list the types of transactions in which a foreign-invested bank is allowed to engage (Law on Foreign-Invested Banks art. 23).

[28] Progressive rates are applied corresponding to different income brackets, which range from 4 percent to 20 percent.

[29] These tax provisions do not apply to citizens of a country that has concluded a tax-exemption treaty with North Korea (Law on Taxes on Foreign-Invested Enterprises and Foreigners art. 7). To date, however, no country has signed such a treaty.

[30] A contractual or equity joint venture must obtain approval to extend the operation beyond the term specified in the contract at least 6 months prior to the expiration of the contract (Contractual Joint Venture Law art. 20).

[31] If the dissolution is carried out under the permission of the body that approved its incorporation at the outset, then the board of directors appoints the liquidators. On the other hand, if the corporation is dissolved pursuant to a court decision,

liquidators are appointed by the court. Specific provisions do not always provide clear and adequate guidance, however. For instance, the law fails to specify the method of evaluating assets and liabilities, not even including applicable accounting principles. Nor are relative priorities among different categories of liabilities adequately defined.

[32] There are two types of arbitration. One is applicable to disputes among domestic parties and the other to disputes involving a foreign party. While there are provisions on arbitration in many laws regulating foreign investments, it is not clear what types of arbitration they are referring to.

[33] The Rajin-Sonbong area is the first FETZ, and the record of investments here has not been impressive, partly because Rajin-Sonbong is located within a remote port city with little infrastructure to support commerce and industry. There are signs that other areas with better locations and infrastructure, most notably Haeju, may be designated as a new FETZ.

[34] For foreign investors, the choice is limited to the three forms of investment discussed above, that is, contractual joint venture, equity joint venture, and wholly foreign-owned enterprise (Law on Free Economic and Trade Zone art. 6).

[35] The North Korean economy appears to have shrunk throughout the 1990s and its GDP per capita is now well below $1,000, although the downward trend might have stopped in 2000. Conflicting reports exist as to the minimum wage in North Korea, partly because there are several exchanges rates, official and unofficial. It also appears that some foreign investors did not have to pay the minimum wage. For instance, one report states that joint ventures in North Korea have paid as little as 70 won per month, notwithstanding the official minimum rate of 160 won per month in the FETZ and 220 won in the rest of the country (see *Economist Intelligence Unit Country Report: North Korea*, 1st Quarter, 1996, p. 46). Further, Noland (2000, p. 136) reports the devaluation that allegedly took place in November 1997 only in the FETZ, substantially lowering the effective minimum wage for foreign investors in the FETZ.
With regard to the location of the FETZ, while Rajin-Sonjong may have an advantage serving as a strategic venue for international trade, its remote location, as noted earlier, hinders it from serving domestic markets. Most tellingly, foreign investors have repeatedly sought to have different locations for their investments, and Hyundai recently announced a plan to establish a special zone in Haeju, a city not far from several major cities in North Korea and from the South Korean border.

[36] Thus, from a policy perspective, it might make more logical sense to separate out measures to better serve domestic markets from those targetted toward serving foreign markets and to establish different plans for different goals.

[37] In this context, provisions giving exorbitant discretionary power to North Korean authorities or provisions that can be interpreted to have several different meanings are especially problematic and clarifications and/or amendments are needed for such provisions.

REFERENCES

Bryan, Greyson, Scott Horton, and Robin Radin (1998), "Foreign Investment Laws and Regulations of the Democratic People's Republic of Korea," *Fordham International Law Journal*, 21, 1677–718.

Noland, Marcus (2000), *Avoiding the Apocalypse: the Future of the Two Koreas*, Washington, DC: Institute for International Economics.

North Korea Quarterly, various issues (for texts of laws and regulations).

Shin, Woong Shik and Sung Cho Ahn (1998), *Foreign Investment Laws and Regulations in North Korea – Investment Guidelines and Practices*, Seoul, Korea: Korea International Trade Association (in Korean).

Yoon, Sang-Jick (1997), "Critical Issues on the Foreign Investment Law of North Korea for Foreign Investors," *Wisconsin International Law Journal*, 15, 325–70.

Table 9.1   Major Laws and Regulations in Foreign Investments in North Korea

Laws and Regulations	Dates Enacted/ Amended
Law of the Democratic People's Republic of Korea on Equity Joint Venture	Sept. 8, 1984/ Jan. 20, 1994
Implementing Regulations for the Law on Equity Joint Venture	Mar. 2, 1985/ Jul. 13, 1995
Law of the Democratic People's Republic of Korea on Foreign Investment	Oct. 5, 1992
Law of the Democratic People's Republic of Korea on Foreign Enterprises	Oct. 5, 1992
Law of the Democratic People's Republic of Korea on Contractual Joint Venture	Oct. 5, 1992
Law of the Democratic People's Republic of Korea on Free Economic and Trade Zone	Jan. 31, 1993
Law of the Democratic People's Republic of Korea on Foreign Investment-Business Enterprise and Foreign Individual Tax	Jan. 31, 1993
Law of the Democratic People's Republic of Korea on Foreign Exchange Control	Jan. 31, 1993
Law of the Democratic People's Republic of Korea on the Leasing of Land	Oct. 27, 1993
Customs Law of the Democratic People's Republic of Korea	Nov. 17, 1993
Law of the Democratic People's Republic of Korea on Foreign-Invested Bank	Nov. 24, 1993
Regulations on Immigration Procedure in the Free Economic and Trade Zone	Nov. 29, 1993
Labor Regulations for Foreign-Invested Business	Dec. 30, 1993
Regulations on Resident Representative Offices of Foreign Business in the Free Economic and Trade Zone	Jan. 21, 1994
Enforcement Regulations for Foreign-Invested Business and Foreign Individual Tax Law	Feb. 21, 1994
Regulations for the Implementation of the D.P.R.K. on Wholly Foreign-owned Enterprises	Mar. 27, 1994
Regulations on Free Trade Ports	Apr. 28, 1994
Regulations on Foreigner's Stay and Residence in the Free Economic and Trade Zone	Jun. 14, 1994
Regulations for the Implementation of the Law of the D.P.R.K. on Foreign Exchange Control	Jun.27, 1994
Implementing Regulations for the Law of the D.P.R.K. on the Leasing of Land	Sept. 7, 1994
Implementing Regulations for the Law on Foreign-Invested Bank	Dec. 28, 1994
Law of the DPRK on the External Economic Contract	Feb. 22, 1995
Insurance Law of the Democratic People's Republic of Korea	Apr. 6, 1995
Customs Regulations for Free Economic and Trade Zone	Jun. 28, 1995
Regulations on Forwarding Agency in the Free Economic and Trade Zone	Jul. 13, 1995
Regulations on Transfer and Mortgage of Buildings in the Free Economic and Trade Zone Annex	Aug. 30, 1995

Table 9.1   (Cont.)

Law of the Democratic People's Republic of Korea Law on External Civil Relations	Sept. 6, 1995
Implementing Regulations for the Law on Contractual Joint Venture	Dec. 4, 1995
Bookkeeping Regulations for Foreign-Invested Enterprises	Dec. 4, 1995
Regulations on Naming of Foreign-Invested Enterprises	Feb. 14, 1996
Regulations on the Registration of Foreign-Invested Enterprises	Feb. 14, 1996
Regulations on Processing Trade in the Free Economic and Trade Zone	Feb. 14, 1996
Regulations on Engraving and Registration of Logos for Foreign-Invested Enterprises in the Free Economic and Trade Zone	Mar. 28, 1996
Regulations on the Development and Management of Industrial Estates in the Free Economic and Trade Zone	Apr. 30, 1996
Regulations on Advertisement in the Free Economic and Trade Zone	Apr. 30, 1996
Regulations on Entrepot Trade in the Free Economic and Trade Zone	Jul. 15, 1996
Regulations on Contract Construction in the Free Economic and Trade Zone	Jul. 15, 1996
Regulations on Tourism in the Free Economic and Trade Zone	Jul. 15, 1996
Regulations on Agent for Foreign Investor in the Free Economic and Trade Zone	Jul. 15, 1996
Bookkeeping Regulations for Foreign-Invested Bank	Jul. 15, 1996
Regulations on Certified Public Accounting for Foreign Invested Enterprise	Jul. 15, 1996
Regulations on Currency Circulation in the Free Economic and Trade Zone	Jul. 15, 1996
Regulations on Border Quarantine For the Free Economic and Trade Zone	Jul. 15, 1996
Regulations on Traffic Inspection at the Boundary of the Free Economic and Trade Zone	Jul. 15, 1996
Regulations on Registration of Vehicles in the Free Economic and Trade Zone	Jul. 15, 1996
Regulations on Foreign Technology Transfer	Aug. 11, 1996
Regulations on Prices in the Free Economic and Trade Zone	Sept. 1, 1996
Regulations on Business Operation in the Free Economic and Trade Zone	Nov. 23, 1996
Regulations on Investments in Real Property and Buildings	Dec. 30, 1996
Regulations on Statistics in the Free Economic and Trade Zone	Apr. 12, 1997
Regulations on Lending in North Korean Won in the Free Economic and Trade Zone	Apr. 12, 1997
Law of the Democratic People's Republic of Korea on International Trade	Mar. 1998

10 The Cost and Financing of Korean Unification

Young-Sun Lee

INTRODUCTION

Many people believe that unification of the Korean Peninsula is fast approaching. Although no consensus exists on exactly when and how it will take place, North Korea is certain to change, and South Korea should be ready to guide it in a desirable direction. Even if unification occurs through disintegration of the North, its form and economic consequences will depend on the response from the South.

The economic consequences of Korean unification have been a frequent object of discussion. Lee (1994), Noland et al. (1996), and Park (1997) estimated unification costs using different theoretical approaches. More estimates have been presented by the media, and were probably calculated using a relatively simple approach. Unfortunately, the diversity and complexity of unification cost estimation have generated confusion in understanding and interpreting the estimates. Furthermore, the mere presentations of the seemingly large cost figures without any appropriate explanation have produced a rather passive attitude toward unification on the part of South Korea people.

This chapter is intended to estimate the unification cost of Korea with theoretically and empirically acceptable concepts, especially in relation to the different forms of unification. It also discusses the financial burden the South Korea people must bear, and how to finance it.

The chapter consists of six sections. Following the introduction, the second section clarifies the concepts of unification cost, discussing various assumptions and characteristics. In the third section, the cost of German unification is explained. An estimate of this cost is then calculated using the computable general equilibrium model (CGE) and compared to the actual cost paid by the West German people after unification. The fourth section presents estimates of the costs of Korean unification also calculated by the CGE model for both rapid unification and gradual unification. The fifth inquires into the feasibility and methods of financing the unification cost, and the sixth completes the chapter by summarizing its findings.

FORMS OF UNIFICATION AND CONCEPTS OF UNIFICATION COST

The concept of unification cost depends upon how we understand the words "unification" and "cost." The speed of unification – broadly cast, whether it is quick or gradual – also affects its cost. We presume that a quick unification or a gradual unification can be an object of our choice. If these two alternatives are not within our choice, it is meaningless to compare them.[1]

Some contend that gradual unification will incur lower costs than quick unification. The former assumes that North Korea can accomplish economic transformation in the long term and gain economic efficiency, minimizing the required transfer of resources from South to North. Those who question such a gradual unification either doubt whether the North can effectively carry out such a system transformation or see in gradual transformation an invitation to interference from the privileged class and hence difficulties in minimizing transformation costs.

Those who favor quick unification over gradual unification hold that the former may incur great initial cost but will result in an efficient economy sooner, thereby resulting in a lower cost in the long run. But those who prefer gradual unification assert that calculating the long-term cost of gradual unification in terms of present value using an appropriate discount rate may lead to a different conclusion. Whether quick unification is politically possible is beyond the scope of this chapter. Let it simply be noted that seeing East Germany collapse may have alerted North Korea and made it more careful to avoid a similar collapse.

Another important question is whether the South Korean people are willing to accept the large albeit short-term financial burden accompanying a quick unification. In the German case, the economic burden of quick unification produced substantial socio-political complaints despite the remarkable strength of the West German economy, as evidenced by a long-term trade surplus. In contrast, South Korea recently faced an economic crisis due to foreign currency shortage and financial difficulties. Whether South Korea, with a foreign debt of $156, 900 million, can deal with the unification cost if unification occurs suddenly is a new question.[2] In such circumstances, gradual unification may be a better choice politically and economically.

The economic concept of unification cost is the income or consumption opportunity we must sacrifice if unification is chosen; its magnitude therefore depends upon the composition of "we." If "we" includes South Korean residents only, everything that is sent to the North from the South for unification is a cost. This narrow perspective applies if South Korean residents can choose between pursuing unification for peace and prosperity or keeping the status quo. If, on the other hand, "we" is viewed more broadly as the residents of a unified Korea, goods sent to the North from the South are no longer costs but merely resource transfers. From a broad nation-minded perspective, "we" may be considered as the Korean people of a unified Korea.

What costs are in store for South Korean residents if unification occurs? Given the present situation, where a great economic disparity exists between the two Koreas, unification will inevitably be accompanied by a transfer of resources from the South to the North. If the border between the two Koreas is abolished, a massive migration of North Koreans into South Korea is expected, given the poverty of the North Korean economy. This will lead to great confusion in South Korea and reduce the South's living standards. Keeping North Korean residents in the North by providing aid or guaranteeing certain living standards while allowing migration may be ideal for social stability. In either case, however, South Korean residents will be required to pay for improving living standards in North Korea.

Unification cost is often defined as the amount of resources South Koreans must spend to bring North Korean living standards up to South Korean levels. Since South Korean residents can spend their resources for other purposes if they do not have to improve living standards in North Korea, it can be said that South Koreans will have to sacrifice for unification, and the size of that sacrifice is the unification cost. How much South Koreans sacrifice depends on how much they aim to narrow the gap in living standards of the two Koreas. Completely equalizing per capita GNP in the two Koreas not only would require a long time, but also would increase the burden on South Koreans. Therefore, a more commonly discussed goal is to increase North Korean per capita GNP to about 60 percent of what South Koreans enjoy. Such an income gap is possible within one nation and is believed unlikely to result in massive migration (see Noland et al., 1996, p. 3).

THE GERMAN CASE

How much did Germany pay for unification? Calculating this cost is not easy because it requires hypothesizing how the German economy would have performed in the absence of unification. Nevertheless, the German case provides valuable lessons for South Korea. Information on how West Germany dealt with the economic burden of unification will help South Korea prepare for the financial burden of Korean unification.

After unification, Germany transferred approximately 1,000 billion DM from the West to the East between 1991 and 1996. As shown in Table 10.1, the size of economic aid from West Germany to East Germany amounted to 63 percent and 95 percent of East German GDP in 1991 and 1992 respectively. It then started to decrease, amounting to 34 percent in 1996. The economic aid was used for projects like social security, deficit payment, privatization cost, and investment inducement.

About 75 percent of the financial input into East Germany was spent for consumption purposes such as guaranteeing living standards, while less than 25 percent was spent for investment purposes such as creating jobs and improving the competitiveness of the East German economy (see Boss, 1998, Table 2). Approximately 50 percent of the total transfer was paid out to households as social welfare expense, and 25 percent took the form of interest payments, public spending, and transfer to the corporate sector (ibid.).

The expenditure on consumption purposes was relatively high because the West German social security system, which was characterized by high benefits and very broad coverage, was applied identically to the East. In particular, currency exchange with overvalued East German currency resulted in increased wages and decreased exports, with the concomitant large increase in unemployment and, ultimately, large expenditures on social security. Since pensions in East Germany were given out according to the same rules as in West Germany, they more than doubled in East Germany between 1991 and 1996. The standard pension in East Germany, which was 40.3 percent of the West German pension before unification, increased to 80 percent of the West German pension after unification. The federal government had to make up for what was lacking in the East

German pension fund with the West German pension fund (ibid.). A great rise in East German unemployment after unification called for a huge financial transfusion from West Germany in order to meet East Germany's employment insurance payment.

Table 10.1   GDP and Domestic Demand in East Germany versus Transfers from the West, 1991–96

	1991	1992	1993	1994	1995	1996
Gross Domestic Product (GDP)	206.6	265.6	323.2	366.1	398.0	414.2
Net Exports	-154.4	-188.0	-192.4	-203.2	–	–
GDP minus Net Exports (Consumption plus Investment)	361.0	453.6	515.6	569.3	–	–
Transfers from West Germany	130.0	252.9	198.7	163.6	139.3	140.7
Transfers in Percent of Consumption plus Investment	36.7	55.8	38.5	28.7	–	–
Transfers in Percent of GDP (East)	63.1	95.2	61.5	44.7	35.0	34.0
To compare:						
GDP of West Germany	2647.6	2813.0	2840.5	2962.1	3061.6	3127.3
Transfers in Percent of GDP (West)	4.91	8.99	7.0	5.52	4.55	4.50

Source: Boss (1998), Sachverstaendigenrat (1997).

Table 10.2 shows that from 1991 to 1995, investment in East Germany reached 756 billion DM, of which 624.5 billion DM, about 83 percent of the total, came from the private sector, and 131.9 DM, about 17 percent of the total, came from the public sector. A substantial part of the investment, some 33 percent, went to the service industry, while an astonishing 70 percent went to housing. Of the rest, 30 percent was invested in the manufacturing industry, and 17 percent in transportation and communication.

The German experience tells us that two kinds of expenditures were made in the unification process: investments aiming at increasing productivity in East Germany and expenditures to maintain the quality of life for residents in East Germany. All consumption expenditures were made from public sources, while investment expenditures came from both the public and the private sectors. Investments from private sources cannot be regarded as public expenditure, since these investments are expected to profit the investors in the future; it can therefore be said that unification costs consist of consumption costs for crisis management and investment made by public institutions.

Table 10.2   Investment in East Germany after Unification, 1991–95 (billion DM)

Industry	1991	1992	1993	1994	1995	Total
Agriculture and Forestry	0.95	1.10	1.30	1.50	1.80	6.65
Manufacturing	32.45	41.10	45.20	49.20	56.20	221.45
−energy/water service, mining	10.35	14.15	17.00	19.10	22.30	82.90
−processing[1]	18.50	22.50	23.70	24.60	27.50	116.80
−construction	3.60	4.45	4.50	5.50	6.40	24.45
Trade	4.35	5.30	5.70	6.00	5.80	27.15
Transport, Communication	16.15	22.50	24.90	26.70	28.80	119.05
Service	23.70	34.60	46.90	63.40	78.90	247.50
−house lease	15.90	23.90	31.40	44.90	56.60	172.70
−other services[2]	7.80	10.70	15.50	18.50	22.30	74.80
Private Total Investment	77.60	104.60	124.00	146.80	171.50	624.50
Public Total Investment	14.90	23.30	26.50	32.20	35.00	131.90
Total Investment	92.50	127.90	150.50	179.00	206.50	756.40

Notes: (1) including construction of gas station.

(2) including banking and insurance.

Source: Shin Dong-Chun (1988, p. 27).

Table 10.3 shows changes in the main economic indicators in East Germany after unification. GDP in East Germany increased from 31.3 percent of West German levels in 1991 to 54.4 percent in 1996. The relatively rapid economic growth in East Germany is a result of a higher rate of investment per capita in East Germany compared to West Germany. Indeed, East Germany's per capita investment in equipment rose from 63.3 percent of the West's in 1991 to 111.7 percent in 1994, and investment in construction rose from 67.2 percent of the West's in 1991 to 184.5 percent in 1996. These numbers suggest that resources were transferred from West

Table 10.3   Main Economic Indicators in East Germany after Unification,
1991–96
(West Germany=100)

	1991	1992	1993	1994	1995	1996
GDP per capita	31.3	38.5	46.2	50.6	52.8	54.4
Investment per capita in Equipment	63.6	75.3	99.5	111.7	–	–
Investment per capita in Construction	67.2	100.8	129.1	164.9	180.6	184.5
Housing	44.5	61.3	81.8	115.8	136.8	146.2
Enterprises	89.4	141.5	195.5	233.3	245.3	239.3
Productivity[1]	31.0	43.1	51.6	54.3	55.2	56.8
Relative wage[2]	150.7	140.9	131.6	129.8	131.2	130.0

Notes: (1) GDP per labor (in market prices).
          (2) Non-self-employed income per capita/ GDP per labor.
Source: DIW, (April 1997, p. 306).

Germany to East Germany at a very rapid rate. But productivity in East Germany did not increase as quickly, reaching only 56.8 percent of the West German productivity level in 1996.

At the same time, however, the relative wage cost of East to West Germany, expressed by the ratio of wage income per capita of employed to GDP per labor, declined from 150.7 percent in 1991 to 130 percent in 1996. This decrease was due to the increase of labor productivity in East Germany. The catch-up was not complete, however, so relative wage costs remain significantly higher in East Germany.

Could the East German economy have enjoyed faster growth if investment allocation in East Germany after unification had been more efficient? To answer this question, we calculate the required amount of investment under the assumption that the optimal allocation of investment could have been made in East Germany. Such a calculation can be made using the computable general equilibrium model (CGE model).[3] This model is based on neo-classical economic theory, which assumes that all markets are perfectly competitive and all production factors are fully employed. The model also assumes that all economic actors regard the market price system as given and try to pursue their goals within their limited constraints, and that all resources are optimally distributed in the initial economic structure. Of course, one may question whether the economic activities of a socialist state like East Germany can be analyzed through a neo-classical model. However, as Lange and Taylor (1998) pointed out, if economic planners were to maximize a society's welfare by allocating resources according to the goals of that particular society, it is at least theoretically possible to achieve a "Pareto optimum" in a socialist state. Without a doubt, lack of information and a rigid bureaucracy make it difficult for the Pareto optimum to be achieved in the real world, but generating an ideal picture of an economy is still useful in providing a benchmark.[4]

The minimum investment cost for East Germany to achieve 60 percent of West Germany's GDP per capita was calculated by using East Germany's 1987 economic data with the CGE model. Under the additional assumption that a large amount of East German capital would become valueless after unification, since East German capital differs greatly from West German capital in terms of productivity or other aspects of quality, we estimated the amount of total investment and optimal allocation of investment throughout different industries under the further premise that only 30 percent of East Germany's capital would be useful after unification.[5]

According to the results shown in Table 10.4, a total of 676.1 billion DM in 1987 prices must be invested in East Germany for its GDP per capita to reach 60 percent of West Germany's level. The results also recommend that 37.3 percent of the total investment be made in the service sector, 12 percent in agriculture and fishery, 9.5 percent in the chemical industry and 7.9 percent in light industry in order to achieve optimal allocation. Considering the industrial structure of East Germany in 1987, these data imply that, for faster economic growth in East Germany, light industry must be reduced, while the chemical and service industries must be expanded.

It is very interesting to compare these results with Germany's actual situation after unification. First of all, the total investment made in East Germany after unification until 1995 was 884.5 billion DM, which was 30.8 percent more than 676.1 billion DM, the suggested amount of minimum investment.

East Germany's GDP per capita remains at 52.8 percent of West Germany's despite this large amount of investment either because investment in East Germany was not optimally allocated or because the real amount of investment was calculated in current prices. Therefore, if the annual amount of actual investment is converted to 1987 constant prices

Table 10.4   Minimum German Unification Cost and Optimal Investment in Each Industrial Sector (investment in billion DM, structure in %)

Industry	Optimal Investment		Industrial Structure (Value Added)	Industrial Structure (Products)
	Amount	Structure		
Agriculture, Forestry and Fishing	80.8	11.96	7.47	8.01
Mining and Quarrying	34.6	5.12	6.92	4.91
Light Industry	53.3	7.90	10.36	17.08
Chemicals	63.8	9.45	14.06	15.89
Ceramics, Stones, Clays	25.0	3.70	2.29	2.78
Primary Metal Products	17.3	2.50	2.80	5.40
Metal Products	27.5	4.08	4.35	4.72
Mechanical Engineering	28.8	4.27	3.58	4.35
Electronics	33.2	4.91	4.98	4.92
Fine Machines	2.5	0.37	0.34	0.31
Transport Machines	15.3	2.27	2.20	2.45
Other Manufacturing	5.3	0.70	0.80	0.70
Electricity, Gas, Water	21.1	3.13	1.02	2.61
Construction	14.7	2.17	1.06	1.32
Service	252.9	37.31	37.62	24.41
Total	676.1	100%	100%	100%

under an assumed average inflation rate of 2 percent, the amount of real investment through 1995 adds up to 786.9 billion DM. The discounted investment volume in 1987 prices still exceeds the minimum investment calculated by CGE model. This adjusted result shows that the investment had not been optimally allocated.

In short, the actual investment of 786.9 billion DM in 1987 prices made from 1991 to 1995 exceeded the required amount of optimal investment to increase East German GDP per capita to 60 percent of West Germany's by a factor of 1.16. And yet, the per capita GDP of East Germany in 1995 was still only 52.8 percent of West Germany's.

Then how much more actual investment is needed for East Germany's per capita GDP to reach 60 percent of West Germany's? If we linearly extrapolate the figures estimated above, we find that 1 trillion and 35.4

billion DM should be invested. This vast sum is 1.53 times the amount that was estimated by the CGE model. In the actual process of investment, inefficient allocation and management appear dramatically to increase the required amount of investment.

It is necessary to point out again that the amount of investment is not entirely public cost. If we apply a 17 percent rate of public investment to total investment between 1991 and 1995, to the total required investment of 1035 billion DM, the public investment cost would be only 176 billion DM. If we assume that East Germany's GDP per capita becomes 60 percent of West Germany's in 1999, and West Germany transfers income to East Germany for crisis management until that time, the total crisis management cost would be 1320.7 billion DM. The result for total unification cost becomes 1497 billion DM, including crisis management cost and investment cost.

Since Germany was unified through a rapid rather than a gradual process, the main fiscal burden of unification was crisis management cost, mainly social security cost. The social security contribution of the German people increased after unification from 16.9 percent of GDP in 1990 to 20.0 percent in 1997, while the ratio of tax burden to GDP changed little – from 23.6 percent in 1990 to 22.6 percent in 1997 (see Table 10.5). These facts indicate that the main fiscal burden of German unification was shouldered by the social security contributions of the West German people.

Another remarkable change in financial situation of Germany after unification has been the increase in the public sector debt. Germany's total outstanding public sector debt increased from 1,298 billion DM in 1991 to 2,140 billion DM in 1996, with an accompanying increase in the debt-to-GDP ratio from 44.0 percent in 1991 to 60.4 percent in 1996. In other words, unified Germany increased public debt by as much as 3 percent of GDP every year in the first five years following unification. We can therefore conclude that the two main, and more or less equally important, financial sources for fiscal burden of the German unification were social security contributions and public debt.

The issuing of government bonds and social security taxes were important means of raising funds for unification. To finance all these costs, however, the German government additionally applied such other measures as cutting the government budget, increasing taxes for West German residents, borrowing from capital markets, and disposing of national assets.

To distribute the burden of unification costs evenly, the German government tried equally to engage the federal, state, and local governments. The costs were distributed equally by enacting a law of financial balance among states, and the funds were basically raised through issuing government bonds. Also, in order to distribute the costs of

Table 10.5   Government Expenditures, Taxes, Contributions to Social
Security, Balance and Public Sector Debt of Germany and South Korea (in
relation to GDP)

Year	Government Expenditures(a)	Taxes	Contributions to Social Security	Other Revenues	Balance	Public Sector Debt (b)
West Germany						
1980	49.0	25.9	16.9	3.3	-2.9	31.8
1985	48.0	25.2	17.6	4.0	-1.2	41.7
1990	46.1	23.6	16.9	3.5	-2.1	43.4
Germany						
1991	50.1	24.1	18.0	3.3	-4.5	44.0
1992	51.9	24.5	18.3	3.7	-5.4	48.7
1993	52.7	24.4	18.8	3.7	-5.8	54.6
1994	51.4	24.4	19.3	3.7	-3.9	57.6
1995	50.7	24.2	19.5	3.6	-3.4	58.0
1996	50.0	23.2	19.9	3.4	-3.5	60.4
1997	49.0	22.6	20.0	3.3	-3.1	61.7
South Korea						
1991	10.3	17.8	1.6	3.2	-1.9	13.4
1992	10.9	18.6	1.7	3.7	-0.7	13.5
1993	10.8	18.8	1.7	2.8	0.3	12.4
1994	10.6	19.8	1.9	2.9	0.5	11.4
1995	10.3	20.5	1.8	2.4	0.4	10.2
1996	10.7	21.1	2.0	2.4	-0.3	-

Notes: (a) NIPA, including Treuhandanstalt.

(b) At the end of the year.

Source: Statistisches Bundesamt(1997a, b), Sachverstaendigenrat (1996), Boss (1998) and the
Ministry of Public Finance and Economy(1997).

unification fairly among the different social classes, the government
imposed a surcharge of 7.5 percent to corporate and income taxes.

ESTIMATES OF THE COST OF KOREAN UNIFICATION

Although the case of Germany affords insight into the cost of Korean unification and how to finance it, the German model cannot be applied directly to the Korean case, since the costs of unification as well as financing methods will depend on the speed of unification as well as on the economic situation. Depending on the form of unification there are two kinds of unification costs. First are investment costs to increase North Korea's productivity to match that of South Korea's. Second are crisis management costs in the form of living expenses to prevent massive migration of North Korean residents to South Korea.

Investment costs will be lower for rapid unification than for gradual unification, because in the former case North Korea's economy will quickly be transformed into a market economy, and the price mechanism will enable efficient investment allocation. However, as in the case of Germany, the costs for rapid unification consist mainly of crisis management costs. If the borders between the two countries dissolve and the income gap is not solved quickly, North Korean residents are expected to swarm into South Korea. To prevent such massive migration, it is necessary to find a way to secure their lives in North Korea. Although investment will gradually increase North Korean productivity, South Korean residents will have to transfer their income to support North Korea as long as North Korea's GDP per capita remains below 60 percent of South Korea's. This is assumed to be the minimum relative level of income for North Korean people to stay in the North.

The case of gradual unification also involves investment costs and crisis management costs. Because gradual unification refers to the unification of North and South Korea's politico-economic system based on the agreement of both countries, North Korea will open and reform its economy slowly with South Korean support until complete economic unification is achieved. Unless integration of the two politico-economic systems is accomplished, borders between the two countries will keep residents from moving freely from one side to the other.

Crisis management costs will be lower with gradual unification. If borders remain and prevent residents from migrating, crisis management funds may not even be necessary. If the borders are eliminated before North Korea's GDP per capita reaches 60 percent of South Korea's, crisis management costs will prove necessary.

Investment costs will, on the other hand, be more burdensome with gradual unification. Because, under this scenario, North Korea's planned economic system will be preserved for a while, even though investment will become more effective with the opening and reform of the economy, it will still remain inefficient as long as the economic system is not a market system. In brief, in the case of gradual unification, crisis management costs will be low, but investment costs high.

Methodology, Assumptions, and Data

We shall now estimate the investment and crisis management costs in both cases. Our first assumption is that the collapse of borders allows South Korean companies to invest in North Korea and North Korean residents to move to South Korea. In this case, how much must be invested in North Korea for North Korea's GDP per capita to reach 60 percent of South Korea's? To find an answer to this question we apply the CGE model that was used for Germany.

As mentioned in the German case, estimating unification costs based on the CGE model involves calculating the minimum resources necessary to increase North Korea's GDP per capita to a certain level for, say, 60 percent of South Korea's per capita GDP. In this case we follow the neo-classical assumption that the current industrial structure enables the best possible allocation and new investments are fairly allocated by the market. Of course, the reality is quite different. As seen in the case of Germany, actual costs of investment were much higher than estimated through this method. We apply this method because giving us insight about the minimum cost of unification is still useful, if only as a starting point.

In order to apply this model to North Korea, we collected data on North Korea's industrial structure, and created a social accounting matrix for North Korea. Doing so required access to an input–output table for North Korea, so we created one based on East German data. The general practice in making input–output tables for North Korea is to use Chinese data, but since North Korea's economic structure is far more dependent on heavy and chemical industry than that of either South Korea or China, its industrial structure can be assumed to have more in common with East Germany's industrial structure before unification.

It is also important to know how much of North Korea's capital stock is usable for actual production. As seen in the German case, most of North Korea's capital stock will become useless with unification. Since most facilities are in bad shape, labor costs are expected to rise after unification, and technological know-how is lacking, it is difficult for most of the capital to be utilized after unification. We therefore assume, as in the case of Germany, that only 30 percent of the existing capital stock will be usable. This assumption is not so heroic as it may at first appear. Although North

Korea is far behind East Germany in terms of technology and capital, so most of its capital stock is likely to be discarded after unification, if North Korea's wages do not increase at the rate of East Germany's, its low-quality capital will not be discarded so completely.

If unification is achieved under these assumptions and South Korea continues to invest in North Korea until North Korea's GDP per capita reaches 60 percent of South Korea's, properly allocating this investment, how much investment must be transferred to North Korea?

Estimating actual numbers with the CGE model requires setting a base year. Although the most recent data are generally best, we chose 1990 as the base year, due to data constraints and the economic situation. In 1990 the North Korean economy was relatively sound, but it started to decline with the collapse of the Soviet Bloc. One may suggest that the costs should be estimated in light of North Korea's current economic situation, but it is more important to analyze whether South Korea is capable of financing unification based on the normal economic structure of the two countries, so we decided to choose 1990, when both economies were in relatively normal condition.

The Bank of Korea estimated North Korea's GNP in 1990 to be approximately 23.1 billion dollars. This means that North Korea's GDP per capita was $1,066. In the same year South Korea's GDP per capita was $5,693, about five times that of North Korea.

Cost of Rapid Unification

In order for North Korea's GDP per capita to reach $3,416, or 60 percent of South Korea's, the minimum amount of required investment according to the CGE model is $88.9 billion. If this sum is well allocated among industries, it can be regarded as the lower limit. Table 10.6 shows the allocation of investment across industries and North Korea's industrial structure in terms of production. Note that not all investments are public expenditures, since a large portion of the investment will come from private sources. In Germany, only 17 percent of total investment came from the public sector, but public investment will probably constitute a much larger portion in Korea since the South Korean economy has a more government-led growth strategy than the West German economy. If the public sector contributes about 30 percent of the investment cost, approximately $26.7 billion must come from public sources.

The CGE model does not take the time factor into consideration. In other words, the CGE model neglects the time it will take for North Korea's GDP per capita to reach 60 percent of South Korea's and assumes that North Korea will achieve the desired economic growth without any adjustment costs. Such is not the case in reality. Such a large amount of investment cannot be made in a short period of time, and even if it were, productivity is unlikely to increase at once. As seen in the German example it will take about 10 years for East Germany's GDP to reach 60 percent of West Germany's GDP.

Table 10.6   The Unification Cost, Optimal Allocation of Investment, and North Korean Industrial Structure after Unification (North Korea's GDP per capita = 0.6 x South Korea's GDP per capita)

Industry	Optimal Investment		Industrial Structure (%) (value added)	Industrial Structure (%) (product)
	Amount (billion $)	%		
Agriculture	14.626	16.50	17.91	16.08
Mining	9.676	10.80	5.40	4.72
Light Industry	5.622	6.34	6.97	14.43
Chemicals	9.956	11.23	3.96	6.55
Primary Metals	4.682	5.28	2.04	5.02
Metals, Machinery	16.322	18.41	13.02	14.95
Other Manufacturing	0.666	0.75	0.77	0.72
Electronics, Gas, Water	3.772	4.25	1.70	2.76
Service	23.427	26.43	48.23	34.78
Total	88.749	100	100	100

If it takes this long for North Korea to catch up to South Korea, North Koreans will probably want to move to South Korea until the North's GDP per capita increases to 60 percent of South Korea's. To prevent migration, South Korea must provide funds for some kind of crisis management or adjustment cost; we therefore assume that South Korea will provide support to North Korea to bridge the economic gap until North Korea's GDP per capita reaches its goal. The amount of the crisis management cost depends on how fast North Korea increases its GDP per capita. The longer the period, the higher the cost will be. We must also consider growth in South Korea's GDP per capita with time, and shall assume that rate to be 6 percent per annum.

The speed of North Korea's economic growth depends on how fast the country opens and reforms its economy in the process of economic integration and as a result establishes an effective market economy. Since this cannot be determined in advance, we conduct simulations for two scenarios.

In the first scenario, we assume that North Korea increases its GDP per capita to 60 percent of South Korea's level within five years. Since North Korea's GDP per capita in the base year is 20 percent of South Korea's, we further assume that the gap will decline by 10 percent every year. The amount of annual investment in crisis management costs, North Korea's economic growth rate, and unification costs are laid out in Table 10.7.

The total amount of investment when optimally allocated is $145.9 billion. This figure is much larger than the results shown in Table 10.6 because the South Korean economy is expected to grow as well and more investment will therefore be needed to bridge the gap between the North and the South. If public investment represents 30 percent of the total needed amount, $43.7 billion will be financed from public sources. However, this amount can also be estimated assuming that investment is properly allocated across industries. Even if a market economy is introduced in North Korea after rapid unification, it will take time for the system to work, and it is unlikely that the investments will be allocated efficiently.

Table 10.7   Unification Costs for Korea According to Scenario 1(billion $)

	Investment Cost	Public Investment Cost (A)	Crisis Managemen t Cost (B)	Unification Cost (A+B)	Growth Rate of North Korea
1st year	2.0	0.6	52.4	53.0	13.2
2nd year	18.0	5.4	41.6	47.0	59.0
3rd year	28.0	8.4	29.4	37.8	41.3
4th year	40.8	12.2	15.6	27.8	32.5
5th year	57.1	17.1	0	17.1	27.2
Total	145.9	43.7	139	182.7	

Assumptions:

(1) Base year: 1990.

(2) South Korean economy grows 6 percent per year.

(3) North Korean GDP per capita grows to overtake yearly 10 percent
    of the income gap to South Korean GDP.

The figure presented above thus refers to minimum costs, and actual expenditures will easily exceed it.

A total of $139 billion in crisis management costs will also be needed to increase North Korea's per capita income to 60 percent of South Korea's per capita income. As in the case of Germany, social security costs will exceed investment costs by a large margin. The sum of public investment and crisis management costs is $182.7 billion, about 60 percent of South Korea's GNP in 1990. In other words, 12 percent of South Korea's GNP must be transferred to North Korea every year for five years after unification. If the figure is too large to be covered by income generated each year, the government can issue bonds or borrow from abroad. If bonds are issued and foreign loans are available, South Korea will have to redistribute a burden of only 5–6 percent of its annual GNP over ten years after unification.

The second scenario is based on the assumption that it will take about ten years for North Korea's GDP per capita to reach 60 percent of South Korea's GDP per capita, as was the case in Germany. In this scenario, the crisis management costs are considerable, because the income gap between the two regions is bridged by rising social security costs for a longer period. Investment costs do not necessarily increase, because the longer the transition takes, the more the facilities that were created with the initial investments will contribute to North Korea's economic growth. If there is little time to bridge the income gap, however, a significant amount of capital will be needed right away. As seen in Table 10.8, the total amount of investment during the 11 years is $121.8 billion. If we suppose that 30 percent of the total investment comes from the public sector, public investment will be approximately $36.6 billion.

The crisis management cost to secure the lives of North Korean residents will be about $524.8 billion. Adding public investment expenditure to this figure means that South Korea will spend about $561.4 billion in public spending to achieve unification within 11 years. The per capita income for South and North Korea in the last year of this time span will be $19,354 and $11,520, respectively. Crisis management costs are much larger than in the scenario that aims at bridging the income gap in five years because South Korea's income level increases with time, ceteris paribus, widening the gap.

These costs are similar in magnitude to the results of the study by Lee (1994), and Noland et al. (1996).[6] Because of social welfare cost, unification is more expensive in the second scenario. The crisis management funds needed to secure the lives of North Koreans include aid for the unemployed, financial support for the elderly, medical insurance, education funds, and financial aid for local governments in North Korea. According to Park (1997, p. 488), financial aid for the unemployed will be about 70 percent of the total crisis management costs.

Table 10.8   Unification Costs for Korea According to Scenario 2(billion $)

	Investment Cost	Public Investment Cost (A)	Crisis Management Cost (B)	Unification Cost (A+B)
1st year	0.4	0.1	52.7	52.8
2nd year	2.6	0.8	55.8	56.6
3rd year	4.0	1.2	58.5	59.7
4th year	6.3	1.9	60.4	62.3
5th year	7.8	2.3	61.1	63.4
6th year	6.5	2.0	60.3	62.3
7th year	10.9	3.3	57.2	60.5
8th year	18.1	5.4	51.0	56.4
9th year	18.5	5.6	40.8	46.4
10th year	21.0	6.3	25.0	31.3
11th year	25.7	7.7	2.0	9.7
Total	121.8	36.6	524.8	561.4

Assumptions:

(1) Base year: 1990.

(2) Yearly growth rate of GDP per capita of South Korea and North Korea are 6 percent and 12 percent, respectively.

(3) South Korea pays investment cost and crisis management costs until North Korea's GDP per capita reaches 60 percent of South Korea's.

How can such crisis management costs be minimized? The best way to cut these costs is to bridge the income gap as soon as possible. In other words, a large amount of investment must be transferred to North Korea. Depending on the will of the government, the volume of public investment may increase within a short period. However, the amount of private investment, which is expected to play a significant role in the unification scenario, depends on the economic situation. Since private investment is stimulated by a market system, the creation of a proper legal order is very important. The establishment of social infrastructure will also encourage private investment in the region. Increased public investment, in sum, reduces crisis management costs.

So far we have discussed the unification costs in the case of rapid unification. How will the unification costs in a gradual unification process be different?

Cost of Gradual Unification

Gradual unification, to repeat, refers to a state where the borders between North and South remain, preventing a massive migration of North Koreans to the South, and North Korea introduces a market system based on an agreement between the North and the South. South Korea is assumed to continue its financial support only until North Korea's per capita income reaches 60 percent of South Korea's. Since there is no massive migration of North Koreans, no additional social welfare expenditures are necessary. However, unless North Korea introduces a market system right away, inefficient investment continues for a long time. Thus, investment expenditures are much larger than in the case of rapid unification. A study of the East European experience shows that the productivity of investment in socialist states is only 2/3 that of capitalist states.[7] North Korea's investment efficiency is expected to be even lower than that of East Europe, since it has a much stronger socialist system. If we assume that North Korea's investment efficiency for the period of gradual unification of ten years is half South Korea's, the total public transfer needed from South Korea will be about $73.2 billion, significantly larger than the public investment costs of rapid unification.

However, even if investment costs are twice as high as those for rapid unification, the total amount of unification costs is much smaller for gradual unification: this scenario eliminates crisis management costs, which exceed investment costs in rapid unification. The question is whether North and South Korea can reach an agreement to pursue gradual unification. Without a firm belief that North Korea will in the long run embrace democracy and a market economy and also open and reform its economy, South Korea is unlikely to continue its financial support. It is also possible that in the process of pursuing gradual unification sudden changes will lead to rapid unification. In this case, the unification costs can be estimated by combining the two cases explained above. In the extreme, a significant portion of transfers from the South to the North may be used for consumption purposes to increase the living standard of North Korea even if unification is gradual. In this case, the cost of gradual unification will be much higher than the figure estimated with the assumption of no crisis management costs.

FINANCING UNIFICATION COSTS

How can the fiscal burden of Korean unification be financed? Increasing tax rates, curtailing government expenditure, issuing government bonds in both domestic and foreign markets, inviting foreign capital, and selling state-run enterprises in North Korea are some of the appropriate measures.

The rate of tax burden to GDP in South Korea rose to 21.1 percent in 1996, as shown in Table 10.5, and is likely to climb further with increases in financial demand, especially for social welfare. Even if the current tax burden ratio is still low compared to that of most OECD countries, it would be difficult to raise it by more than 2.0 percent in order to meet unification costs, since it is already close to that of Japan, a country with an economic structure and cultural background similar to Korea's. Once peace takes root in the Korean Peninsula as a result of unification, the size of defense expenditure may be reduced by 1.5 percent of GNP.[8] Expenditures other than defense can also be spared for unification financing by, say, 0.5 percent of GDP. Issuing government bonds was regarded as another measure for securing the fiscal burden until the 1997 financial crisis broke out in South Korea. Until then, the financial position of the South Korean government was fairly sound, with a budget surplus of about 0.4 percent of GNP from 1993 to 1995, and a deficit of 0.3 percent in 1996; these figures are quite low compared to other OECD countries. Nor has the outstanding stock of government debt been a serious problem in South Korea, the government debt-to-GNP ratios having decreased from 14.9 percent in 1990 to 10.2 percent in 1995, again quite low, at least as compared to the German case of 45.5 percent in 1991 and 60.4 percent in 1996, as shown in Table 10.5. It was once thought that the South Korean government could increase the public debt by at least 3 percent of GNP every year for five years, making the outstanding public debt ratio to GNP about 25 percent.

The 1997 financial crisis made the possibility of debt financing very uncertain. It is now difficult to predict how much foreign debt should be repaid by the government in the future. If we assume that about 50 billion US dollars in addition to the existing foreign debt before the crisis will be paid by the government, the public debt-to-GNP will soar up to about 30 percent. Since this ratio is still lower than Germany's in 1991, there may still be room for the government to issue bonds to cover the fiscal burden for unification. Raising about 2 percent of GNP per year would make the debt-to-GNP ratio over 40 percent within five years. Although this ratio is still lower than in the German case, the rapid increase in the public debt will increase interest rates, which may reduce private investment so that economic growth would slow down, which in turn would make it difficult to mobilize resources for the fiscal burden of unification.

Issuing government bonds to finance the construction of production-related facilities in North Korea is clearly preferable to printing money. It minimizes such effects of financial deficits as inflation and increased interest rates.

Foreign capital can also contribute to this financing of unification costs. Foreign investors may find social infrastructure such as communications and electricity profitable and therefore attractive uses of their funds. However, since most of the foreign capital invested in North Korea will be on a commercial basis, the fiscal burden for public purposes will not be reduced as much as the incoming foreign investment, and the government must take over most of the public investment in social infrastructure. As we saw in the German case, state-run enterprises cannot eventually be sold to earn net revenue, because most of them are old-fashioned and obsolete.

In short, increasing the tax rate and curtailing financial expenditures will allow about 4 percent of yearly GNP to meet unification costs, and this sum satisfies the investment requirement of gradual unification. This scenario therefore involves no significant financial difficulties. Quick unification, however, depends additionally upon government bonds and foreign deficits to meet the high initial costs of crisis management, amounting to over 4 percent of GNP. In this case, financial difficulties present a significant problem.

CONCLUDING REMARKS

We have examined how unification costs vary with the form of unification, finding that quick unification incurs lower investment costs and higher crisis management costs than its gradual alternative. Total unification costs in case of rapid unification are estimated to be about 60 percent of South Korea's 1990 GNP, a sum that can be transferred to North Korea by sending 5–6 percent of GNP each year to the North for ten years after unification. If gradual unification is possible, the lower crisis management costs reduce this figure significantly.

The estimated cost of unification can be financed through higher taxes, reduced expenditure, and borrowing. However, there remains the question of how to deliver the financial resources temporarily required by unification and how to distribute the burden of unification across generations and income groups. This is a political rather than an economic question, and is beyond the purview of this chapter.

Resource mobilization and distribution of the financial burden will be the most urgent problems in the case of a quick unification, while efficient transformation of the North Korean system will be most important in the case of a gradual unification. If system transformation is slow, the political management of various interest groups will emerge as a hot issue.

Unification costs may also be controlled through appropriate policy choices. Quick unification requires policies like minimizing crisis management costs, while gradual unification calls for policies that accelerate transformation of the North Korean system, thereby speeding up the realization of unification benefits.

Finally, the author wants to emphasize that the recent economic crisis in South Korea can have an important impact on the course of Korean unification. The South Korean government's deteriorated financial position makes gradual unification more financially feasible than quick unification.

NOTES

[1] For the purposes of this chapter, "quick unification" means that South Korea can take over North Korea in a very short period of time after the political collapse of its government. "Gradual unification" means that the Korean Peninsula becomes united through an agreement between South and North Korea to recreate a single country over a much longer period of time involving political and economic system transformation.

[2] This is a gross figure for the end of 1997. Since Korea's claims on the rest of the world are estimated at about $60,600 million, the net foreign debt of Korea at the end of 1997 was $96,300 million.

[3] The computable general equilibrium model (CGE model) has been used for calculating unification costs by Noland et al. (1996) for the North Korean case, and by Shin (1998) for the German and Korean cases.

[4] For more information on the estimation of unification costs with the CGE model, refer to research by Dong-Chun Shin of the Institute for Korean Unification Studies, February, 1998.

[5] This assumption is based on Sinn and Sinn's (1992, p. 102) estimation of capital stock.

[6] In the study by Young-Sun Lee (1994), government spending and the reduction of consumption expenditure to balance the per capita income between North and South were considered as unification costs. In the 40 years after 1990, they were estimated at about $330–$841 billion. Bridging the income gap requires South Korea to transfer about 6 percent of its GNP every year for 10 years. Noland et al. (1996) based their study on the assumption that in order for North Korea's per capita income to reach 60 percent of South Korea's per capita income, North Korea will have to adopt a market economy and will need $415–$2,242 billion for unification costs, depending on the speed of unification.

[7] This is the result of empirical analysis performed by Gregory and Stuart (1985),

who compared the productivity growth between GDR and FRG from 1960 to 1981.
[8] With regression analysis using cross-country data, Cho (1997) estimated the normal level of defense expenditure when Korea is in peace, and came up with this figure.

REFERENCES

Boss, Alfred (1998), "How Germany Shouldered the Fiscal Burden of the Unification," *Kiel Working Paper* No. 851, Kiel: The Kiel Institute of World Economics.

Cho, Dong-Ho (1997), "The Estimation of Benefit of Korean Unification," in Young-Yun Kim (ed.), *Division Costs and Unification Costs*, Seoul: Korea Development Institute (KDI).

Deutsches Institut für Wirtschaftsforshung (DIW) and Institut für Weltwirtschaft an der Universität Kiel (IFW), Gesamtwirtschaftliche und unternehmerische Anpassungsprozesse in Ostdeutschland, Diskussionsbeiträge, No. 168, 169, 176, 178, 183, 190/191, 198/199, 205/206, 218/219, 231, 236/237, 245, 257.

Deutsches Institut für Wirtschaftsforshung (DIW) (1997), *Die Lage der Weltwirtschaft und der Deutschen Wirtschaft im Frühjahr 1997*, Berlin: DIW Wochenbericht 17/97.

Dornbusch, Rüdiger, Holger C. Wolf (1994), "East German Economic Reconstruction," in Olivier Blanchard (ed.), *Transition in Eastern Europe*, Bd.1, Washington, pp. 152–182.

Gregory, Paul R. and Robert C. Stuart (1985), *Comparative Economic Systems*, second edition, Boston: Houghton Mifflin Company.

Lange and Taylor (1998), *On the Economic Theory of Socialism*, The University of Minnesota Press.

Lee, Young-Sun (1994), "Economic Integration of the Korean Peninsula: A Scenario Approach to the Cost of Unification," in Sung Yeung Kwack (ed.), *The Korean Economy at a Crossroad*, Westport CT: Praeger.

Noland, M., S. Robinson and M. Scatasta (1996), "Modeling Economic Reforms in North Korea," mimeo.

Park, Tae-Kyu (1997), "Estimating unification costs and ways to raise funds," in Chun, Hong-Taek and Young-Sun Lee (eds), *Economic Integration Strategies and Unification on the Korean Peninsula*, Seoul: Korea Development Institute (KDI).

SVR (Sachverständigenrat zur Begutachtung der

Gesamtwirt-Schaftlichen Entwicklung) (1991), Die wirtschaftliche Integration in Deutschland. Perspektiven Wege Risiken, Jahresgutachten 1991/92, Stuttgart, 1992.

SVR (Sachverständigenrat zur Begutachtung der Gesamtwirt-Schaftlichen Entwicklung) (1997), Wachstum, Beschäftigung, Währungsunion-Orientierungen für die Zukunft, Jahresgutachten 1997/98, Stuttgart.

Shin, Dong-Chun (1998), *Economic Cooperation and Unification Costs: A Comparative Analysis between Germany and Korea*, Seoul: Samsung Economic Institute.

Sinn, Gerlinde and Hans-Werner Sinn (1992), *Jumpstart: the Economic Unification of Germany*, translated by Juli Irving, MIT Press.

The Ministry of Public Finance and Economy (1997), *Public Finance Statistics of Korea.*

11 The Implications of Increased Economic Integration[*]

Marcus Noland

INTRODUCTION

Today there is relatively little economic interaction between North and South Korea. Most of what does occur takes the form of unilateral transfers from the South to the North, with food assistance and KEDO being the most prominent examples. Genuine exchange is less important.[1] In significant part, exchange takes the form of processing on commission, whereby the low cost of North Korean labor is exploited in the fabrication of light industrial goods, though North Korea also exports some minerals and other natural resource-based products to the South.

Historically, economic integration has been limited by the impediments created by the mutually wary North and South Korean regimes. In 1994 and 1995, the government of Kim Young Sam, concerned about a possible collapse in the North following the death of North Korean leader Kim Il-Sung, removed some restrictions on exchange. For its part, the government in Pyongyang tried to channel inter-Korean economic activity through the unattractive special economic zone (SEZ) established in the remote Rajin-Sonbong area, where contact with South Korean firms could literally be quarantined from the rest of the North Korean economy.[2]

The South Korean government's stance shifted noticeably with Kim Dae Jung's inauguration in 1998.[3] Kim proclaimed a "sunshine policy" later rechristened the "Constructive engagement policy," toward the North. In essence, the policy seeks to engage the North in a wide range of contacts in the hope of creating a set of interdependencies that in the long run would discourage the North from external aggression and perhaps even promote the internal transformation of the regime. Initially, President Kim identified three principles in outlining this policy: no tolerance of Northern military provocation, no attempt on the Southern side to engineer North Korea's collapse or containment, and the separation of politics and economics. And in a clear departure from his predecessors, Kim has encouraged other countries to increase their engagement with the North, for example by calling on the US to end its economic sanctions against North Korea. Since then, the South Koreans have added reciprocity to the policy mix.[1]

This perspective appears to come from the conviction that the South lacks the economic, social, and political capacity to handle a collapse of the North and that peaceful coexistence is a preferable state of affairs. At the same time, it amounts to an implicit criticism of past Southern unification policy, which had put an overwhelming emphasis on high-level government-to-government talks and, with the exception of emergency food relief, had generally discouraged nonofficial contacts.

In the economics sphere, the government had immediately announced a number of business facilitation measures (mainly in the form of cutting red tape) aimed at opening opportunities for South Korean firms in the North.[2] The North reportedly responded by stationing working-level commercial officers at its embassy in Beijing and is reportedly considering a UN proposal for establishing direct rail links between the North and South (Flake, 1999).

Since the inauguration of this policy, business contact has increased between the North and South, though it is unclear how much of this change should be attributed to policy.[3] In June 1998, Hyundai founder Chung Ju Young visited North Korea, driving 500 head of cattle through the demilitarized zone (DMZ). After a second visit in October and a meeting with Kim Jong Il, an agreement was subsequently reached for a tourism project at Mt Kumgang (discussed in greater detail below) and the possible development of a second SEZ, in the Haeju District on North Korea's western coast just north of Inchon. The Haeju location would be vastly preferable to Rajin-Sonbong. This plan calls for Hyundai to develop the infrastructure and then lease sites to SMEs. Hyundai claims that the industrial park would take ten years to complete and could produce $4.4 billion worth of goods a year and generate $400 million in wages for North Korean workers.[4] The *chaebol* and Pyongyang also reached an agreement by which Hyundai would supervise the construction of railroad cars at North Korea's Wonsan plant. It imported the first 44 of these cheap cars in May 1999. Hyundai has also reportedly discussed other projects as well, including an automobile assembly plant, a power plant in Pyongyang, a ship repair yard, off-shore oil exploration, a roofing tile factory, and plans to contract North Korean workers on projects in third countries.[5] Chung returned to the North with 501 head of cattle (and 20 cars) in November. One of the tenets of the policy has been the separation of business and politics. In this regard, the Kim government has been less forthcoming with official assistance than its predecessors, allowing the private sector to carry a greater share of the burden. This change may in part reflect domestic politics: Kim has been tarred in the past as being "soft" on the North, and, in any event, the South Korean economy has been in difficult shape since his inauguration.

Nevertheless, the notion that politics and economics have been separated is not entirely credible. Take, for example, Hyundai, which has been the most prominent in North–South exchange. Given its weak financial condition, it is highly questionable whether it was in any condition to commit nearly $1 billion in payments to North Korea, as called for in its agreement with the North. When questioned about this matter, Hyundai officials have indicated that the government would "make it up to us", a claim that has been verified in private conversations with government officials. Hyundai has already arguably benefited from government largesse. Government-controlled banks significantly increased loans to Hyundai in 1998, and the government managed to steer the bankrupt automaker Kia out of Ford's hands and into Hyundai's.[6] Many in South Korea suspect that the government helped Hyundai take over LG Semiconductor for similar reasons.

Probably the biggest impact of the constructive engagement policy has been the dramatic increase in the number of North and South Koreans coming into contact with one another. Excluding the Mt Kumgang tourists, nearly 3,500 South Koreans have traveled North since the inauguration of the policy – a number more than during the entire period since the war. In addition, nearly 90,000 tourists have visited Mt Kumgang, though their contacts with Northerners have been highly circumscribed.

Kim's constructive engagement policy has put Pyongyang on the defensive. While the existence of a prosperous South Korea is surely an enormous advantage in terms of the North's economic development, Pyongyang is afraid of what it accurately understands as the "Trojan horse" of increased contact with the South.[7] This being so, for South Korea – like the US – official transfers in the form of support for KEDO (estimated price tag for South Korea of roughly $3 billion) will continue to outweigh private commercial exchange in its economic relationship with North Korea in the near future. If North Korea were to overcome its reticence and accept the "package deal" offer from South Korea, the US, and Japan embodied in the

Perry initiative, this action could lead to a dramatic increase in commercial exchange.

The remainder of this chapter takes this latter possibility as its starting point and examines the possible implications for the economies of the two countries if North Korea were substantially to liberalize its economy and permit a significantly greater degree of economic integration with its neighbors. (Alternatively, one could think of this integration coming through a process of collapse and absorption.) The main conclusions are as follows. Liberalization and reform of the North Korean economy could have a tremendous impact: incomes could rise significantly; domestic food availability could increase dramatically, ending the famine; and the sectoral composition of output and employment could change profoundly. However, even if these changes were to occur in the North, integration through trade could have little impact on the macroeconomic performance of the South Korean economy. The reason is simple: North Korea is just too small economically to have much of an impact on the South. One might think of the integration of the Mexican and American economies through the North American Free Trade Agreement (NAFTA) or the accession of a small Eastern European economy to the European Union (EU). While integration might have some significant effect on particular firms or industries, at the level of the overall economy, the impact could be imperceptible.

This conclusion could change radically, however, if factor markets were allowed to integrate, especially in the case of a scenario of collapse and absorption. In this case, integration could have a major impact on the South Korean economy. Depending on the specific integration scenario, factor-market integration could significantly affect the rate of growth of the South Korean economy, its sectoral composition of output, and its distribution of income and wealth.

REFORM IN THE NORTH

The North Korean economy is in crisis. Although the regime has undertaken some reforms in response to the crisis (like establishing the Rajin-Sonbong SEZ and the Mt Kumgang tourism project, permitting limited private initiative in agriculture, allowing greater scope for private markets outside the plan in the distribution of consumer goods), the consensus of a wide range of observers is that the current reforms are insufficient to pull North Korea out of its predicament. Current polices arguably amount to a series of short-term tactical adjustments without any overarching vision or rationale. If these moves prove inadequate to cope with the crisis at hand, the regime will be forced to make a choice whether to accelerate and widen the reforms, or to stand pat and try to ride out the current difficulties, risking collapse if the situation worsens. Either path could result in significantly greater economic integration with the South.

The question naturally arises of what the North Korean economy would look like if it were to undergo successful reform. One change would involve a reallocation of factors according to comparative advantage. Were reform accompanied by a reduction of political hostilities with the South, there could also be a significant demobilization of the military and the concomitant release of productive factors for alternative uses. Based on the experiences of other transitional economies, one would expect significant reorientation of international trade away from socialist allies and toward natural trading partners.

One way to get a clearer sense of how North Korea might look as a "normal" country is to use a standard "gravity" model of bilateral trade to simulate its post-reform trade pattern. The regression model, originally estimated by Frankel and Wei (1995), characterizes the volume of trade as a function of size, income level, proximity, adjacency, participation in regional economic integration schemes, and cultural similarity. North Korean values of these explanatory figures are then substituted into the gravity model regression to generate North Korea's "natural" pattern of trade. According to this analysis, North Korea's natural trading partners would be South Korea, Japan, China, and the US, in that order. South Korea and Japan alone would account for nearly two-thirds of North Korean trade. Moreover, the share of international trade in national income would roughly quintuple, though the resource reallocation associated with such a large increase in trade would almost certainly boost income significantly as well. The scope for change in North Korea is dramatic.

North Korea's prospective comparative advantage has been analyzed using disaggregated trade and investment data for North Korea, South Korea, and Japan.[8] This analysis concluded that North Korea's sectors of prospective comparative advantage would largely be in the primary products sectors in which North Korea's natural resources convey a comparative advantage, as well as in the light manufacturing industries which, although in decline in Japan and South Korea, could be competitive in lower-wage North Korea. Overall, these sectors are consistent with the sectors identified by Hyundai for its prospective Haeju SEZ.[9]

These results, along with the huge increase in trade derived from the gravity model calculation, would predict an enormous change in the composition of North Korean output away from heavy and toward light industry. Recovery of land damaged in the natural disasters of the 1990s could be expected to lead to increased agricultural output and employment. The implication is significant adjustments for many North Korean workers and enterprises. At the same time, the expanding industries would be labor intensive, facilitating the transition by absorbing displaced labor. This benefit could be especially important if military demobilization were to release a large number of workers for non-military activities.[10]

A GENERAL EQUILIBRIUM PERSPECTIVE ON REFORM

Noland et al. (2000a, 2000b, 2000c) use a series of computable general equilibrium (CGE) models to analyze the economy-wide repercussions of the recovery of land damaged in the flooding, the provision of food aid, the liberalization of international trade, the change in technology, the "obsolescence shock" associated with opening to the outside world, and the potential "peace dividend" from military demobilization. These models have a standard neoclassical specification, except that they incorporate disequilibrium in grain markets and severe quantity controls in exports and imports with concomitant distortions in domestic product and factor markets.[11] The markets for goods, factors, and foreign exchange are assumed to respond to changing demand and supply conditions, which in turn are affected by government policies, the external environment, and other exogenous influences. The model can be considered medium-to-long run in that all factors are assumed to be intersectorally mobile. It is Walrasian in that only relative prices matter. Sectoral product prices, factor prices, and the exchange rate are determined relative to an aggregate consumer price index, which defines the *numeraire*.[12]

The models have eleven sectors: rice, maize, other agriculture/forest/ fisheries, mining, light manufacturing, industrial intermediates, capital goods, construction, public administration, the military, and services. There are three "demanders": a single aggregate household that buys consumer goods, a government that spends on goods and public administration, and an aggregate capital account that purchases investment goods. The government is the sole and completely price-inelastic demander of military services. All goods and services are traded internationally with the exceptions of construction, public administration, and the military. Domestically produced and traded goods are specified as imperfect substitutes, thereby providing for a realistic continuum of "tradability" and allowing for two-way intersectoral trade.

Primary factors of production include three types of land, capital, agricultural labor, high-skill urban labor, and low-skill urban labor. Aggregate production functions are estimated for aggregate capital and labor using data reported in Hwang (1993) and Y.S. Lee (1994). The results are remarkably robust and plausible given the quality of the underlying

data.   Constant elasticity of substitution (CES) specifications yield
estimates of the substitutability between capital and labor of around unity.
The hypothesis that the aggregate production function is Cobb–Douglas
could not be rejected. In most specifications, North Korea exhibits slightly
negative total factor productivity (TFP) growth, which is typical of many
pre-reform socialist economies.   In the CGE model, sectoral production
technology is represented by a set of Cobb–Douglas functions of the
primary factors, with the exception of the mining and military sectors which
use CES functions with lower substitution elasticities.   Intermediate inputs
are demanded according to Leontief, fixed input–output coefficients. Labor
and capital are intersectorally mobile; land is specific to agriculture, but
mobile within the three agricultural sectors. Migration is permitted between
rural and urban low-skill labor markets.[13]

In Noland et al. (2000a), the model is used to run five basic scenarios. In
the first, North Korea costlessly recovers land damaged in the 1996–97
floods. In the second, quantity rationing of international trade is removed.
The next three scenarios are in some sense extensions of the second. In the
third, the North Korean economy experiences an 18 percent sectorally
uniform increase in TFP as a result of its economic opening and importation
of capital equipment embodying new technologies from abroad.[14] The
fourth scenario subjects the North Korean economy to an "obsolescence
shock" to its capital stock as a result of economic opening, exposure to new
technologies, and changes in relative prices of inputs and outputs. Finally,
Noland et al. (2000a) examine the issue of military demobilization and the
"peace dividend." In this scenario, the North Korean military is
demobilized by 70 percent, until the share of the military in national income
approximates the 3 percent exhibited in South Korea.[15] Each of these
scenarios is implemented in ten steps or experiments. In addition to
scenario 1 ("land recovery") and scenario 4 ("systemic reform"), in a paper
focused on the famine, Noland et al. (2000b) report additional scenarios
involving the provision of international food aid and more and less limited
reforms in the agricultural sector.

The rehabilitation of flood-damaged lands would have a relatively minor
impact on GDP, increasing it by less than 2 percent. Domestic production
of rice and other agricultural commodities would increase by around 4
percent and corn production would rise by 12 percent, but domestic food
availability would remain below the minimum needs quantitative target
established by the UNDP, the FAO, and the WFP.[16] At first glance, this
might seem odd – that increasing the arable land endowment of a famine-
afflicted country had so negligible a macroeconomic impact. Two things
should be kept in mind, though. First, North Korea already had been
experiencing famine prior to the floods that commenced in July 1995.

Second, only around 15 percent of the arable land was affected by the floods. So, while natural disasters may have exacerbated the problem of food availability, the famine is not just a product of bad weather. Rather, systemic mismanagement and a lack of intermediate inputs such as fuel and fertilizer are its proximate cause. The latter, in turn, has been due to severe balance-of-payments constraints and policy decisions about the use of foreign exchange – areas which are fundamentally outside the agricultural sector. Nevertheless, this result underlines a critical issue: if only a relatively modest component of the decline in output can be attributed to flood-related declines in agriculture, then what explains the rest?

Impediments to international trade could have been a major impact on this decline. The gravity model results suggest that in 1990 the total share of imports and exports in North Korean GDP would have been roughly 70 percent if North Korea had exhibited the economic behavior of a "normal" country. With a now smaller economy, the expected trade share should be even higher. A complete freeing of this constraint would increase GDP by 40–60 percent due to static reallocation of factors alone, depending on the precise specification of the model and whether liberalization is on a non-preferential or preferential basis. (Qualitatively similar results are obtained in Noland et al. (2000c) when North Korea liberalizes preferentially and forms a customs union with South Korea.)[17] Domestic availability of rice and corn on commercial terms would increase by 80–90 percent.

This static reallocation effect would not be the only impact of liberalizing trade. Results derived from Coe et al. (1996) indicate that TFP might increase by 18 percent. These gains could offset losses occurring through an obsolescence shock to the capital stock of up to 25 percent.

One should not attach too much weight to the exact figures derived from this modeling exercise. Rather, these results are probably best interpreted as an indication that, in an economy as distorted as North Korea's, even a relatively simple move such as an increase in the economy's openness to international trade could have enormous macroeconomic effects, dwarfing the impact of a flood.

The final scenario is a 70 percent military demobilization in which North Korea's expenditure on the military is reduced to a share of GDP similar to that of the South's. Major diplomatic breakthroughs would be prerequisites for this to occur, but the experiment is presented as a heuristic exercise to illustrate the size of potential pay-offs. In some sense, this experiment too is dependent on the trade liberalization experiment. Without liberalization it is unclear where the demobilized resources would be redeployed; with it, however, they could be redeployed to their highest efficiency uses.

Redeployment of resources on this scale could add at the margin another 8–10 percent to GDP. The five scenarios undertaken together increase real

GDP by 40–80 percent from the base, depending on specification and whether liberalization was undertaken on a preferential or non-preferential basis. Domestic food availability would exceed the UNDP/FAO/WFP target for "normal total demand" in the unilateral liberalization scenario and the "normal human demand" in the customs union scenario.[18] With non-defense government spending held constant in nominal terms, the other components of GDP would rise: real consumption would nearly triple, investment would nearly double, and international trade would expand enormously. With the trade balance held constant, the real exchange rate would experience modest appreciation; if the real exchange rate was held constant, the trade deficit would expand somewhat.

The composition of output would change enormously as light manufacturing, mining, construction, and services expanded, while industrial intermediates, capital goods, and the army contracted in response to changes in the relative price structure and the decline in government demand for military services.[19] Light manufacturing would experience an export explosion with exports increasing 40-fold and mining exports more than three-fold. Imports would rise in all traded-goods categories, led by a 15-fold growth in capital goods imports. Even in the case of large financial inflows from abroad, which would drive up the real exchange rate, the traded-goods sector of North Korea would expand relative to the base (Noland et al., 2000c). These qualitative results hold whether liberalization was on an most-favored-nation basis or on a preferential basis with South Korea. Within agriculture, maize output would fall, and then expand, as the highly inefficient production of rice was abandoned and land was increasingly devoted to the production of maize.

These changes in composition would have profound effects on factor usage and returns. Up to 2.5 million workers could leave the agricultural sector and another 350,000 could leave the army, with the bulk re-employed in the light manufacturing sector. (Even in the agricultural sector, the employment and wage changes would be greater under economic reform than through land recovery.) Employment would also increase in the mining, construction, and service sectors. The real wages of all three classes of labor would more than triple, with the largest increases experienced by the high-skilled. The rate of return on capital would also more than triple, but the rate of return on land would fall, as the increased availability of imported agricultural goods reduced domestic scarcity, and with it the implicit returns to land. There would be some shift in the distribution of income away from land and toward urban high-skilled labor.[20]

These results are speculative and subject to a certain degree of spurious precision. Nevertheless, the modeling work conveys a number of important points. First, even when defined narrowly in terms of domestic food availability, the pay-offs to reform dwarf the impact of more narrow efforts to raise productivity in agriculture. Second, the provision of aid may have unintended consequences. Third, there would be massive shifts in the composition of output under reform. Millions of workers would switch jobs, for example. Fourth, the importance of international trade would increase tremendously with reform. Fifth, demobilization of the military could have significant economic benefits because the military acts as a significant drag on the North Korean economy.

A GENERAL EQUILIBRIUM PERSPECTIVE ON NORTH–SOUTH INTEGRATION

Noland et al. (1998a, 1998b, 1999 and 2000c) add South Korea to the mix. They find that a key variable affecting virtually every issue of interest would be the magnitude of cross-border labor migration from North to South. Migration would act as a substitute for capital transfer. The more labor was allowed to migrate, the lower the amount of capital investment necessary to reconstruct the North Korean economy. If no investment were undertaken and North Koreans were able to move south freely, North Korea would be virtually depopulated before differences in income levels were sufficiently narrowed to choke off the incentive to migrate. Conversely, if incomes in North Korea were raised solely by infusions of capital investment, the amount needed to choke off the incentive to migrate could be as high as $1 trillion. Presumably neither of these outcomes is acceptable to South Korea, so the real issue is the form of an intermediate solution that would involve a combination of cross-border movements in both labor and capital.

And, of course, efficiently allocated investment yields returns, not just costs. Noland et al. (1998b) in fact identify a scenario, based on cross-border factor flows derived from the German experience, in which South Korea would benefit relative to the no-unification base case: the present discounted value of the South Korean future consumption stream with unification would exceed that of the no-unification baseline.

Noland et al. (2000c) re-examine this result using a model calibrated to 1996 and find that the earlier result rested on two problematic foundations. First, the situation in North Korea had deteriorated more than originally thought, and as a consequence, the income gap had grown appreciably. Second, the result rested critically on the rapidity of technological convergence between the North and the South. In the potentially Pareto-improving case, the North adopts South Korean technology over a decade, attaining not only the South Korean level of productivity, but its input mix as well. This is a more rapid rate of technology upgrading than has been observed in the case of Germany. Even in the optimistic case in which North Korea attained the rates of technological convergence observed in the German case and attracted sufficient investment to equalize the rate of return on capital between North and South Korea, per capita incomes in North Korea would remain well below those in the South, creating an ongoing incentive for cross-border migration.

The second important message of this work is that factor-market integration could have significant distributional implications. With factor-market integration, income would shift toward capital and away from labor, and within labor toward higher skilled groups. To the extent that the highly skilled were the predominate owners of capital, this analysis suggests that absent some compensatory policies, factor-market integration would cause greater income and wealth inequality in the South.

Put crudely, in the collapse and absorption scenario, the economics come down to the movement of Southern money north, or the movement of Northern people south. The policies that are ultimately adopted will be a function of politics. Possible cleavages include those between the North and the South, and within South Korea between capital and labor (owners of capital viewing Northerners as a new source of cheap labor, and labor regarding the North as a potential source of labor market competition). Cleavages within the South Korean labor force, between the high-skilled and low-skilled, could also occur. Depending on the macroeconomic policies applied, the internationally traded- and non-traded goods sectors could be affected in very different ways, opening up another cleavage. Policies that deny North Koreans some of the economic gains of unification (such as proposals to maintain the DMZ and administer North Korea as a Special Administrative Zone, which would prevent the equilibration of wages and rates of return on capital between the North and South, or proposals for the South Korean government to retain rights to all assets in the North) would be sustainable only if North Koreans were denied political rights.[21] In this scenario, the key issue is the North Koreans' ability to participate in political decision making.

CONCLUSIONS

North Korea is both larger in population and smaller in economic size (and hence poorer in per capita terms) relative to South Korea, than was East Germany compared to West Germany, though by exactly how much no one really knows. The population of North Korea is roughly half that of South

Korea. Enormous uncertainty exists as to the value of output and per capita income. Suffice it to say that, in relative economic terms, North Korea is quite small.

As a consequence, the impact of integration of product markets between North and South Korea, while critical to the North, would have trivial effects on the South. The analogy would be to the formation of NAFTA, or perhaps accession of a small Central European economy to the EU – tremendously important for the smaller economy (Mexico), virtually imperceptible to the larger one (US).

The story changes enormously if factor markets are allowed to integrate. Cross-border movements in labor and capital could have an enormous impact on the South Korean economy. As noted in the introduction, migration could act as a substitute for investment: the more that labor was allowed to migrate, the lower the amount of capital transfer that would be necessary to reconstruct the North Korean economy. Noland et al. (1999), using a model calibrated to 1990, present the results of a thought experiment in which rehabilitation of the North Korean economy occurs solely through internal reallocation of factors of production, technology upgrading, and migration. With no additions to the capital stock, nearly three-quarters of the North Korean population would head South if given the opportunity. More recent work, incorporating the rapidly widening income differential since 1990, indicates that North Korea would be nearly depopulated before equilibrium was attained (Noland et al., 2000c). Conversely, incentives for migration could be reduced through the maintenance of employment and wage increases, though the necessary investment could be enormous – as much as $1 trillion – if the incentive to migrate were eliminated solely by capital investment (Noland et al., 1997, 1998a, 1998b).[22]

The key point overlooked in most discussions of "the costs of unification" is that efficiently allocated investment yields returns, not just costs. Using figures derived from the German experience, Noland et al. (1998b) find that in a scenario with relatively small amounts of private capital investment combined with relatively high levels of North–South migration, South Korea actually would come out ahead. The present discounted value of future consumption would be $35 billion higher with unification compared to the no-unification baseline. (However, in the worse case scenario of large grant transfers combined with low levels of migration, South Korea is approximately one half trillion dollars worse off.)

However, as shown by Noland et al. (2000c), this result depends critically on North Korea achieving full technological convergence with the South within a decade. This assumption represents a more rapid rate of convergence than has been identified in the German case. Applying rates of technological convergence estimated from the German experience and assuming that the rate of return on capital in North Korea could not fall below that observed in South Korea, Noland et al. find that, even under relatively optimistic conditions, the North would not attain the 60 percent per capita income target within a decade. This result suggests that Northerners will face economic incentives to migrate south for a prolonged period of time.[23]

Factor-market integration between North and South Korea could have significant distributional implications. In South Korea, income would shift toward capital and away from labor, and within labor toward higher skilled groups. The higher skilled are predominately the ultimate owners of capital, and as a consequence, without some offsetting policies, factor-market integration would generate greater income and wealth inequality in the South.

These economic changes would have political implications as well. Several cleavages would be likely: regionally between the North and the South, within South Korea between capital and labor, and within the South Korean labor force, between the high-skilled and the low-skilled. If integration were accompanied by increased capital inflow from abroad and an appreciation of the real exchange rate, another cleavage could result, in this instance between the internationally traded and non-traded goods sectors.

In the event of collapse and absorption, a host of unification issues (conversion rate of North Korean won to South Korean won, assignment of property rights, etc.) have enormous implications for the economic welfare of current residents of the DPRK. The extent to which they are afforded a voice in politics will be a critical aspect of the unification process. Effective participation by Northerners would appear to rule out some policies, such as proposals to maintain the DMZ and administer North Korea as a Special Administrative Zone, which would prevent the equilibration of wages and rates of return on capital between the North and South, or proposals for the South Korean government to retain rights to all assets in the North. Conversely, policies that would deny to Northerners gains from the unification process would only be sustainable if their participation in democratic politics were circumscribed. Thus, the key economic issue is the extent to which the North Koreans would be full participants in the political system of a unified Korea.

NOTES

[1] South Korean government statistics put two-way trade turnover at just over $200 million through the first seven months of this year, though this overstates actual *trade*, by counting KEDO oil deliveries (a transfer) as an export from South to North Korea.

[2] See Noland (2000) for details.

[3] According to Flake (1999), government-to-government initiatives include exchange of weather information, joint development of a television special on North Korea's cultural heritage, possible South Korean investment in one of the failed joint-venture banks, the construction by a South Korean NGO of a pharmaceutical factory in the Rajin-Sonbong trade zone, and cooperation in the agricultural field, including the provision of "Super Corn" seed. Kim Dae Jung also proposed a swap of North Korean spies held in the South for Southern prisoners of war still in detention in the North. Furthermore, the South Korean government announced that it would permit the sale of non-political North Korean videos.

[4] One example is its willingness in April 1998 and June 1999 to allow "fertilizer for family reunion" talks to break down rather than acceding to Northern demands (though announcing afterwards that private fertilizer donations would be permitted). See Council of Foreign Relations (1999) for more details on the evolving engagement policy.

[5] See Flake (1999) for a list of these measures. Small and medium-sized enterprises (SMEs) could be a major beneficiary of the reduction in red tape. Several industry associations have made exploratory visits to Pyongyang or Rajin-Sonbong.

[6] Park (1998) goes so far as to argue that current policy for a variety of reasons will actually discourage investment in the North by the *chaebol*, but he does accept the notion that there could be increased investment by SMEs. One news report (*Chosun Ilbo*, 21 March 1999) indicated that there had indeed been a decline in applications to the South Korean government for "economic cooperation" projects, though this could simply be a reflection of the depressed state of the South Korean economy at the time.

[7] Associated Press, February 4, 1999.

[8] Hyundai announced in June 1999 that it would hire the first batch of 300 North Korean workers to work on a project in Turkmenistan.

[9] At the same time, one could argue that the government's August 1998 intervention in the Hyundai Motors strike (in which it effectively sided with the strikers) and its 1999 investigation into Hyundai's "Buy Korea Fund" were against the *chaebol's* interests.

[10] The May 31, 1999 joint editorial of *Rodong Sinmun* and *Kulloja* described "opening" as a "Trojan horse tasked to destabilize socialism."

[11] The data set included 465 sectors. See Noland (1996, 2000) for details of the computation, and a list of sectors of prospective North Korean comparative advantage.

[12] At a press conference on November 1, 1998, Hyundai Chairman Chung Mong-hon identified light industrial products, shoes, clothes, needlework, woven goods, spinning, toys, kitchen wares, assembled metal products, precise machines, metal

machine tools, plain operating machines, leather goods, bags, and textile goods as promising sectors for investment in the North on the basis of their labor intensity. In addition, TV assembling, radio, fans, electronics parts, plastic goods, synthetic rubber processing, and machine parts have been declining in terms of competitiveness in the South and could be produced "with mutual cooperation." Beverages, food, cigarettes, and pulp for which raw materials are "easy to obtain" could also be produced in the North. See also S.Y. Lee (1998), who performed an analysis similar to the one above and obtained results quite like those reported above.

[13] Perhaps half of the military is already engaged in non-military activities, so the other half is available for effective demobilization under supportive political circumstances.

[14] Coles and Hammond (1995) develop a rigorous general equilibrium model of famine. They demonstrate that famine is possible even in a perfectly competitive Walrasian economy, and that all of the classical existence and efficiency theorems apply. Noland et al. (2000b) is, to the present author's knowledge, the first application of CGE modeling to an actual famine.

[15] The exchange rate variable in the model can be seen as a price level deflated (PLD) real exchange rate, with the *numeraire* cost-of-living index as the deflator.

[16] More technically-oriented readers are referred to the original sources for complete algebraic renditions of the models, detailed descriptions of data construction techniques (including the actual social accounting matrices used), and model parameterization.

[17] The possibility of sectorally non-uniform increases in TFP is analyzed in the models of North–South integration discussed in the next section.

[18] In the model, it is assumed that half of the army is engaged in activities (construction, manufacturing, etc.) that normally would be performed by the civilian sector of the economy, while the other half of the army is engaged in "war fighting" activities. Demobilization is modeled as a reduction of resources devoted to strictly military activities.

[19] The impact of the floods could be underestimated through two possible channels. First, with high substitutability among primary inputs, labor and capital could simply substitute for land. Second, recalling that some of the capital stock in the agricultural sector had been destroyed in the floods, as a mental experiment and check on robustness, we ran a variant of the first experiment in which the agricultural capital stock is augmented as land is recovered. The addition of capital along with land would indeed increase the output response, but the impact on GDP would be still only around 2 percent.

[20] In the customs union scenario, integration with the North would have a modest positive impact on South Korea. Trade with North Korea would mostly substitute for trade with other countries and, given the small size of North Korea relative to South Korea, trade creation and diversion would have a trivial impact on South Korea. Only three sectors would experience percentage changes in output of more than 1 percent, and South Korean GDP would rise by less than 1/2 of 1 percent. Formation of the customs union would be a Pareto improvement: returns to all factors would either increase or remain unchanged. The distributional implications would be trivial. This conclusion would change dramatically,

however, if factor markets are allowed to integrate – an issue explored in the collapse and absorption section of this chapter. In contrast, formation of the customs union would amount to a significant movement toward free trade for North Korea relative to its previous external barriers. This would generate results similar to those discussed above for the non-preferential opening scenario. Trade with both South Korea and the rest of the world would increase, and, from the standpoint of the whole peninsula, the customs union would be strongly trade-creating. GDP for the peninsula as a whole would rise by 1.5 percent.

[21] Noland et al. (2000b) also report a "complete recovery" scenario in which agricultural yields are raised to their pre-crisis level as a function of the increased availability of intermediate inputs. The main difference between this and the previous "systemic reform" scenario is that, due to the increased yields, rice production in North Korea would actually rise, increasing 20 percent from the base. Maize production would more than double. (The production increase would be tilted toward maize, because North Korea's comparative disadvantage is less intense in its production. Under free trade, some land formerly used to grow rice would be converted to maize production.) The increase in grain yields would boost the agricultural wage, thus moderating some of the rural–urban migration and reducing the increase in income inequality that would arise from the happy fact that all three categories of labor more than double their wage rates relative to the base.

[22] For the sake of brevity, the remaining discussion refers to scenario 5, experiment 10–the maximum reform case.

[23] Noland et al. (2000b) report one additional scenario of interest under which, in the absence of reform, North Korea is provided food aid until the UNDP/FAO/WFP "normal human demand" target is reached. The result would be a crowding out of both domestic production and imports on commercial terms. The aid in effect would act as implicit balance-of-payments support, and import demands for all traded goods would increase. Public administration and military expenditures are held constant by construction. If this modeling assumption were relaxed, however, presumably these activities too would expand in response to the provision of aid. Food is fungible.

[24] See Young et al. (1998) for a proposal along these lines.

[25] It cannot be overemphasized that these figures are highly speculative in nature. Two assumptions are key. The first is the extent to which North Korea is subject to an "obsolescence shock" in which the value of its capital stock declines when exposed to international competition; and the second is the extent to which it achieves gains in technical efficiency as foreigners transfer capital, technology, and management in the context of a reform and opening policy. In both cases a fairly broad set of outcomes are plausible. Prudent estimates of the magnitude of cross-border factor flows in a plausible unification scenario would be in the order of millions of workers and hundreds of billions of dollars.

[26] Of course, this line of analysis does not exhaust the economic effects of unification. Presumably there would be a "peace dividend" associated with military demobilization. Noland et al. (2000a, 2000b) report estimates of economic efficiency gains associated with partial demobilization in the range of $1 billion to $3 billion annually. (These estimates were obtained under variations of the assumption that with unification (or at least peaceful coexistence) military

expenditures on the Korean peninsula as a share of national income could be reduced to some international benchmark such as the OECD average.) There may also be negative "congestion externalities" associated with migration of North Koreans south. I am unaware of any estimates of the potential magnitude of these costs.

REFERENCES

Coe, David T., Elhanan Helpman, and Alexander Hoffmaister (1996), "North-South R&D Spillovers," *Economic Journal*, **107** (440), 134–49.

Coles, Jeffrey L. and Peter J. Hammond (1995), "Walrasian Equilibrium Without Survival: Existence, Efficiency, and Remedial Policy," in K. Basu, P. Pattanaik, and K. Suzumura (eds), *Choice, Welfare, and Development: a Festschrift in Honor of Amartya Sen*, Oxford: Clarendon Press.

Council on Foreign Relations (1999), "U.S. Policy Toward North Korea: A Second Look," http://www.foreignrelations.org/public/pubs/NKoreaTask.html.

Flake, L. Gordon (1999), "Patterns of Inter-Korean Economic Relations," Washington: Atlantic Council of the US, processed.

Frankel, Jeffrey A. and Shang-Jin Wei (1995), "Is a Yen Bloc Emerging?," *Joint U.S.–Korean Academic Studies*, **5**, 145–75.

Hwang, Eui-Gak (1993), *The Korean Economies*, Oxford: Clarendon Press.

Lee, Shi-Young (1998), "Prospects for Trade Between the Two Koreas," in Yang Un-Chul (ed.), *The Political Economy of Korean Unification*, Seoul: The Sejong Institute.

Lee, Young Sun (1994), "Economic Integration of the Korean Peninsula: A Scenario Approach to the Cost of Unification," in Sung Yeung Kwack (ed.), *The Korean Economy at a Crossroad*, Westport CT: Praeger.

Noland, Marcus (1996), "The North Korean Economy," *Joint U.S.–Korea Academic Studies*, **6**, 127–78.

Noland, Marcus (2000), *Avoiding the Apocalypse: The Future of the Two Koreas*, Washington: Institute for International Economics.

Noland, Marcus, Sherman Robinson, and Monica Scatasta (1997), "Modeling Economic Reform in North Korea," *Journal of Asian Economics*, **8** (1), 15–38.

Noland, Marcus, Sherman Robinson, and Ligang Liu (1998a), "Calibrating the Costs (and Benefits) of Unification," in Marcus Noland (ed.), *Economic Integration of the Korean Peninsula*, Washington: Institute for International Economics.

Noland, Marcus, Sherman Robinson, and Ligang Liu (1998b), "The Costs and Benefits of Korean Unification," *Asian Survey*, August.

Noland, Marcus, Sherman Robinson, and Ligang Liu (1999), "The Economics of Korean Unification," *Journal of Policy Reform,* 3, 255–99.

Noland, Marcus, Sherman Robinson, and Tao Wang (2000a), "Rigorous Speculation: The Collapse and Revival of the North Korean Economy," *World Development*, 28 (10), 1767–87.

Noland, Marcus, Sherman Robinson, and Tao Wang (2000b), "Famine in North Korea: Causes and Cures," *Economic Development and Cultural Change*, forthcoming.

Noland, Marcus, Sherman Robinson, and Tao Wang (2000c), "Modeling Korean Unification," *Journal of Comparative Economics*, **28**, 400–21.

Park, Jin (1998), "Inter-Korean Economic Relations in the IMF Era," *Korea Focus*, March–April, 66–80.

Young, Soogil, Chang-Jae Lee, and Hyoungsoo Zang (1998), "Preparing for the Economic Integration of Two Koreas: Policy Challenges to South Korea," in Marcus Noland (ed.), *Economic Integration of the Korean Peninsula*, Washington: Institute for International Economics.

12 Costs and Benefits of Unification

Young Back Choi

INTRODUCTION

The rather sudden unification of Germany in 1990, along with the collapse of socialism, caused much excitement and conveyed a strong sense of urgency about the future of two Koreas. Since then, many economists have tried to calculate the potential costs of Korean unification in light of the experience of German unification.[1] These estimates are high enough, however, to quell some of the initial excitement over the prospect of Korean unification. The 1997 financial crisis in South Korea has probably further dampened enthusiasm for a German-style unification of the two Koreas, as well reflected in the current South Korean "Sunshine Policy" (Kim, 1999).

The principal aim of the Sunshine Policy is not to push for immediate unification, but instead to establish a durable peace based on the coexistence of two Koreas. Many have criticized it as merely helping the North prolong its sickly regime, but the rationale has been to avoid either a total collapse of the famine-stricken North or military adventures undertaken with desperate bravado. The intentions of the South Korean policy are: (1) to assure the North that the South has no interest in seeing the North Korean government fall; (2) to provide certain economic assistance, including food for famine relief and the financing of nuclear power plants construction in exchange for the renunciation of ambitions for nuclear weapons, viz., KEDO; and (3) to assist the North in reforming its moribund economy by lifting economic sanctions against the North, allowing South Koreans to do business with North Korea. To date, the most notable business deal between the North and South has been the "Diamond Mountains Tourism", which promises the North revenue of up to $930 million through 2005.[2]

North Korea has behaved unpredictably (Flake, 1999). Instead of reducing tension in the Korean peninsula and focusing on improving its economy, the North appears intent on escalating tension in the peninsula – threatening to develop nuclear weapons, provoking a series of naval conflicts, launching medium-range ballistic missiles, and so on. Some of these moves may be seen as calculated by the North to gain bargaining leverage (to get the greatest amount of foreign aid, especially from the US and Japan, as it can no longer rely on its erstwhile ideological allies, Russia or China, for bailouts.) Even if the North has been successful to some extent in achieving its goals, the extortionist policy is unsustainable in the long run. The North has projected itself as an increasing menace, uninterested in peace. In some respect it appears to regard the Sunshine Policy itself as one of the most significant threats to its survival.

A number of reasons may explain the perverse behavior of the North. For example, it may reflect a dilemma facing the North Korean leaders as they see both the necessity of revitalizing its economy through reform and the danger these actions pose for their power. The North's economy has collapsed, operating at about 20 percent of the level it had in the late 1980s (See Table 12.1). Famine has devastated the country. Millions have died, and millions more are threatened. Contributing factors for this disastrous outcome include the decades-long adherence to the mistaken policy of *juche* (self-sufficiency), the failure of central planning, and the disappearance of foreign aid from Russia and China – all compounded by a string of floods. North Korea needs to reform and open up the economy. But reform threatens the very foundation of the regime. The power of the North Korean rulers is based exclusively on the cult of personality and the militarized sector of the economy, distinct from the rest of the economy. Any attempt to reform the economy, which requires loosening the rigid regimentation and introducing economic incentives, threatens their power

Table 12.1 North Korean Economic Indicators, 1992–96

	1992	1993	1994	1995	1996
GNP*	20.8	20.9	15.4	12.8	10.6
Real Growth Rate	--	0.3	-26.3	-17.0	-17.3
Government Revenue	15.8	16.2	16.6	9.7	8.1
Government Expenditure	15.7	16.1	16.6	9.7	8.2
External Debt (NK estimate)	--	--	--	--	3.6
External Debt (Outside estimate)	--	--	--	--	12.0

Note: *In billions of US dollars at US$1 = NK Won 2.5.
Source: Data provided by the North Korean authorities to IMF, IMF (1997)

base. The erratic behavior of the North may largely reflect its difficulty in resolving the dilemma: they are, as it were, "riding on the back of the tiger."

This problem, I believe, is compounded by the deeply held suspicion on the part of the North that the ultimate aim of the South is unification (annexation or absorption in other parlance), and the South, therefore, is a threat to the regime in the North. In fact, the term "sunshine" – adopted from Aesop's fables – could be interpreted as betraying the ultimate intention of the South. The North Korean leaders could easily support, at least to their own satisfaction, their suspicions about the nature of the Sunshine Policy. First, the Sunshine Policy faces strong opposition in the South, so, however innocent in motive, it may be short-lived. More importantly, most public debates on the future of the two Koreas appear to rest on the presumption of their eventual unification. The discussions, consequently, focus on different scenarios of unification and on how to deal with their associated problems. The estimation of the costs of a German-style unification is one genre. Others include issues of monetary union, legal structure (for the North), property claims, and balanced regional development.

The presumption of unification rests on both strong emotions and compelling economics. It may seem natural that the eventual unification of two Koreas is nearly universally accepted as a matter of course. After all, Korea was arbitrarily divided in 1945 by the super powers. Ever since, re-unification has been the stated national goal of both Koreas. Generations of Koreans on both sides have been raised to believe that to think otherwise is to commit one of the worst treacheries. In addition to the emotional appeals, the economic benefits from the unification of two Koreas are much anticipated. It is widely expected that the unified Korea would benefit from the presence of many complementary resources – cheap labor, mineral deposits, timber, etc. In addition, the unification would create a larger national economy, allowing for a greater division of labor, greater scale economies, and even superior bargaining position *vis-à-vis* foreign countries. Given these appeals of unification, the North Korean leaders may reason, the ultimate aim of the Sunshine Policy must be unification.

The principal aim of this chapter is to assess the verity of the widely held expectations about the gains from Korean unification, by analyzing the associated costs and benefits. Though their estimation is fraught with difficulties, it should be one of the cornerstones of the policy formulations about the future of the Korean peninsula. First, there is the question of whether the expected gains from unification have any validity. I happen to believe that they are grossly overstated. If the unfounded optimism about the gains from unification in the South can be deflated, there is a better chance for peace by making people in the South more cautious about unification and by allaying the North's fear about the South's hidden motive in proposing peace in the peninsula. A fair understanding of the costs and benefits of unification is also the basis for the exploration of alternatives.

The outline of the chapter is as follows. First, I examine the expected benefits from unification, and find them greatly overstated by the popular view. The real potential gains are associated with peace. Second, I examine the expected costs of unification, and find them grossly understated by the popular view, which ignores not only the possibility of cost over-runs, but also the costs associated with the growth of government and the potential for regional conflicts. Based on this analysis, it is not at all clear whether there would be any net gain. Third, since most of the putative benefits of unification can be achieved without it, I argue that "no unification" is a superior alternative. The gains between unification and no unification are not significantly different, but the latter will cost a lot less. Therefore, there is not much for the South to gain, and it can do better without unification. Fourth, I consider the development prospects for the North with and without unification. I argue that the North would have a better future without unification. Fifth and finally, I consider possible difficulties of no unification from political, ethical, and other economic points of view. I conclude that the anticipated difficulties are not insurmountable, and the outcomes are superior to other alternatives. If these arguments prevail, South Koreans would be less eager to demand unification (at any cost) and the North Korean leaders would worry less about the South's hidden motive and more about reviving the economy. Based on a careful consideration of expected benefits and costs, therefore, I propose "no unification" as a win-win solution to the difficult situation in the Korean peninsula.

Of course, a sudden collapse of North Korea may force South Korea to take over the North. South Koreans should not rule out such a possibility and must be prepared for the contingency. But such an event should be dreaded by everyone. If enough people on both sides are convinced that unification is not the way to go (and that the other side is so convinced), perhaps, steps can be taken to avoid such a collapse. This chapter aims to contribute to the exploration of one more reason to dread unification.

GAINS FROM UNIFICATION

The anticipated gains from unification of Korea are broadly the following: (1) complementary resources, (2) cheap labor, (3) enhanced bargaining power, (4) reduced defense spending, and (5) gains from trade. Let us briefly consider them in turn.

Complementary Resources

Many in South Korea believe that the unification of Korea would widen the range of complementary resources, mentioning, for example, rich mineral deposits, forests, and hydroelectric potential in the North. I believe that they are in error, grossly overestimating the *value* of resources in the North. As for mineral deposits, the popular view has come down to us from the Japanese colonial period when the South was largely agricultural and the North had heavy industries that took advantage of mineral deposits and hydroelectric power.

But things have changed since, and by now this story is basically a myth. Today the mineral deposits in North Korea are not so significant economically as many people believe them to be. The secular trends of declining commodity prices in the global market and declining transportation costs have rendered the location of mineral deposits largely irrelevant. North Korea's minerals may be mostly depleted, and what remains can be obtained more cheaply in the international market. The value of hydroelectric power potential is not clear when low-cost nuclear power is available. After all, KEDO is building two nuclear power plants, not hydroelectric dams. As for timber, we increasingly learn that North Korean mountains are denuded from over-harvesting.

Low-cost, High-quality Labor

It is true that currently wages are low in North Korea. However, the attractiveness of relatively low wages in North Korea is likely to evaporate in the process of unification, as South Korea will be forced to provide a welfare provision comparable to what prevails in the South. The reasons are as follows. If northern wages were kept low after unification, North Koreans would move south, looking for greener pastures, competing for jobs and seeking welfare benefits. The government could not restrict movement within the unified national boundary. Nor would it be possible legally to discriminate against North Koreans with respect to welfare provisions. Moreover, South Korean labor is likely to behave like West German labor, demanding the generous provision of welfare to its less fortunate new compatriots to avoid losing jobs to a flood of cheap labor. Consequently, low wages in the North must become a thing of the past.

The judgment that labor is high quality is questionable as well. If the quality of labor is judged only by years of schooling, one may be led to conclude that the North has a high-quality labor force. But if consideration is given to the kind of education, work habits, and attitudes people acquire under socialism, the judgment must be tempered a great deal. A lot of retraining, formal and informal, would be necessary to convert socialist workers into free workers.

Enhanced Bargaining Power

Many seem also to expect that a larger national market will mean greater bargaining power in international trade negotiations. This could be an important consideration for trade negotiators who feel that South Korea has been bullied by bigger economies in trade negotiations. But the prospect of gaining from greater bargaining power is more imagined than real. First, the unification would not bring about a significantly extended market, at least in the short to medium term, and would add little to the bargaining power. Although the North Korean population is around 27 million, the North is currently a subsistence economy on the verge of mass starvation and suffering from years of "industrial cannibalization." The increase in purchasing power after unification, therefore, would not be significant. The situation would be somewhat altered if the South provided a generous wealth transfer to the North. The increased purchasing power in the North, however, would come at the expense of South Koreans. In either case, there will be no significant extension of the market in the near future due to unification.

Moreover, if politicians and bureaucrats feel that unification would enhance Korea's bargaining power in trade negotiations, against whom can South Korea use it? Against the US, or the EC, or Japan, or China, each of which has a much larger national market? Given their heavy dependence on trade with these powers, South Koreans probably have more to lose than to gain from playing hardball in trade negotiations.

Reduced Defense Spending

Because the two Koreas currently devote substantial resources to deterring the other side from gaining a decisive military advantage, the unification of the Koreas would significantly reduce spending on national defense.[1] The potential gain is great. First, a two-thirds reduction on both sides over time would release a staggering seven or eight hundred thousand young men from military duty each year. Closing military bases and eliminating inter-Korea combat zones would make a great amount of land available for civilian use. The peaceful use of the DMZ that has been no-man's-land for nearly a half a century is a tantalizing prospect. In addition, reduced military expenditure could lead to a significant reduction of tax burdens from the present levels. Currently, South Korea spends about 3.4 percent of GNP on defense.[2] If defense spending can be cut by 50 percent, several billion US dollars a year would be saved. In other words, there will be significant "peace dividends."[3]

But the real question is whether unification is the only way to reduce defense spending. If the two Koreas could come to agree on peaceful co-existence, then similar benefits can be gained without unification. While the peace dividends are real, they are not unique to unification. Rather, they are by-products of peace in the Korean peninsula.

Gains from Trade

The gains expected from trade rest on the possibility of greater scale economies and division of labor. But gains from trade follow naturally from a peaceful relationship and do not require unification. Since the 1960s, South Korea has benefited significantly from increased trade with other countries. Trade follows price differences and profit opportunities. It is not necessary to form a political union to benefit from trade, especially in today's world where trade barriers have been significantly lowered through multi-lateral agreements since World War II. Certainly, there is the potential for gains from trade between the North and South, especially in the long run. Again, the expected gains from trade are not unique to unification. They are what is expected from a peaceful relationship.

A brief consideration of the anticipated gains from unification thus far seems to suggest that the anticipated gains are greatly exaggerated. The advantage of cheap labor is likely to be more elusive as the South will be compelled to provide generous welfare programs for the North. The alleged advantages of the North's complementary resources – mineral deposits and lumber – appear to be grossly overstated. The trumpeted advantage of gaining bargaining power, if exercised, is more likely to be harmful than beneficial. It appears that the most significant expected gains – reduction in military expenditures and gains from trade – would follow naturally from the elimination of the inter-Korean hostility. Unification is not a pre-requisite for the real parts of the expected gains from unification.

COSTS OF UNIFICATION

The unification of the two Koreas would entail significant costs. Since the magnitude of the costs would depend on the specific manner of unification, my discussion dwells necessarily on generalities. The most obvious costs of unification would involve developing the North and providing for North

Koreans during the transition. There are other costs, perhaps less obvious, but not less serious; they include the almost certain expansion of government and the potential social conflicts. Let us consider them in turn.

Costs of Development and Welfare Provisions

The cost of raising the North's economy to the level of the South's would be staggering, as many have estimated. The North Korean economy has almost completely disintegrated, and it faces a major famine. Millions have died, and many more millions are threatened with starvation. The North blames a string of bad weather for the famine. But the real reason for the current state of affairs is the decades-long pursuit of the doctrine of *juche*, resulting in economic backwardness and severe industrial cannibalization. In the 1960s, the North boasted of a successful industrialization, in the fashion of communist Russia. However, after the potential of the forced mobilization (and the patience of ideological allies in avuncular Russia and China in supplying the North with aid) had been exhausted, the North Korean economy steadily declined for nearly two decades. If the Korean peninsula is unified, the South is basically taking over an area larger than itself and populated by some 20 million destitute people, lacking substantial industry or resources. (The only sector in any decent shape would be the fairly well-equipped and well-trained North Korean army, one-million-men strong, see Table 12.2).

Table 12.2 Real GNP: North and South, 1992–97

	1992	1993	1994	1995	1996	1997
North*	20.8	20.9	15.4	12.8	10.6	–
South**	305.7	315.2	341.0	386.2	395.3	350.9***

Notes:
 * In billions of US dollar at US$ 1 = NK Won 2.5.
 ** The Bank of Korea, *Statistics*.
 *** This figure reflects the financial crisis in Korea in the late 1997.
Source: Data provided by the North Korean authorities to IMF, IMF (1997).

The costs of developing the North would be staggering – a great burden if the South alone is to bankroll it. Broadly, costs are of the following kinds: costs of restructuring and privatizing uneconomical state enterprises, costs of building up infrastructure, costs of cleaning up environmental degradation, costs of assuming the North Korean external debts (largely to Russia, China and Japan), and costs of providing welfare for the North Koreans during the transition. In addition, there will be costs associated with settling the property claims by millions of North Korean refugees in the South and elsewhere. In light of the German experience, we should expect massive cost overruns.

The "peace dividends" accruing mainly from reduced defense spending may therefore fall far short of the required expenditure. The gap, then, must be filled either by government borrowing (or printing money) or by additional taxes. Financing the development costs would introduce a great deal of distortion in the economy.

Alienation and Social Conflict

Unification is likely to breed mutual resentments between the North and the South. As it stands now, South Koreans will most likely take charge – they will handle the financing and have the expertise. But North Koreans will resent the dominance of South Koreans in all areas – finance, business, politics, academics. South Koreans, in turn, are likely to be frustrated with slow progress and resent the fact that they shoulder enormous expenses when many North Koreans seem to prefer relying on welfare provisions to working. (Indeed, such seem to be the prevalent sentiments between West and East Germans.) There are other possibilities. For example, if North Koreans are given certain property claims for assets as a part of the privatization process, then, as a large part of the assets is likely to be accumulated by South Koreans, they will be blamed for having schemed to defraud the people of the North.

Koreans are not the most tolerant people. There are already strong regional prejudices and resentment between the Kyungsang provinces and the Cholla provinces, and this conflict has been politicized since the 1960s. Regional resentment and prejudices between the North and South could be much worse than anything we have seen to date. Although placing a dollar figure on these sentiments is difficult, they would definitely reduce whatever benefit we could expect from unification, and do so significantly.

Growth of Government

A seldom considered but important cost of unification is the guaranteed expansion of government. Some people may see no problem there; they ignore a serious problem. Already, many South Koreans feel that their centralized and bloated government is overly intrusive and hampers changes necessary to improve their lives. The process of searching for the causes of the 1997 financial crisis in the South made it clear to many that the overbearing government is the root of the evil. Yet, South Korea has not been able to roll back the government. Two of the chief difficulties are the politician's tendency to look for popular solutions and the bureaucrat's reluctance to let go of "iron bowls." Unification would be a god-sent opportunity for them to expand government, as it presumes to feed and develop the North. Not only will the government grow bigger, but it will become even more intrusive than now as it strives to meet certain arbitrarily set targets for development. Many would regard the further expansion of government in Korea as a definite minus in terms of personal freedom and economic efficiency.

From the above consideration of the costs of unification, we must conclude that common estimates significantly understate the costs of unification. When all the costs are fully considered, it is not at all clear whether there would be much, if any, net gain from unification. The argument for unification loses much of its rationale.

Even so, the sentimental appeals of unification will tempt a good many people to insist that unification is somehow beneficial. (Keep in mind that neither the gains nor the costs are, or can be, precisely estimated.) For them, moreover, there is no alternative. They want unification at any cost. At this point, I suggest that we think about the unthinkable – "no unification" – and see whether it might be a credible alternative.

A BETTER ALTERNATIVE: NO UNIFICATION

By no unification, I do not mean "no unification now"; nor do I mean "no unification in the near or distant future." By no unification, I mean ruling out any thought of merging the two Koreas into one nation, just as there is no thought of merging Korea with Russia, China, Japan, or the US. I mean that South Korea and North Korea should regard each other as foreign sovereign states – in the same manner they regard the Philippines, Japan, or Thailand.

Here, I wish to argue that no unification is a better alternative. The reasons are as follow: (1) it is more conducive to peace and (2) it promises a greater net gain than unification. Let me explain.

"No Unification" is More Conducive to Peace

A clear statement of "no unification" will induce the policymakers in the North to be less suspicious about the intentions of the South toward their country. The survival of their regime will be less threatened on that account, and they will worry less about the South's instigating to undermine their power and/or being dominated by the South in the reform process. Being less suspicious about the South, the North is more likely to focus on the imperatives for its survival – putting its house in order and developing its economy. The North will soon realize, it is hoped, that a lasting peace in the peninsula is much better suited for their purpose (of staying in power) than erratic extortionist tactics, from which the net gain is small and diminishing marginal return sets in rapidly.

Until a lasting peace in the peninsula is attained, the South should maintain a credible defense capability like any other country facing a hostile and belligerent country. The combination of a strong defense posture and a clear and formal renunciation of the goal of unification (after building a consensus in the South) should soon convince the North of the extravagant foolishness of escalating tension in the peninsula.

"No Unification" Promises a Greater Net Gain than Unification

No unification would reduce costs without reducing gains. No unification has fewer costs than unification. As North Korea will be in charge of its own destiny, the South need not shoulder most of the costs of transforming the North – costs of restructuring and privatizing uneconomical state enterprises, building up infrastructure, cleaning up environmental degradation, and providing welfare for the North during the transition. In the interest of its own survival, the North must, sooner or later, reduce its belligerence and try to attract a package of foreign aid for its development. The South can take a part, but not as the only partner. With other countries wanting stability in the region and therefore joining in the deal, the South's role may be even less significant. What is important is to convince North Korea that it must proceed pretty much on its own, without counting on substantial economic transfers and food relief. That is, the North should be persuaded to earn its own way. If and when the North succeeds in creating an environment hospitable to business, foreign capital and know-how will surely flow in. The North, considering the experiences of other LCDs and former socialist economies, will do whatever is necessary to attract them. Although initially undertaking the minimal reforms deemed necessary for its survival, the North will embark on a long march of economic development. Over time, there is no reason it cannot develop into a prosperous economy in its own right. In the meantime, the byproduct of reduced tension in the peninsula is a boon to the South.

The preceding section revealed that the most significant expected gains – the peace dividends and the gains from trade – can be had by securing peace without unification. For example, consider the gains from trade. It was not necessary for South Korea to become a part of a larger entity for it to derive much benefit from trading beyond national boundaries. Peace dividends accompany peace with or without unification. Because some of the anticipated benefits more directly tied to unification – for example, the North's natural resources and enhanced bargaining power – are grossly exaggerated or elusive, there is no clear superiority of unification over no unification in terms of expected gains. The main difference is the emotional appeal of unification.

The argument that no unification promises greater net gain than unification does not rest on the precise estimation of the relevant costs and benefits. Given the insufficiency of data, if I were to base my arguments on precise estimations, the foundation of my arguments would be shaky indeed. Rather, I assert that the costs of the latter exceed those of the former. All that is then needed to make the case is that the gains from either are roughly equivalent.

A BETTER DEVELOPMENT PROSPECT FOR THE NORTH

What is good for the South is not necessarily bad for the North. "No unification", in fact, promises better development prospects for the North. In order to appreciate this assertion, we must compare the development prospects under unification with those under "no unification."

Development of the North with Unification

The development of the North after unification would be characterized by the imposition of the South Korean system and government-directed development programs. I see much waste, inefficiency, corruption, and social conflict for the following reasons.

Imposition of the South Korean System

Given the vast differences in their resources, unification would foist on South Korea the full responsibility for integration. In carrying out this task, the South Korean system will be imposed on the North, and it may not be the most suitable for this development. First of all, even if the system has greatly benefited the South – ignoring for the moment the increasing call to reform the system within the South itself – it may not best serve the development of the North, which faces very different conditions. South Koreans have first-hand knowledge of the difficulties of adopting institutions evolved elsewhere.

Moreover, the South Korean system itself is not without problems, many of which have been pointed out in the aftermath of the financial crisis in 1997. Why should the North be limited to adopting the South Korean system, when it can learn from the varied experiences of developmental and transitional economies and experiment with various possibilities? There are plenty of examples of successes and failures from which to draw lessons – not only in South Korea, but also in Japan, China, Russia, Vietnam, Taiwan, Cuba, Romania, Albania, and other countries. Imposing the South Korean system would needlessly restrict the North's opportunity to experiment with suitable institutions. Not only is the imposition of the South Korean system on the North dreaded by the North for political reasons, but it should be dreaded for economic reasons as well.

Government-promoted Development

The efficacy of government-directed development efforts is at best questionable. Massive foreign aid since the end of World War II has seldom succeeded in bringing about the meaningful economic development of the recipient. Rather, these programs tend to be counter-productive, merely proliferating rent-seeking groups, breeding corruption and inefficiency, and making an economy dependent on a constant (or even increasing) infusion of aid (Bauer, 1990). There is little doubt that, given the chance, North Koreans will excel in the rent-seeking game, doing their utmost to frustrate the development effort.

Various plans for internal development have not fared much better. They tend merely to create the growth of government, massive waste, and regional dependency. For all its effort, for example, the South Korean government has not succeeded in bringing about balanced regional development within its own country. Can we reasonably expect it to accomplish this difficult task in the North?

If anything, there is the danger of transforming the program to develop the North into "corporate welfare" for Southern business interests. Given the underdevelopment in the North, and the South Korean government's willingness to foot the bill in the event of unification, there will be a great deal of demand for capital goods. Many South Korean producers will envision a captive market for their investment goods. South Koreans who foot the bulk of the bill for unification/integration may feel that they have good reason to expect that they should also supply the bulk of the capital goods used in the North. The unification process is therefore likely to turn into a golden opportunity for South Korean producers of capital goods. The consequences of the direction of economic development in the North will be for the worse. They include increased costs of developing the North, more corruption, and more corporate welfare. Waste will be rampant and corporate welfare will lead to frictions with other countries that covet the market.

Some in the South may object to this reasoning. They will argue that the *dirigiste* South Korea has successfully developed its economy and therefore has the expertise to develop the North. It is, indeed, true that the South has accumulated a certain amount of knowledge of and experience in economic development and policymaking. Through various channels it should be willing to share this expertise with the North if such is desired. However, there is a problem in applying the lessons learned from its experience: the situation is different now. The kind of practices – of growth at any cost – that propelled the South along the path of rapid growth in the 1960s, 1970s, and even 1980s cannot be effectively carried out under the current South Korean system, in which the government can no longer exact near-total submission from people. Ironically, what expertise the South can offer based on its own developmental experience could be more easily put into practice with effect if the North stayed separate.[4]

Development Prospects for the North Without Unification

The development of North Korea with no unification will be characterized as self-reliant and self-determining – not in the sense of following the misguided policy of *juche* or self-sufficiency, but in the sense of having its future depend largely upon its own actions.

Once the principle of no unification is firmly established, North Korea will be pretty much on its own. Given its dire economic situation, the North should be able to solicit a package of aid from other countries, in a combination of famine relief and other economic aid. But the aid will be different from what Russians or Chinese used to provide, or for that matter what the US used to provide for other LDCs. It is hoped that everyone has learned a lesson or two from the futile past attempts of showering LDCs with aid packages. The future foreign aid will come with more strings attached – requiring the North to behave in certain ways that may be contrary to the wishes of their rulers. Moreover, the aid will be grossly inadequate for the development of the North Korean economy, since it has degenerated into something less than a subsistence economy. The North Korean rulers must, therefore, make up the shortfall in revenue needed to retain their power. They face broadly two choices.

One choice is to follow their traditional extortionist approach of exacting additional transfers from grudging donors. The North used to exploit its geo-political position to receive substantial transfers at various times from Russia and China by playing them against each other. Now, the transfers from the erstwhile ideological allies have been either cut off or reduced to trickles. Currently, the North is trying to cultivate new donors in the US, Japan, and South Korea by becoming a nuisance. But this tactic is nearsighted. It garners barely enough resources for the rulers to stay in power, and does little or nothing to improve the lot of the already struggling people. The circle is vicious. It cannot be sustained for long. Either the population will be drastically reduced and, God forbid, there soon will be few left to dominate, or the rulers will be ousted in a riot, or coup – as in Romania, Albania, or Uganda. The new ruling group would then face the same choices again.

A better choice for the North Korean leaders is to adopt certain changes to generate needed revenues on both a sustained basis and (one can always hope) an increasing scale. Other countries, including South Korea, have chosen this course – when all other options seemed to have been exhausted – and have done well since; there is no reason why the North should not enjoy similar success.

The realization that there is no place to fall back on will, sooner or later, lead to reform, if only because the rulers of the North need to generate revenue to govern and retain their power. The reforms will not be textbook pretty, but the regime will do whatever it takes to earn enough to stay in power. Although a degree of stability is necessary to retain power, as the encompassing interest group, they must experiment with various schemes to generate needed revenue (Olson, 1982; Choi, 1994). Such schemes will not succeed unless a significant portion of the people also benefit and adjust their behavior to conform to the market. The requirement to earn a profit, therefore, will induce the North Korean economy gradually to become market conforming. The potential is tremendous, if only because the North Korean economy has so long been suppressed and distorted. A sustainable developmental path will be embarked upon, with much better prospects than the one under unification. Over time, North Korea could turn into a rapidly growing economy. Its rulers would have not only a better chance of staying in power, but also a good chance of getting credit for rebuilding the nation and bettering the lot of the people.

Of the two development prospects – with or without unification – I think no unification is more attractive. The North will not necessarily grow faster or develop better on its own, but it has a chance to do better on its own, if it tried.

DIFFICULTIES OF "NO UNIFICATION"

No unification is not without its own difficulties, however. They include: (1) the political viability of advocating no unification; (2) the moral dilemma of tolerating a dictatorial developmental state in the North; and (3) the problem of refugees. The relevant question is whether these are severe enough to render no unification an unattractive option.

Political Viability

Introducing the concept of no unification may involve certain political risks. Many South Koreans have a strong sentimental attachment to unification and may react negatively to the idea. But would people really want unification, at any cost? Their enthusiasm for unification has already moderated after seeing the high cost estimates of the German-style unification and experiencing the financial crisis in 1997. The real issue is how to persuade people of both the stupendous costs of indulging in their gut feelings and the existence of a better alternative. How to implement them lies in the realm of political leadership. But it does not seem impossible.

The Moral Dilemma

Once the principle of no unification is accepted and the North tries to embark on a course of development, the conditions there may not be pretty to witness – not by US standards, and not even by South Korean standards. Political repression would continue and working conditions are likely to remain sub-par for a long time. Conditions in the North will be difficult to ignore and some in the South will raise the question: how can we let fellow Koreans in the North suffer under ruthless dictatorship and severe economic hardship?

The correct way to see the situation is as follows. The premise, let us not forget, is that North Korea is a foreign country. Citizens in South Korea should not expect their government to intervene in North Korean affairs, just as they find it imprudent to intervene to rectify conditions in Indonesia or Iraq. Nevertheless, anyone in the South who feels morally compelled to aid anyone or any group in the North should be free to do so – as an individual, or in collaboration with other like-minded individuals.

Refugees

Reform in North Korea will mean less regimentation and greater movement of people. Its conditions will not improve overnight. Many in the North will be tempted to emigrate wherever the wage level is substantially higher. Though many places will qualify under this criterion, the South will be especially attractive because of its the common language and proximity. A mass migration can result, possibly with large-scale disruption in the South.

Few countries with any moral scruples have ever succeeded in preventing people seeking to settle in their countries from doing so. What to do?

A rapid improvement in economic conditions in the North can, to some extent, reduce the incentive to migrate. Unfortunately, there is no known method of engineering the rapid economic growth of a country from outside. The South should not even attempt to do so. It would only waste resources and, in the process, induce the misallocation of resources in the North and retard its development.

A partial solution lies within the South itself – a set of reforms. Especially important are a reduction in welfare provisions and deregulation of the labor market. If welfare provisions are sufficiently cut, the South would become somewhat less attractive to settle in, and the inflow of people from the North would be reduced. But given the vast differences in prevailing wages, migration would still be large in scale. The labor market therefore must be reformed. If it is made more flexible and welfare provision is meager, then the influx of people is not necessarily so bad – all of the newcomers will earn their keep and contribute more to the South Korean economy than they consume. With appropriate reforms in the South, refugees may be even welcomed.

CONCLUDING REMARKS

The main argument thus far is that for both North and South Koreans no unification is superior to unification because it promises much greater net gains. Yet, hardly anyone, anywhere, seems to entertain no unification as a serious option. Koreans on both sides have for too long taken for granted the eventual unification. To think otherwise may seem too treacherous even to contemplate. If the analyses presented here are even half-correct, however, the option of no unification merits serious consideration. According to the analyses presented above, the presumed destiny of unification is too costly. A clear articulation of the principle of no unification could allay the suspicions of North Korean leaders regarding the true motive of the South. Comforted by the thought of their greater security, they may become more willing to cooperate and promote peace in the peninsula. From this everyone would benefit.

NOTES

[1] Lee (1992). Through 1998 the total amount of West German subsidies to East Germany came to $560 billion. In 1999, there will be additional subsidy of $22

billion.
[2] In 1998 alone, Hyundai paid the North $190 million, not counting another $90 million invested in the North for the infrastructure, hotels, etc.
[3] Even after unification, Korea cannot eliminate its defense, as it would still be surrounded by much bigger neighbors, i.e., China, Russia and Japan.
[4] As of 1997, the South spent U$15.1 billion (or 3.4 percent of GNP) on defense. The figure for the North is less clear. The National Unification Board estimates for 1996–1997 is U$5.2 billion, (or 23 percent of GNP). Note however, the estimate is not consistent with the data in Table 12.1, provided by the North to the IMF. One must consider the statistics with much caution.
[5] There is a distinct possibility, however, that the "peace dividends" would be significantly reduced as career military officers object to a drastic reduction of the armed forces. In both Koreas, the military has a great deal of power. It can easily find reasons to maintain strong military capabilities against "external threats" and justify them to the satisfaction of politicians. Protecting the interests of career military officers could diminish the size of the peace dividend significantly.
[6] I do not mean to imply that such is the only way to go.

REFERENCE

Bank of Korea (1999), *Statistics.*

Bauer, Peter (1991), *The Development Frontier: Essays in Applied Economics*, Cambridge, MA: Harvard University Press.

Choi, Young Back (1994) "Industrial Policy as the Engine of Economic Growth in S. Korea" in *The Collapse of Development Planning*, (ed.), Peter Boettke New York University Press, NY: 231–255.

Flake, Gordon (1999), "Inter-Korean Economic Relations Under the 'Sunshine Policy," *Korea's Economy 1999*, Korea Economic Institute of America: 100–106.

IMF (1997), "Democratic People's Republic of Korea – Fact Finding Report", EBS/97/204, Nov. 12.

Kim, Sung-Han (1999), "South Korean Policy Toward North Korea," *Korea's Economy 1999*, Korea Economic Institute of America: 94–99.

Lee, Kie Bok (1992), "Equalization of Income in an Unified Korea" in T. Chen, Y.B. Choi, and S. Lee (eds), *Economic and Political Reform in Asia*, Institute of Asian Studies, St. John's University: 213–34.

Olson, Mancur (1982), *The Rise and Decline of Nations,* New Haven: Yale University Press.

Index